This book is going to be perhaps the most lethal weapon in the arsenal against the so-far partially successful attempts (thanks to social media) to tout the 20-year Marcos era (January 1966 to February 1986) as a "golden age" in Philippine history. Specifically, JC Punongbayan relentlessly examines every one of 50 claims that have been made regarding that period—from the faintly ridiculous (that Imelda Marcos did not use public funds to build her "bopis" hospitals) to the utterly insane (that nobody was poor during the Marcos regime). And he debunks every one of them with a mountain of data and past studies, all footnoted, referenced, and acknowledged so anyone can check and see for themselves the accuracy of JC's rebuttals. The joy of it is that he combines seven years of scholarly research with simple, clear, compelling writing. Bravo!

—SOLITA C. MONSOD
PROFESSOR EMERITUS
UNIVERSITY OF THE PHILIPPINES
SCHOOL OF ECONOMICS

The countless lies and disinformation on social media about the so-called golden age of martial law have created a huge divide in our country. This book will help put a stop to the spread of false narratives and bring to light what really happened during one of the darkest periods in Philippine history. JC Punongbayan has done a splendid job of setting the record straight and upholding the truth.

—ATTY. CHEL DIOKNO
HUMAN RIGHTS LAWYER AND
CHAIR, FREE LEGAL ASSISTANCE GROUP

Punongbayan stepped out of the ivory tower and immersed himself in conversations taking place in social media to bring us this illuminating book. He deftly collapses the false Marcos and martial law narratives on the Philippine economy using facts backed by authoritative references. *False Nostalgia* is truly a useful and easy-to-read myth buster.

—MARITES DAÑGUILAN VITUG
AUTHOR AND JOURNALIST

FALSE NOSTALGIA

FALSE NOSTALGIA

JC PUNONGBAYAN

FALSE NOSTALGIA

THE MARCOS "GOLDEN AGE" MYTHS AND HOW TO DEBUNK THEM

bughaw

Published by BUGHAW
An imprint of Ateneo de Manila University Press
Bellarmine Hall, Ateneo de Manila University
Katipunan Avenue, Loyola Heights
Quezon City, Philippines
Tel.: (632) 8426-59-84
E-mail: unipress@ateneo.edu
Website: https://unipress.ateneo.edu

Cover art and design: Albert Raqueño
Book design: Ace Vincent Molo

The National Library of the Philippines CIP Data

Recommended entry:

Punongbayan, JC.
False nostalgia : the Marcos "golden age" myths and how to debunk them. — Quezon City : ATENEO DE MANILA UNIVERSITY PRESS, [2023], ©2023.
xxiv, 377 pages; 20.32 cm

ISBN 978-621-448-246-7 (pb)
ISBN 978-621-448-247-4 (pdf)

1. Marcos, Ferdinand E. 2. Philippines. President (1965–1986 : Marcos) 3. Philippines — Politics and government — 1965–1986. I. Title.

959.90564 DS686.6.M35 2023 P320230004

For mom and dad

CONTENTS

PART 2 CRISIS MISMANAGEMENT

PART 3 CRAZY RICH FILIPINOS

LIST OF FIGURES

LIST OF TABLES

FOREWORD

EMMANUEL S. DE DIOS
PROFESSOR EMERITUS
UNIVERSITY OF THE PHILIPPINES
SCHOOL OF ECONOMICS

THE PROBLEM OF CONTESTED LEGACIES, especially of dictators or authoritarians, is not unique to the Philippines. Even affluent societies and mature democracies have had to confront political divisions over the evaluation of leaders of their recent and even distant past. At one extreme, Hitler's horrific crimes against humanity and the devastation and human toll caused by his wars of choice against other nations left no choice but for Germans as a people to confront their problematic past, a process known as *Vergangenheitsbewältigung*. This process has led to a clear and official prohibition of symbols and propaganda that advocate or glorify Nazism (e.g., nowhere in Germany is even a *Hitlerstraße* to be found). While this has not prevented the rise of fringe right-wing political groups that surreptitiously advocate Nazi-related ideas (e.g., racist anti-immigrant policy), the whole German education system, mainstream media, official cultural institutions, political party system, the police, and the justice system are constantly mobilized to bring pressure to bear to prevent a Nazi recrudescence.

Results are slower and less clear-cut in other cases. The remains of Spanish dictator Francisco Franco, who ruled Spain from 1935 to 1975, were exhumed only in 2018, after his earlier burial in the Valle de los Caidos (the equivalent of our Libingan ng mga Bayani), and reinterred instead in a private family vault. It took more than four decades after Franco's death for the Spanish government to decide that it was incompatible for a modern democracy to memorialize a dictator. Only in 2007 was a "historical memory law" passed that proposed to remove all public references honoring persons associated with the Franco regime (the last statue of Franco was removed only in 2018) and instead to memorialize the victims of the dictatorship. These moves did not come without vehement political debates over Franco's legacy—and even today the political process is controversial—but it does tell us that historical and political amnesia is neither inevitable nor irreparable.

More distant is the example of Napoleon Bonaparte, the "emperor of the French," whose legacy after two odd centuries remains the subject of lingering dispute. His contested legacy consisted, on the one hand, of restoring law and order in revolutionary France and introducing reforms and the civil code in many countries of Europe that previously suffered under despotic princes—but also a record of devastating wars and invasion of neighboring countries and the installation of puppet rulers. Despite the subsequent lionization of Napoleon in public monuments, Charles de Gaulle, France's outstanding wartime leader, remained a fervent non-admirer who wrote that Napoleon "left France crushed, invaded, drained of blood and courage, and smaller than he had found it."

As such instances show, it is by no means unusual if different groups in society hold conflicting assessments of past political personalities and events over long periods before coming to a final judgement that is acceptable to most citizens—or at least learning to live with their remaining differences enough to move on with their national future. Some societies succeed at it better than others, making a break with the past sooner rather than later, more completely rather than partially and tepidly. In all these processes, however, one thing is clear, to paraphrase a US statesman: while people are free to choose their judgments and even hold on to these over long periods of time, they cannot choose to ignore facts.[1] An indispensable condition for overcoming problematic periods in a nation's life is an agreement on fundamental facts and events. In the natural course of things, national reflection, political debate, the media, the education system—but, above all, scholarship—should be expected over time to distill fact from fiction and pave the way for an appreciation of the past that can serve as a sound rational basis for moving on.

From this perspective, the Filipinos' effort to grapple with the legacy of the authoritarian rule of Ferdinand E. Marcos Sr. has truly been remarkable: rather than leading to final clarity and conciliation, the passage of time has instead only produced increased distortion and dissension. Rather than putting paid to the issues raised by the dictatorship and relegating these to history books, these have only cropped up in new forms and repetitive debates that time and again threaten to crowd out more debates over more urgent national concerns.

An important underlying difference for the Philippines is precisely that historical fact itself has been distorted, disputed, and manufactured. Werner Sombart wrote famously that facts are like beads requiring a string to connect them, emphasizing the need for a theoretical narrative of history.[2] In our case, however, Sombart's well-known aphorism must be reversed: it is not that we merely need the string of a national narrative to tie the beads of facts together; we lack even the genuine beads to work into a narrative. The "beads" of fact our people are given to work with today are pieces of stale pastry that crumble upon closer handling and scrutiny. Without facts, no reliable narrative can be woven.

This situation has arisen owing to several weaknesses: political, intellectual, and institutional. The political failure is that numerous vested interests, careers, and political reputations of people continue to depend on a misrepresentation of the Marcos era, most notably the Marcos-Romualdez family itself and its hangers-on. This can ultimately be traced to the political fragility and lack of will of post-EDSA governments, which failed to seize the opportunity to make a clean sweep of and hold to account the enemies of democracy with their illiberal agendas. The second—for which we as scholars must bear responsibility for our complacency—is the failure to provide a coherent and definitive fact-based account of the country's social history and development that could provide a rallying point for society. Such an account would have properly put the period of the Marcos dictatorship in its place as a definite backward step in the country's development. None of these is helped by the chronic weakness and corruption of some of the country's important institutions: the justice system, which failed time and again to prosecute the crimes under the Marcos regime to the fullest extent; the education and media, whose low quality and obsequiousness prevented them from taking any initiative in affirming even the most basic facts, not to mention providing the context, of important events in the nation's history;[3] and not the least, there is the low ethical level of the country's commercial and industrial elites for whom wealth—from whatever source—appears to be the only criterion for social acceptance and respectability. This must include the advertising and public relations industry, which has shown a peculiarly amoral perspective on truth and facts in its servicing of political campaigns.

These preconditions have rendered the mass of Philippine society (already poorly informed, poorly educated, and politically disengaged) vulnerable to what was a new phenomenon of the weaponization of social media. Trolls, influencers, microcelebrities, and other spreaders of fake news—cynically organized and paid for by operators in a "network of disinformation"—have rushed to fill in the vacuum left by deficient politics, scholarship, education, and elite culture.[4] It has since become known that the now-pervasive Marcos "golden age" myth, the subject of this book, was the result of a well-organized campaign of "positive branding" cascaded down from political strategists to digital influencers.[5] While that campaign achieved its immediate objective of returning the Marcos family and its cohorts to the country's highest positions, it also wreaked long-term havoc on the minds of many Filipinos whose understanding of Philippine history and their own condition has, as a result, become even more confused, fragmentary, and misdirected. Beyond political campaigns, it is this deeper damage that must be repaired.

This book is a bold step in that direction. It is the signal service of JC Punongbayan to take the step of directly confronting misinformation—in its existing shape and form—and using the cold eye of scholarship to correct it point by point. In doing so, JC breaks out of the mold of those academics who look with disdain on correcting popular misconceptions as something beneath them or as something too obvious or banal to engage their attention. Such an attitude is what left the field free for purveyors of disinformation in the first place.

JC would no doubt fall into the category of what used to be known as a "public intellectual." But where the old quip about public intellectuals was, "The more public they are, the less intellectual they get," JC is part of an emerging generation of academics who are remarkably just as nimble in the trenches of social media as in the rarefied atmosphere of academic discourse. (The closest models might be Paul Krugman or Tyler Cowen.) JC's highly active social-media accounts are keenly followed by tens of thousands; yet he is a bona fide quant, a wonk who is up to speed with cutting-edge methods in his field—e.g., machine-learning techniques applied to economics (a topic of his pioneering dissertation)—and much else in economics.

JC's double credentials are reflected in this book's approach. It is a unique juxtaposition of populist misconceptions as propagated in social media, on the one hand, and serious academic research debunking these, on the other, with full respect and seriousness paid to both. As JC himself points out: "Some of these myths might appear shallow or absurd, but these are useful springboards that we will use for a deep dive into various aspects of the Marcosian economy." True to his concern for undoing the damage caused by the network of disinformation, JC directly enumerates the false memes that have proliferated regarding the Marcosian "golden age"—already too well-known to him and which he has frequently combatted in a tit-for-tat manner in his social media persona. But his approach to debunking them in this volume takes the "long form" of thoroughly grounded scholarly research thus mustering history, economics, politics, and political economy in the explanation, and, in some cases, even presenting new factual material. This has the advantage not only of a summary "fact-check" but also the presentation of a larger narrative. Extending Sombart's simile, JC crushes fake beads, supplies more durable ones, as well as provides a strong string.

This work by its example thus throws an implicit two-sided challenge: scholars are asked to show serious concern for the state of mind of the broader society they live and work in and to devote efforts to dispel myths and reverse disinformation. To the general public, the invitation is look beyond memes, facile judgments, and smart comebacks, and begin the hard work of confronting the unvarnished truth of the country's history.

May our responses be worthy of the efforts and engagement of JC and the successor generation he represents.

INTRODUCTION

"Perception is real, the truth is not."

—Imelda R. Marcos in
The Kingmaker

"There was truth and there was untruth,
and if you clung to the truth even against the
whole world, you were not mad."

—George Orwell,
Nineteen Eighty-Four

ON 9 MAY 2022, THE UNTHINKABLE HAPPENED. More than 31.6 million Filipinos elected Ferdinand "Bongbong" Marcos Jr., second child and only son of the deposed dictator Ferdinand Marcos Sr., to become the seventeenth president of the Philippines. That number represented a whopping 59 percent of the votes, making

Marcos Jr. the Philippines' first majority president after the EDSA People Power Revolution in 1986. Marcos Jr.'s votes were also more than twice the votes that went to his top contender for the presidency, then vice president Leni Robredo.[1]

The Marcoses' return to Malacañang in 2022, backed by such a massive mandate,[2] is at once utterly unsurprising and surprising.

It is utterly unsurprising because virtually all statistical indicators pointed to such an outcome. Pulse Asia, one of the country's two most trusted survey outfits—and the only one that came out with monthly surveys in the last electoral cycle—reported in April 2022 that 56 percent of voting-age Filipinos preferred Marcos Jr., which is pretty close to the 59 percent of votes he actually got.

More significantly, the Marcoses have been playing the long game and working to reclaim Malacañang since their return from their exile in Hawai'i in 1991.

Recall that Imelda, wife of the dictator, tried to run for president twice: first in 1992, where she lost, and in 1998, where she withdrew. In 1992, Imelda in fact placed fifth in the race, garnering 10.3 percent of the votes. Meanwhile, Marcos crony Eduardo "Danding" Cojuangco placed third with 18.2 percent. Together, Imelda and Danding's percentages beat the 23.6 vote-percentage garnered by the winner, Fidel V. Ramos. Jovito Salonga, statesman and first chair of the Presidential Commission on Good Government—tasked to go after the Marcoses' ill-gotten wealth—also ran in the same race but placed a mere sixth, gaining just 10.2 percent of the votes.

The fact that Imelda won 2.34 million votes a mere five years after the EDSA Revolution that ousted her husband from power should already have given us a hint of their enduring popularity—notwithstanding everything that had happened throughout the dictatorship and their family's eventual downfall.

Meanwhile, after his own return from exile, Marcos Jr. ran and won as representative of Ilocos Norte's second district (1992–1995), then became Ilocos Norte governor (1998–2007), and again as congressman (2007–2010). He finally landed a national position in 2010, when he won a Senate seat and served there until 2016. After that, he ran for vice president but was beaten by Robredo, although only by a hairline. Thus, Bongbong *nearly* won the vice presidency in 2016.

One might therefore reasonably say that Marcos Jr.'s victory in 2022 was the culmination of a more-than-three-decades effort toward political redemption, restoration, and rehabilitation—whatever you want to call it.

But Marcos Jr.'s win was also utterly surprising, at least in one respect: the enormous crowds that attended Robredo's campaign sorties all over the country—peaking at about 700,000 to 800,000 people in the *miting de avance* in Makati City and exceeding most of Marcos Jr.'s rallies—gave hope that the opposition leader could present a credible and worthy challenge to Marcos Jr.'s sizable lead in the surveys. Robredo's campaign, awash in pink, was also historic since it was driven in large part by volunteerism that was never seen before in the country. Using their own money, so-called Kakampinks printed all sorts of campaign paraphernalia, from posters and banners, to shirts and stickers. Organizers of sorties across the country were openly competing to get larger crowds than the last big rally. And by the tail end of the campaign period, many people—even celebrities who were otherwise silent throughout the administration of outgoing president Rodrigo Duterte—came out in support of Robredo and even participated pro bono in activities ranging from mob performances to house-to-house campaigns.

Lo and behold, the huge crowds provided but illusory hope: the people who attended just happened to be active and invested, but were not at all representative of the voting population. Apparently, there was a vast silent majority of Marcos Jr. supporters who kept their cards close to their chests and did not display their support until election day.[3]

BUT HOW DID MARCOS JR. SNAG THE PRESIDENCY, with 31.6 million votes to boot? I think it boils down to identity politics, which is manifested in two ways: an intense sense of regionalism that has always characterized Philippine politics and intense polarization on social media.

One Pulse Asia survey in March 2022 found that support for Marcos Jr. correlated well with people's region of origin.[4] No doubt that Marcos Jr. would capture northern Philippines, especially his home province of Ilocos Norte. But by teaming up with Sara Duterte—mayor of Davao City and the feisty daughter of then incumbent President Duterte—Marcos Jr. was able to capture southern Philippines as well, both its voters and local leaders. In hindsight, the regional alliance was a match made in heaven, and this was advertised as such in posters and online ads: Marcos was portrayed as the "tiger" of the north, while Sara Duterte was the "eagle" of the south. This was accompanied by a fitting slogan of "unity" throughout the campaign period. Although often overused (to the point that their plans for the economy also hinged on unity and literally nothing else), this simple yet clear message resonated with millions of voters.

The success of this regional team-up is evident in the map of the election results: only a handful of provinces (including Robredo's home region of Bicol, as well as Western Visayas) turned "pink," and these areas were sandwiched by much of Luzon, Central Visayas, and Mindanao—all awash in red. Although Marcos Jr. enjoyed a landslide victory in most of the country, some analysts are doubtful if he would ever win the presidency had he not secured Sara Duterte's clout in Mindanao—the same Duterte clout that catapulted her father to the presidency back in 2016.[5]

Besides the prevailing sense of regionalism among Filipino voters, however, Marcos Jr.'s win should also be credited to his campaign's aggressive use of social media geared toward disinformation and the poisoning of political discourse.

LET'S BACKTRACK A BIT: THE MARCOSES ARE NO strangers to lies. Heck, the Marcos dictatorship was built on and thrived in it.

On the way to gaining power, Marcos Sr. and Imelda consciously built an entire mythology about themselves. For instance, they co-opted the folk tale of "Si Malakas at si Maganda," which told the story of the first man (the strong Malakas) and the first woman (the beautiful Maganda) emerging from a bamboo stalk. Later, Marcos Sr. commissioned a painting depicting him as Malakas and Imelda as Maganda—essentially, the Filipino Adam and Eve, the country's father and mother.[6] Many other images depicting themselves as such have appeared in edifices built during the dictatorship. In her tell-all book, Beatriz Romualdez Francia, Imelda's niece, wrote:

> Imelda had also busied herself with building a number of palatial resthouses for their family,

> many of them featuring images of Malakas and Maganda. The Sto. Niño Shrine in Leyte has a painting of Malakas and Maganda. The University of Life features a towering statue depicting the same legendary features. New fake stained glass doors of resin featuring Malakas and Maganda were installed at the entrance of the remodeled Malacañang Palace.[7]

Apart from these images, Imelda also commissioned a 300-page book titled *Malakas and Maganda*, where the first couple was depicted as "god-like beings, looming like giants on the horizon over their diminutive subjects." The epilogue also claimed boldly that only the first couple could save the country.[8]

The declaration of martial law in 1972 was also built on the patently fake news that defense minister Juan Ponce Enrile was "ambushed" in his car. Marcos Sr. blamed this attack on communist rebels, but in the dying days of the regime, Enrile admitted that the ambush was in fact staged. Still, Marcos's men, especially his top propagandist Primitivo Mijares, wrote press releases about the ambush (even before the attack happened) in a bid to bolster the case for martial law.[9]

Marcos's propaganda was so effective that even the very date of the declaration of martial law has been shrouded in a veil of lies. Officially, Marcos insisted that he declared martial law on 21 September 1972. But in fact, martial law did not take effect—oppositionists were not rounded up and Congress was not locked up—until two days later, 23 September. Nonetheless, Marcos stuck to the earlier date because he found it especially auspicious, with seven being a special number for him and that 21 (not 23) is divisible by seven.[10] To this day, the official declaration is remembered on 21 September, and very few people remember that it is not at all the real date to commemorate.[11]

In the 2010s, the Marcoses' mythology and propaganda found a new home in the vast and deep recesses of the internet—and in no time, it would unsettlingly take on a new and much larger life of its own. As social media use in the Philippines flourished, so did the opportunities for the Marcoses to rebrand their image in the 21st century, especially among a new generation of voters who neither lived during martial law nor were taught about it well in schools. Only the naïve would find it difficult to see that the current exponential spread of lies about the Marcoses online—primarily portraying the Marcos dictatorship as nothing short of a utopia and a golden age—has something to do with their bid to regain political power.

Disinformation about the Marcoses is now rife in more popular social media platforms like Facebook (on which most Filipinos have an account and even free access), YouTube, and Twitter, as well as in newer ones like TikTok. Lies have also penetrated Wikipedia, where loyalists and trolls constantly edit articles related to the Marcos family to put them in the best possible light.[12]

Evidence suggests that the Marcoses were, in fact, early adopters of social media; they realized pretty quickly the potential of the internet to spread their lies in ways that were unprecedented in scope and speed. For instance, the journal *Kasarinlan* published in 2013 screenshots of Bongbong Marcos's Friendster account.[13] Created as early as March 2004, the account featured in 2010 a portrait of the Marcos family alongside the cartoon image of a boy holding up a pinwheel. In the background, there is also a larger windmill set against a blue sky. There was also a link to an online game called "Windmill City." Thus, as early as then, Bongbong was already leveraging the Bangui Windmill Farm in Ilocos Norte for his political image—even if the said project was initiated not by his provincial government but by a private corporation called NorthWind Power Development Corporation[14] (now fully owned by Ayala Corporation) and funded in cooperation with the World Bank[15] and the Danish government.[16]

The Marcoses' savvy use of the internet for their political project has extended well into the 2010s. For instance, a whistleblower from political data firm Cambridge Analytica confessed to news outlet Rappler that their company had received "a request straight from Bongbong Marcos to do a family rebranding," and that their CEO Alexander Nix saw this as an irresistible "financial opportunity."[17]

According to an investigative report by Rappler, there exists an "extensive" network of influencers in various social media platforms that "appear to be part of a systematic campaign to burnish the image of the Marcoses and pave the way for their further rise in Philippine politics."[18] Around September 2019, Rappler detected at least 360 pages and 280 groups on Facebook that were supportive of the Marcos family. Certainly, there is a lot more of such pages and groups now. But many were created back in 2014, two years before—and therefore in the run-up to—the 2016 elections. It was around this time that Imelda made press statements wishing for her son Bongbong to run for president. During her 85th birthday in 2014, Imelda said, "I still have a vision and hope to bring more help to the Filipino people," and that her son Bongbong, who was then still a senator, was "qualified" to run for the presidency in 2016. Bongbong, following the pressure from his mother, did run for the vice presidency in 2016.

On the face of it, Bongbong's defeat that year would seem to suggest the disinformation network set up by his camp came to no avail. But note that Robredo's lead over Marcos Jr. was a slim one: a little over 263,000 votes. This lead would climb to more than 278,000 following Marcos Jr.'s electoral challenge and the recount of votes in some provinces.[19] But it was still a narrow lead for Robredo. The fact is, Marcos Jr. *almost* snatched the vice presidency in 2016, nearly stepping closer to the presidency.

In 2019, the Marcoses—stronger than ever since EDSA and backed by a robust machinery offline and online—won a lot more positions in the national and local levels.[20] Bongbong's sister Imee won a senatorial seat for the first time. Imee's 29-year-old son Matthew became governor of Ilocos Norte, while Matthew's aunt Cecille Araneta-Marcos became vice governor. Matthew's uncle, Eugenio Marcos Barba, was the province's vice governor but went on to become the province's second district representative, replacing Imelda. Meanwhile, Ferdinand Marcos Sr.'s nephew Michael Marcos Keon, who was once Ilocos Norte governor, also won as mayor of Laoag City, the province's capital.

Fast-forward to October 2021, Bongbong Marcos, having been finally defeated in his electoral dispute with Robredo, announced that he would be running for president in the pivotal 2022 elections.[21] Two days later, Robredo also announced her own presidential bid, having said previously that she would perhaps be enjoined to run for president if Bongbong officially runs for the presidency. Alas, her campaign—aside from preparing too late in the game—proved no match to the Marcoses' money and their strategic investments over the past decades.

THE EFFECTIVITY OF THE MARCOSES' ONLINE disinformation network rests of course on the narratives that pervade such network. The chief objective of these narratives is to perfume and rebrand the Marcoses' image and put Marcos Sr.'s "legacy" (as they would be the last to admit that his reign was a dictatorship) in the best possible light—especially in the eyes of the youth.

Arguably the most prominent and believable[22] of these narratives is the myth that the Philippines attained its "golden age" during the dictatorship: that under Marcos's rule, the country experienced unprecedented growth and prosperity, and this unambiguously improved the lives of Filipinos. This golden age myth takes on many forms: for example, that we were one of the richest countries during martial law (second only to Japan); that the numerous grand roads, bridges, and edifices built by the Marcoses did the country good; that the strength of the peso against the dollar was an unalloyed boon; and that the economic crisis in the mid-1980s occurred after the Marcoses fled the Palace and not before.

The thing is, many people believe such lies, or at least accept a vague notion that the Marcos era was indeed the Philippines' golden age. In a 2016 *New York Times* article, some people said martial law "was when the Philippines was the leader of Asia," "a time when our economy was booming," and that "life was easier under Marcos . . . [W]e have to tell our children and grandchildren about these times."[23] Fast-forward to 2021, a person interviewed by the BBC said in Filipino: "I would like to experience the good life that people were saying when Ferdinand Marcos Sr. was still the president. We need to have that back." (In the same report, another person was quick to push back against the reporter's description of

FIGURE 0.1 The idea of a Marcosian golden age (or golden rule) has been there a long time. (Photo from the 1983 funeral procession of Ninoy Aquino by Gabriel U. Iglesias; reprinted with permission)

Marcos as a "dictator": "Excuse me, please correct the word 'dictator.' ")[24]

Over the years, the Marcoses have assiduously peddled their versions of what the former Donald Trump adviser Kellyanne Conway would call "alternative facts." In 2016, when Bongbong was asked by media about his father's spotty record, he said:

> Will I say sorry for the thousands and thousands of kilometers that were built? Will I say sorry for the agricultural policy that brought us to self-sufficiency in rice? Will I say sorry for the power generation? Will I say sorry for the highest literacy rate in Asia? What am I to say sorry for?[25]

At any rate, by hammering home this "golden age" myth today—in whatever form—the Marcoses want today's youth to cherish and remember the legacy of Ferdinand Marcos as a utopian age, whitewashing the regime's atrocities and cultivating what might be called "false nostalgia." More importantly yet very subtly, they wish to implant into the minds of voters that only another Marcos in the Palace can bring about another golden age for the country and deliver us from all the woes and troubles our country is suffering from today.

On 9 May 2022, 31.6 million believed such a message. And thus the Marcoses' political restoration was completed. The triumph of the Marcosian lies was presaged by Nobel Peace Prize winner Maria Ressa in one of her grim but sunny tweets. In 2019, Maria said: "A lie told a million times becomes a fact. Without facts, we can't have truth. Without truth, we can't have trust. If we don't do anything substantial now, democracy as we know it is dead."[26]

BUT JUST BECAUSE MANY PEOPLE BELIEVE something, that doesn't make it necessarily true or right.

Since the rise of Marcosian disinformation on Facebook around 2016, I have been studying and researching what happened to the Philippine economy during martial law, giving talks and writing articles here and there. I saw, through a mountain of data and past studies, that the Philippines suffered its worst postwar recession or economic crisis during martial law (specifically in the mid-1980s) and that this crisis was directly traceable to the economic mismanagement brought about by Marcos's dictatorship. The combination of profligate spending and wanton borrowing snowballed into a full-blown debt crisis, which exploded and tanked the economy. It was so bad that it pulled down the upward trajectory of the economy and led to two decades of missed opportunities—hence what economists call the "lost decades of Philippine development."

This book aims to debunk this "golden age" myth once and for all. Each chapter starts with a common myth or misconception about martial law and economic aspects of Marcos Sr.'s rule, then followed by a quick rebuttal. Some of these myths might appear shallow or absurd, but these are useful springboards that we will use for a deep dive into various aspects of the Marcosian economy—from the infrastructure spree and trade and industrial policy, to poverty and hunger—and provide more context and detail about the economic and political milieu of the time. The common theme threading the chapters is that the martial law years were emphatically *not* the golden age of the Philippine economy. And despite some gains in some years, we should not lose sight of the bigger picture that paints Marcos as a profligate and corrupt spender who drove the economy to bankruptcy and collapse and led millions of Filipinos to decades of suffering.

Throughout the book, the use of data from various sources is also emphasized. Contrary to the aphorism that data cannot lie, they can do so; it is not at all true that data are infallible. For instance, lots of government statistics during the martial law era—to the extent that they were published—should be taken with a huge grain of salt. In a number of instances, government officials themselves have manipulated statistics to make the economy appear more robust or resilient than it really was. Notable examples are the Central Bank's bloating of statistics about the country's international reserves and their discontinuation of a wage survey.[27] The deeper the Philippines was in crisis, the more that the regime was willing to fudge the numbers. Thus, we will make sure to compare and contrast data from various sources (including those from international groups, think tanks, and scholars) to triangulate the truth. Another good thing about data is that you don't have to take my word (or anybody's word) for it: you can always check and verify them yourself. This book will generously provide links and references to these data.

I am well aware that there is a limit to using data, especially if the purpose is to nudge people to think differently about their previously held beliefs. Many studies, in fact, show that throwing data at people is not particularly helpful in changing people's minds: people tend to clam up and hold on to their prior beliefs more even when presented with data. Data alone won't work; they need to be embedded in stories and narratives. This is not to say that we are trying to persuade anyone to change any view. My goal here is modest: I just want to contribute to the ongoing conversations by providing a book-length space in which we can collect facts that will counter the Marcosian "golden age" myth; at present, no book does that. We also do our best here to provide a clearer and more accessible presentation of facts vis-à-vis other references on martial law economics, such as extremely academic book chapters or journal articles, which most students and teachers find unreadable and inaccessible. In doing so, I hope this book is instructive, helpful, and handy not just for students and teachers, but also for casual readers and truth-seekers.

More generally, I hope that this book will help us Filipinos find common ground on which we can give a critical, fair, and honest reckoning of the Marcos dictatorship. At the very least, I hope that this book gives all of us, especially the youth, a firmer grip on the facts surrounding what really happened during that fateful episode in our history—to anchor us to the truth before our addiction to new media completely drowns us in a sea of lies and makes us collectively lose our grip on reality altogether.

June 2022
Quezon City

PART 1

CAREFREE UTOPIA

01 The Philippines was the richest country in Asia?

CLAIM 1	VERDICT
The Philippines was the richest country in Asia during the Marcos dictatorship.	FALSE

CLAIM 2	VERDICT
The Philippines was the second richest country at the time, next to Japan.	FALSE

PERHAPS NO BIGGER MARCOSIAN "GOLDEN AGE" myth exists than the one that claims that the Philippines was the "richest" country in Asia during the dictatorship. Other versions of the myth claim that we were the *second* richest country, next to Japan,[1] or that it was actually Japan that was second to us.[2]

It is easy to understand why this myth persisted. How can the Marcos family and their loyalists claim Marcos Sr.'s eternal greatness if the Philippine economy had in fact stagnated during his reign or was otherwise left in the dust by the dizzying growth of its neighbors?

This myth can be easily debunked by looking at the Philippines' economic record. To measure the size of any economy, economists have traditionally looked at gross domestic product (GDP), or the total value of all goods and services produced in the country in a given span of time. GDP measures not just total spending in the economy, but also total income—the idea being that whatever we spend becomes the income of the people we buy from. But simply comparing GDP over time and across countries can be tricky. First, different countries obviously use different currencies: the Philippines has the peso, Thailand the baht, Malaysia the ringgit, and so on. So, GDP figures need to be converted to a single currency and, in practice, this is usually the US dollar. Second, rising prices erode the value of our income over time: for all we know, GDP is increasing not because a country is indeed producing more goods and services, but just because prices are rising so fast. This is why economists prefer looking at *real* GDP, or its version that removes the effects of rising prices (otherwise known as inflation). Third, one also needs to adjust for the different costs of living across countries. If you earn the equivalent of PHP 100,000 a month in the US, that may not seem much. But if you earn the same amount in the Philippines, that goes a long way. This is why expats love going to the Philippines to spend their vacation or retirement money. In the same manner, what nations' incomes can buy in their respective jurisdictions must be controlled for.[3]

Looking at GDP alone, it is easy to see that the Philippines was not the richest country in Asia back then. Table 1.1 shows that in 1965, when Marcos first came into power, Japan was already the richest country in Asia—as far as the records tell us—followed by China, India, and Indonesia.[4] More and more economies overtook us since

TABLE 1.1 Asian economies that were richer than the Philippines in 1965, 1975, and 1985

	1965	1975	1985
In terms of real GDP	Japan China India Indonesia	Japan China India Indonesia	Japan China India Indonesia South Korea Pakistan Thailand
In terms of real GDP per person	Japan Hong Kong Singapore	Brunei Japan Macau Singapore Hong Kong Malaysia Taiwan	Brunei Macau Japan Singapore Hong Kong Taiwan South Korea Malaysia Maldives Thailand Mongolia

Source: Penn World Table 10.0
Note: Economies listed in order of decreasing GDP or GDP per person.

then: by 1985, the economies of South Korea, Pakistan, and Thailand were all larger than ours. In fact, at no point during the Marcos dictatorship was the Philippines the richest country in Asia; that is plain to see from the data.

But of course, an economy may seem large just because there are more people in it transacting day in and day out. China's economy, for example, was already large back in 1965 chiefly because it boasted a population that was 721 million strong (that figure would double by 2021, or in just 56 years). Hence, economists prefer looking at GDP divided among a country's population, otherwise known as GDP per person or GDP per capita (*capita* being Latin for "head").

Here, again, the Philippines' status among Asian countries is unremarkable. On a GDP-per-capita basis, Japan, Hong Kong, and Singapore were already richer than us in 1965. Ten years later, four more countries would be added to that list: Brunei, Macau, Malaysia, and Taiwan. And in another ten years, by 1985, even more countries became richer than us: South Korea, Maldives, Thailand, and Mongolia.

Zooming in on the countries now forming the Association of Southeast Asian Nations (ASEAN), the Philippines was in fact the region's economic leader in the 1950s.[5] Sure, income data back then was only available for the Philippines, Malaysia, and Thailand. Economic data for other countries (including Singapore and Brunei) came in only later. But, alarmingly, the Philippines steadily lost its standing in the region throughout the Marcos dictatorship. When Marcos took over the presidency in 1965, only Singapore was richer than us on a per-capita basis. Not long after, by 1968, neighboring Malaysia already overtook us. In 1984, at the height of the Philippines' severest economic crisis since World War II, Thailand outstripped us. Indonesia did so as well in 1991.

The relatively flat growth trajectory of the Philippines vis-à-vis the rest of ASEAN is self-evident in figure 1.1. Compared to our neighbors, it took us far longer to grow our economy. Our early head start in the 1950s was wasted. We lagged behind our neighbors. Fast-forward to 2019, the only countries poorer than us are the CLMV countries of

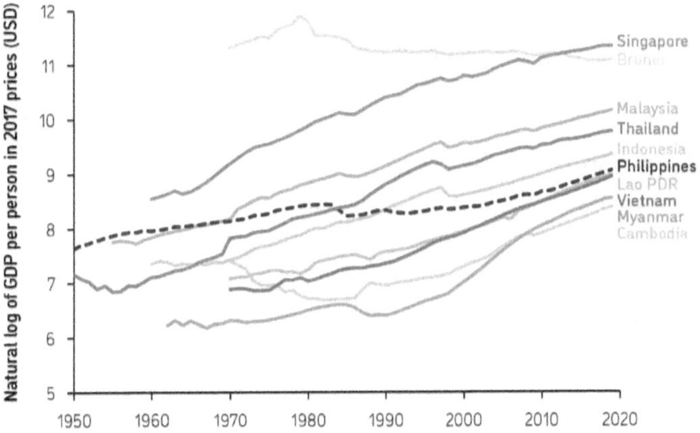

FIGURE 1.1 Income trajectory of ASEAN, 1950–2019 (Source of data: Penn World Table 10.0; data until 2019)

Cambodia, Lao People's Democratic Republic (Lao PDR), Myanmar, and Vietnam. These countries have been grouped together as the region's economic late bloomers. But at the turn of the century, these countries have quickly managed to catch up. Vietnam and Lao PDR in particular have grown spectacularly and their gap with the Philippines has narrowed a lot to the point of almost being on par with one another. (There are, in fact, projections that Vietnam has already outstripped the Philippines in 2020, in the middle of the COVID-19 pandemic.[6] Lao PDR is not far behind.)

In sum, because of the record economic contraction during martial law, the Philippines lost its standing in the region throughout the Marcos dictatorship. Apart from turning into Asia's laggard throughout the period, in 1984 and 1985, the Philippines also experienced its worst economic downturn (or recession) in its postwar economic history.

Traditionally, a country is considered in a recession if its real GDP shrinks in two consecutive quarters. But during the Marcosian economic crisis, the Philippine economy shrank in *nine* consecutive quarters. In both 1984 and 1985, the economy shrank by about seven percent each year, for a total of nearly 14 percent. The decline was so bad that it was not even toppled by the COVID-19 recession, which lasted for only five consecutive quarters (from 2020 to 2021) and where the economy shrank by *just* 9.6 percent from 2019 to 2020.

We can put things in better perspective by looking at GDP per capita (figure 1.2). From 1960 to 1982, GDP per capita rose steadily, peaking at PHP 94,102 per Filipino in 1982. But GDP per capita slipped since then and did not return to its 1982 level until *21 years later*, or after more than two decades. In other words, the average Filipino's income in 2003 was just about the same as the income they had enjoyed back in 1982. This lamentable episode in our economic history has been called the "lost decades of Philippine development"[7] and is directly attributable to the economic crisis that Marcos had allowed to happen in the last few years of his reign. Put another way, Marcos's rule of more than two decades disrupted and pulled down our otherwise promising economic trajectory.

THE FACTS ABOVE RAISE A LOT OF QUESTIONS. FOR instance, if we had just continued our growth path in the 1950s and 1960s, where would we be now? Would the Philippines be one of the largest—if not the largest—economy in ASEAN?

In 2016, my statistician friend and colleague Manuel Albis and I looked at the GDP data and strove to answer

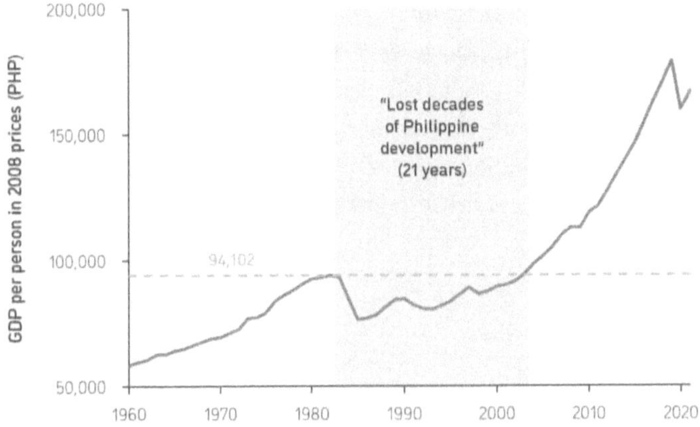

FIGURE 1.2 "Lost decades of Philippine development" (Source of GDP per capita data: Philippine Statistics Authority)

this last question.[8] We found that if the Philippines had just copied the average growth rates of its neighboring countries, our average incomes in 2014 would be about three to four times larger than it actually was—depending on the assumptions one used. Moreover, even if we had just copied the growth rate of the worst-performing neighbor in the region, our average income in 2014 would still be about 30 percent larger than its actual level. These figures are at once amazing and depressing, and these give us a sense of the lost opportunities we missed in the decades during and after the dictatorship.

In sum, the Philippines was never Asia's richest country during the Marcos years. But in the first place, why did the Philippines lag behind in Asia at large and in ASEAN in particular in the 1960s and 1970s? How come our growth trajectory was much flatter than those of our neighbors? The answers to these questions are very much rooted in the economic mismanagement and corruption of the Marcos dictatorship. The Marcoses not only deprived Filipinos of their incomes during martial law, but also future generations' potential incomes due to the regime's profligate spending and mismanagement of the Philippine economy. We will explore the details throughout this book.

02 The exchange rate was PHP 1.5 or PHP 2 per US dollar?

CLAIM 1	**VERDICT**
During the Marcos dictatorship, the peso was very strong against the US dollar, with an exchange rate of PHP 1.5 or PHP 2 per US dollar.	FALSE
CLAIM 2	**VERDICT**
A strong peso automatically means that the economy is strong.	FALSE

APOLOGISTS OF THE DICTATORSHIP HOLD DEAR the idea that the Philippine peso during the dictatorship was quite strong vis-à-vis the US dollar. They claim it was as strong as PHP 1.5 a dollar; some say it was PHP 2 a dollar.[1] A strong peso, to their minds, equated to a strong economy. And this version of the "golden age" myth has been endlessly repeated and shared on various social media platforms.

This myth can be busted on two grounds.

First, although the peso was generally strong for the most part of the dictatorship, it was actually not *that* strong

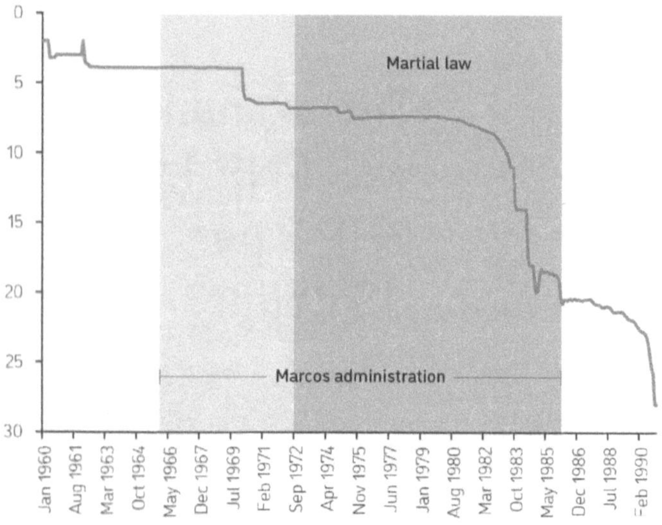

FIGURE 2.1 Peso-dollar exchange rate (PHP per USD), 1960–1990 (Source of data: Bangko Sentral ng Pilipinas)

(figure 2.1). When Marcos first took his oath as president on 30 December 1965, a US dollar was already equivalent to PHP 3.90. That's 95 to 160 percent weaker than what apologists make it out to be. Since then, the exchange rate progressively worsened: abruptly dropping to PHP 6.10 a dollar in 1970, further plummeting in the early 1980s, until it reached a low point of PHP 20.46 in February 1986—the month the Marcoses were ousted from Malacañang. Never in Marcos's many years in office did the exchange rate become PHP 1.50 or PHP 2 a dollar.

Second, and more importantly, a relatively strong peso during the Marcos years was by no means an indication that all was well or that the economy was in tip-top shape. To be fair, it is quite easy to fall for the trap of thinking that a strong currency equals a strong economy—something that should automatically be celebrated. Many people, even "experts," still get it wrong these days. But in basic economics, one is taught early on that any exchange rate is just like any other price: the price of a particular currency is expressed in terms of another. And just like any other price, there are winners and losers whenever the exchange rate rises or falls.

When the price of pork increases, for example, it is good news for pork sellers and traders—but bad news for those who *buy* pork. Likewise, when the price of the peso increases (that is, when the peso becomes scarcer or dearer with respect to the US dollar, and therefore becomes stronger), it is good news for dollar spenders (like importers of US chocolates or designer bags) or anyone who sells pesos to buy dollars: they all have to shell out fewer pesos for every dollar. But a stronger peso is necessarily bad news for dollar earners (like exporters of Cebu furniture and Zambales mangoes), or anyone who sells dollars to buy pesos: they receive fewer pesos in return for every dollar.

By this logic, we can surmise that not everyone was happy with the exceptionally strong peso during the early Marcos years—and even before that. Above anyone else, exporters were complaining and railing against it the most.

EVEN IF THE PESO WAS NOT AS LOW AS PHP 1.5 OR PHP 2 per US dollar during the Marcos years, one can still validly ask: why was the peso exceptionally strong back then compared to, say, the present?

Let's go back in time.

During American colonial rule, specifically in June 1903, new Philippine coins came to Manila from the US and the "parity of the new coins" was initially maintained at the exchange rate of PHP 2 to USD 1. This was made official when the Philippine Commission passed the Philippine Gold Standard Act in 1903 and fixed the peso-dollar at the said exchange rate.[2] This rate prevailed until after World War II, when it was again explicitly codified in the US government's 1946 Bell Trade Act, to which the Philippine government acceded. Records show that the US government's peg of the Philippine peso was actually unique at the time: the US did not fix its dollar to any other currency by law or treaty.[3]

Keeping the exchange rate that way was, in fact, rather ironic. The whole point of the Bell Trade Act was to give the Philippines "breathing space" as it transitioned from US dependence to independence, and to prevent total economic collapse while the Philippines made that transition.[4] With the Philippine economy in shambles after the war, things could easily get worse if our trading relations with the US were to collapse as well. To prop up trade, the Act stipulated that there ought to be preferential (lower) tariffs on products imported from the US.

There were three problems with the fixed exchange rate embedded in the Bell Trade Act. First, even if we wanted to, we cannot make the peso cheaper vis-à-vis the US dollar (that is, we could not devalue it). Second, between 1940 and 1949, local prices went up a lot more than they did in the US. This meant that far from the PHP 2 to USD 1 exchange rate, a more realistic rate would have been somewhere between, say, PHP 3 to PHP 4 to a dollar.[5] Third, by maintaining a fixed exchange rate—where the US dollar is made artificially cheap vis-à-vis the peso—the law incentivized Filipino traders to deal with US counterparts and not those from other trading countries.

Therefore, instead of ensuring economic independence from the US, the peso peg had an opposite effect, keeping alive the Philippine economy's dependence on America.[6] The Bell Trade Act, in other words, contravened the spirit of independence the Americans were ostensibly pushing for. If you were a self-proclaimed nationalist at the time, you would have argued against the overly strong peso.

Despite the drawbacks of the peg, it was maintained for a number of reasons. For one, the expensive peso promoted imports and discouraged exports, leading to a huge trade deficit with the US. This only means we were exporting a lot less than what we were importing from them. Despite this, the trade deficit was filled nonetheless by substantial economic aid from the US by way of "grants, credits, direct investments, and settlement of war claims"—all of which buoyed our supply of dollars or *international reserves*.[7]

Crucially, nationalist sentiments also served as an argument to keep the artificially strong peso. Even before the war, politicians came to prioritize the welfare of Filipinos above anyone else. This came to be expressed in many forms, such as the provision in the 1935 Constitution that prevented foreigners from gaining access to select industries. After the war, nationalist sentiments were further amplified and expressed in policies like the "Filipino First" policy of former president Carlos P. Garcia in the 1950s. Of course, pushing Filipino interests above anything else wasn't necessarily bad. So-called infant industries could use the special attention and care given to them by the government in order to grow and mature and become solid competitors in the global stage. The peso's peg to the dollar, owing to the Bell Trade Act, made imports cheap, and the government used the strong peso to spur the importation of cheap machinery, equipment, and raw materials from abroad—which in turn fed the factories and turned the wheels of domestic industry. In other words, nationalists realized that domestic industry (manufacturing in particular) can be boosted through massive importation, but only if the peso was kept artificially strong against the US dollar.

This trade strategy—also known as *import substitution industrialization* or ISI—was a hallmark of Philippine economic policy, especially from 1954 to 1961. Through massive importation, all sorts of reassembled or "recombined" goods were produced in Philippine soil: from consumer goods like liver spread and condensed milk, to more durable and sophisticated goods like televisions and cars.[8]

In short, although the peso's peg to the dollar initially had a negative effect, it was transformed into something that could be good for the country through ISI.

However, this further led to problems for the economy. The country's heavy dependence on imported goods from the US meant a huge demand for dollars, which, according to basic microeconomics, should result in a relative glut and weakening of the peso. But by keeping a fixed exchange rate—and preventing the normal workings of supply and demand—this meant that the Philippines was constantly on the brink of running out of dollars to pay for its imports.

This perennial dollar shortage posed a threat of an economic disaster because the country could possibly not pay its imports and other dollar obligations.[9] By 1949, in fact, the Philippines fell into a full-blown balance-of-payments crisis,[10] which prompted the government to institute a policy of import control: essentially controlling how much imported goods could be brought into the country. At the same time, the government instituted a policy of foreign exchange control:

dollar earners had to make sure that their transactions went through authorized government channels, essentially surrendering their dollars to the government. The government, in turn, allocated those dollars to payments for key or priority imports. Essentially, it would hand local industries dollars so the latter can buy raw materials from abroad needed for their growth. (As we will see later, Marcos would inherit and encounter much the same problems throughout his dictatorship, especially in the 1980s.)

At first, politicians thought that this policy of controls was sustainable; it was not. By focusing on the domestic economy's growth, such a nationalist policy came at the expense of integration into the world economy. The infant industries we gambled on remained infants and never learned to stand on their own feet.[11] And importers did not turn into exporters later on. The inward-looking trade policies of the time also shunned the inflow of foreign capital, which could have accelerated economic growth—just as our Asian neighbors (specifically the "Asian tigers") had experienced. All the while, the Philippine economy kept bleeding its dollar reserves, because the government had kept the PHP 2-per–US dollar exchange rate in the 1950s—even if the Bell Trade Act was already superseded in 1955 by the Laurel-Langley Agreement, which removed any obligation for the Philippines to follow the US-imposed exchange rate peg. We could have let go of the exchange rate peg, but we did not because of tremendous political pressure and lobbying from the country's industrialists. Politicians, too, were wary that a sudden devaluation of the peso might make imports a lot more expensive, sending inflation through the roof, and therefore hurting their political image. Abruptly letting go of the strong peso would amount to political suicide.[12]

By 1957, the Philippines experienced yet another balance-of-payments crisis, again prompting exchange rate controls and policies that discourage importation in general.[13] By then, even more people realized that the currency peg was no longer sustainable and that it was time for the government to finally devalue the peso. Exporters were the ones clamoring for such devaluation, while importers—who had enjoyed the artificially strong peso for a long time—resisted it strongly.

Controls were also evolving to become a favorite policy of politicians: although initially used to combat the drain in international reserves, such controls were later justified as "a device needed to restrain the Filipino's fondness for foreign luxury goods"—again evoking nationalist sentiments.[14] However, controls also spawned corrupt practices, as public officials leveraged import licenses to nudge certain businesspeople to avoid criticizing the government.

THIS "DECONTROL" ISSUE CAME TO BE ONE OF THE major political issues in the 1960s and was said to be a key point of debate in the 1965 elections that led to Marcos Sr.'s first term as president. Although his predecessor Diosdado Macapagal had allowed a partial decontrol of the peso, many influential groups in the business sector saw this as a lukewarm response and clamored for a stronger policy. Enter Marcos, who had promised the business sector during his presidential campaign *full* decontrol if he wins the election.

Years prior, in 1960, the Philippine government decided to pursue decontrol in phases. The most advanced stage happened right after President Macapagal was elected to office in December 1961. By January 1962, he had implemented a "freely fluctuating exchange rate" for current and capital transactions and the total abolition of exchange controls—except for a requirement that exporters surrender a fifth of their export earnings to the Central Bank at the old rate of PHP 2 to USD 1.[15]

On the whole, this decontrol turned out to be successful, halting the balance-of-payments crisis and somehow replenishing our reserves. At first, there were fears that decontrol would be inflationary: that a suddenly weaker peso (for example, the exchange rate for "essential imports" jumps from PHP 2 to PHP 3.90 per dollar) would induce more expensive imports and therefore jack up domestic prices. But the price increases after decontrol were relatively modest.[16]

For exporters, a politically important bloc, the 20-percent dollar retention scheme stuck out like a sore thumb. Right before the 1965 elections, the pivotal First National Congress of Producers and Exporters saw President Macapagal and Senate President Marcos Sr. wooing the business community by presenting their respective positions about the government's dollar retention scheme. Exporters found this restrictive and clamored for its abolition. Macapagal, too, wanted to abolish this scheme, but said that sudden decontrol would cause inflation to skyrocket. To soften the blow on prices, Macapagal proposed a new export tax. But as expected, this did not sit well with the business community.

In contrast, Marcos announced his intention to unconditionally abolish the 20-percent dollar retention scheme altogether—and hammered home his proposal with his excellent oratorical skills. Aside from promising that he would never approve the proposed export tax as long as he was Senate president, he also proclaimed that Macapagal's dollar retention scheme "should have been wiped out on July 16, 1963" and "that the administration has failed to do so is a stark accusation the President must answer before in public forum."

Marcos won the debate. As recounted by National Artist and writer-journalist Nick Joaquin:

> [President] Macapagal declared himself in favor of abolishing the 20 percent dollar retention scheme. It was one of his finest speeches: cool, clear, forthright, unemotional. It should have guaranteed him headlines. But Marcos stole the show. The President spoke in the morning, Marcos in the afternoon. And when Marcos was through, the President's speech might as well have been on crocheting.[17]

Note that while loyalists today boast about the strong peso during the Marcos years, Marcos Sr. was in fact moving (at least promising the public) to devalue the peso and make it weaker.

Notice as well in figure 2.1 that the peso-dollar exchange rate did not budge during Marcos's first term. He kept the peso artificially expensive at PHP 3.90 until his second oath-taking on 30 December 1969 and in the month after that. It was not until February 1970—right in the middle of the social upheaval of the First Quarter Storm—that the peso suddenly dropped to PHP 5.63 a dollar, and in March, it further dropped to PHP 6.1 a dollar.

This sudden devaluation was not of Marcos's own accord: it was in fact one of the preconditions laid down by the International Monetary Fund (IMF) to "stabilize" our economy in exchange for loans. During Marcos's first term as president, the government was already spending in excess of its means. Nowhere was this profligacy more obvious than in the extravagant reelection campaign of Marcos Sr. in 1969.[18] At the same time, the country kept running out of dollars because Marcos had largely continued the ISI policy of his predecessors as well as the exchange rate peg. As a result, the country ran significant deficits,[19] which Marcos's government financed by incurring huge new loans. This presented a borrowing crisis—not at the scale of the debt crisis in the 1980s, but a crisis nonetheless. The IMF agreed to intervene and lend us much-needed dollars, but on the condition that the Marcos government let go of its unsustainable exchange rate peg, which was the ultimate reason for the chronic dollar shortages. Hence, the peso was significantly devalued in 1970. Since then, Marcos's economic managers shifted from a fixed exchange rate to a "managed float": the exchange rate would still be relatively steady, but it was partially allowed to change with the ebb and flow of supply and demand.[20]

The 1970 peso devaluation was not without a price. By making imports more expensive, such a policy led to a massive spike of inflation that eroded people's incomes and wages—thus feeding further into the growing sense of discontent of Filipinos (which Marcos would later leverage for his declaration of martial law). The huge spike in prices in the 1970s (which was compounded by powerful typhoons like Titang and Yoling, as well as world oil price hikes) did not help promote exports: although the peso was weakening (and, in theory, helping promote exports), prices at home were rising much faster, making the *real* or inflation-adjusted exchange rate effectively stronger in the process (thus making exports even less attractive than before). The cycle would be repeated more than a decade later: the Marcos dictatorship racked up even huger sums of debt. And in the 1980s, the IMF would intervene once again to stabilize the economy, ordering yet another round of significant peso devaluation in 1983 and 1984—leading to another round of economic crisis that was worse than before.

IN SUM, DURING THE MARCOS YEARS, THE Philippine peso was never as strong as boasted by today's loyalists and fanatics. Marcos kept the peso artificially strong far longer than needed and his refusal to devalue it much earlier led to abrupt devaluations that spelled economic misery for Filipinos.

Interestingly, Marcos's economic managers (including economist Gerardo Sicat) advocated for a weaker peso to promote the country's export industries. But Marcos failed to abide by his advisers' proposal:[21] he realized that an artificially strong peso helped boost the revenues and profits of the import-dependent businesses to which he appointed his cronies (primarily family and friends). In other words, the fixed exchange rate provided a cozy environment in which the businesses of Marcos's cronies thrived. By implication, Marcos himself thrived in that environment, too, since he milked these myriad businesses in one way or another. Is it any wonder the peso remained artificially strong throughout the dictatorship—like a zombie that just refuses to die?

03 "Golden age" of agriculture?

CLAIM 1 Marcos established the International Rice Research Institute (IRRI).	**VERDICT** FALSE
CLAIM 2 The Philippines was the world's top exporter of rice during the Marcos dictatorship. Alternatively, the country was a rice exporter during the Marcos years, but became a rice importer starting with former president Corazon Aquino's term.	**VERDICT** FALSE
CLAIM 3 Marcos's agricultural credit program called Masagana 99 was an unbridled success.	**VERDICT** FALSE
CLAIM 4 Marcos introduced the tilapia to the Philippines.	**VERDICT** FALSE

THE SUPPOSED CONTRIBUTIONS OF MARCOS TO Philippine agriculture hold a special place in the hearts of loyalists and apologists. They consistently paint a picture of a flourishing agricultural sector during the dictatorship.

The son of the dictator himself, Bongbong Marcos, posted in a vlog on 11 September 2021 (on the occasion of Marcos Sr.'s 104th birthday) that his father had established the International Rice Research Institute (IRRI) in Los Baños, Laguna. Bongbong said, in Filipino, "First and foremost, the people need to eat so [my father] formed the IRRI, International Rice Research Institute, to research what is the best seedling, the best technology, expanding irrigation systems."[1]

Meanwhile, supporters claim that the Philippines was the world's top exporter of rice and sugar at the time of the dictatorship. Others even claim that from being a top rice exporter, the country was degraded to being a rice importer during the administration of former president Corazon Aquino.

One of the dictator's daughters, Imee, claimed in a Senate hearing that the Masagana 99 program of her father was a rousing "success"—only to be rebutted in public by former president Rodrigo Duterte's finance secretary Carlos Dominguez III, who once served as agriculture secretary during the time of Aquino.

Finally, Marcos's supposed wonders extend to fisheries too: some say that he was even the one who introduced the tilapia in the country.[2]

LET'S DEBUNK THE IRRI CLAIM FIRST. THE IRRI was in fact established by the Ford and Rockefeller Foundations in 1960, a full five years before Marcos was elected to his first term as president. Marcos, though, was the one who signed in November 1985 the executive order creating the Philippine Rice Research Institute (PhilRice) located in Muñoz, Nueva Ecija.[3] PhilRice was meant to focus on more localized issues in the Philippines' rice industry (vis-à-vis IRRI's more international scope). But the establishment of PhilRice took so long. According to M. S. Swaminathan, former IRRI director-general from 1982 to 1988 and considered as the "Father of the Indian Green Revolution," Marcos resisted for a long time the idea of setting up a *national* rice research institute, thinking "it was IRRI's responsibility to look after the country's problems too, which were quite localized with so many thousand islands making up the Philippines."[4]

While Marcos hardly had anything to do with the creation of the IRRI, he did have an interest in making the Philippines rice self-sufficient during his first term as president. This was by no means a unique aspiration, for his predecessors aspired for it as well.

In 1966, IRRI scientists developed a new rice variety called IR8-288-3 (later renamed as simply IR8), which produced significantly larger yields. Whereas average yields then were about one metric ton per hectare, IR8 produced an average of 9.4 metric tons per hectare (at one trial, it even produced as much as 10.3 metric tons per hectare). Marcos got wind of this remarkable development and reportedly flew by helicopter to the IRRI in June of that year.[5] He since requested the ramping up of production of IR8 seeds, and not long after, thousands of Filipino farmers were flocking to the IRRI to get seeds of their own. This rapid adoption of modern rice varieties is reflected in figure 3.1: from nearly none in 1966 to almost 50 percent of farmers by 1970, or in the span of just four years. Also, there was a steady and

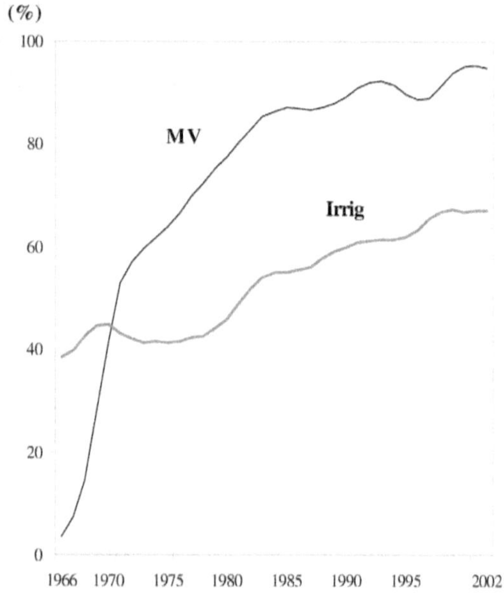

FIGURE 3.1 Trends in adoption of modern rice varieties and rate of irrigated areas, 1966–2002 (Reprinted from Arsenio M. Balisacan and Majah-Leah V. Ravago, "The Rice Problem in the Philippines: Trends, Constraints, and Policy Imperatives," MPRA Paper, no. 24865, 2003, 17.)

significant increase in the total area of rice farms from 1970 to about 1976 (figure 3.2).

Apart from the adoption of modern varieties (IR8 was later called "miracle rice"), it cannot be denied that there was, at the time, a sizable expansion of the irrigated rice farms across the country: from a little over 30 percent in 1965 to about 44 percent in 1970. Note, however, that the expansion of irrigated rice lands later on was slower than it is touted to be: by 1985, right before the dictator's ouster, a

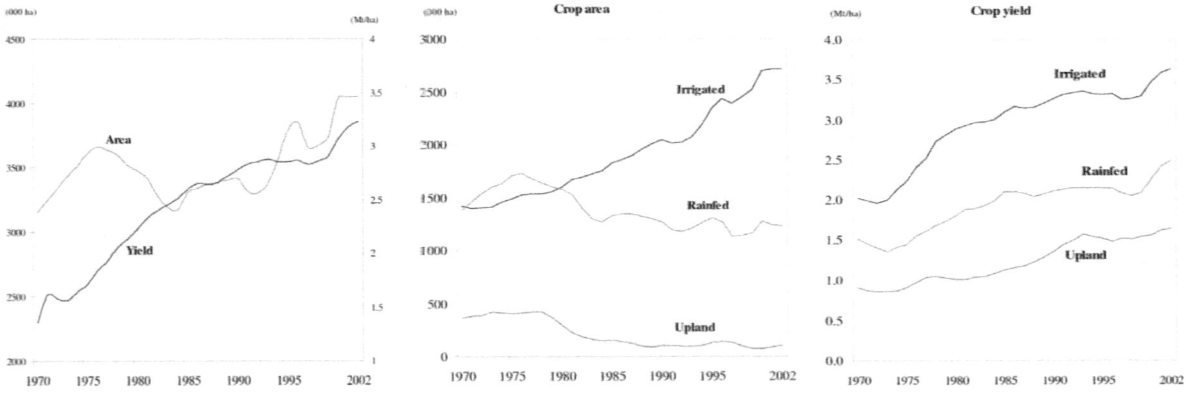

FIGURE 3.2 Trends in rice area and yield, 1970–2002 (Reprinted from Arsenio M. Balisacan and Majah-Leah V. Ravago, "The Rice Problem in the Philippines: Trends, Constraints, and Policy Imperatives," MPRA Paper, no. 24865, 2003, 16.)

little more than half of all rice farms were irrigated (figure 3.1). Still, there was an undeniable rapid increase in the crop yield of irrigated farmlands vis-à-vis rainfed farms and uplands.

Miracle rice, coupled with the expansion of irrigation, naturally led to a boom in rice production. Whereas total production grew by only 2.1 percent from 1960 to 1965, that growth more than doubled to 4.6 percent on average between 1965 and 1980. We even produced enough rice to become a net exporter of rice in some years: from 1968 to 1970, and then again in 1977 through 1983 (figure 3.3).[6] So, there's an iota of truth to the idea that we exported rice during martial law.

It was also during Ferdinand Sr.'s first term that the government made a serious commitment toward agrarian reform, especially farmers' ownership of the rice or corn lands they tilled.[7] A mere three days after martial law was declared, Marcos signed a presidential decree declaring the entire country under land reform.[8] By 21 October of the same year, Marcos signed Presidential Decree No. 27, which stipulated that tenants could own three hectares of the land that they till if it is irrigated, and five if non-irrigated. Beneficiary farmers had to join farmers' cooperatives through which payments for their land will be coursed.[9] Moreover, landowners can own or retain no more than seven hectares of their land (also called the "retention limit"). This is much lower than the previous 75-hectare retention limit.[10]

DESPITE THESE GAINS IN AGRICULTURE, IT'S EASY to overstate Marcos's contribution to Philippine rice production during his time.

First, although we exported rice in nine out of the two-decade dictatorship of Marcos, we still imported rice in

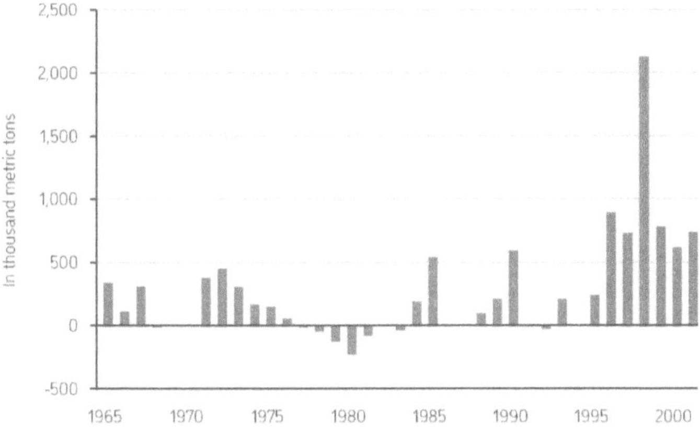

FIGURE 3.3 Amount of imported rice, 1965–2001 (Source of data: Arsenio M. Balisacan and Majah-Leah V. Ravago, "The Rice Problem in the Philippines: Trends, Constraints, and Policy Imperatives," Munich Personal RePEc Archive Paper Paper, no. 24865, 2003.)

eleven other years. In addition, we never became a "top rice exporter" during the dictatorship, as boasted by loyalists. According to Dawe (2002), we never made it to the list of top ten rice exporters in 1965 to 1981, or even during the periods before or after that (see table 3.1). Sure, there were spurts of high rice production, but they were short-lived. Marcos reduced—but by no means eradicated—the country's need to import rice.

One of the biggest reasons for this is that the Philippines inherently does not have a comparative advantage in rice production, contrary to what politicians or activists claim. For instance, we do not have the mighty Mekong River of our continental ASEAN neighbors, which naturally irrigates rice lands there and thus brings costs of production down. Seeing that no amount of government policy can change this

TABLE 3.1 Top 10 rice exporters in the world (in terms of million tons of milled rice)

	1950–1954	1965–1981	1985–1998
Countries	Myanmar Thailand USA China Cambodia Egypt Italy Vietnam Pakistan Brazil	USA Thailand China Myanmar Pakistan Italy Egypt Japan Australia North Korea	Thailand USA Vietnam India Pakistan China Italy Australia Uruguay Myanmar
Share of top 10 countries to total world rice exports	80 percent	71 percent	72 percent

Source: David Dawe, "The Changing Structure of the World Rice Market, 1950–2000," *Food Policy* 27 (2002): 355–70.
Note: Countries listed in order of decreasing rice exports.

fact, some economists think that maybe we ought to disabuse ourselves of the delusion of achieving rice self-sufficiency to begin with. Nevertheless, rice self-sufficiency has long and always been a favorite goal of politicians. Even Marcos himself was wont to proclaim that his administration had combatted the chronic food shortage. As early as his third State of the Nation Address in 1968, he prematurely said:

> We have succeeded in solving our chronic food shortage. The country has attained self-sufficiency

> in rice and corn one year ahead of the deadline set for it by our administration. This fulfills a historic dream of several generations of Filipinos who equated the solution of the rice problem with the nation's self-esteem.[11]

This is perhaps the source of the myth that is circulating today.

Second, some of Marcos's interventions in the rice market backfired. Most notably, three days after he declared martial law—aside from declaring the entire country as a land reform area—he established the National Food Authority or NFA (originally called the National Grains Authority). Essentially, the NFA served as the country's monopoly in rice importation; it was the only agency that could bring in rice from abroad. If the NFA foresaw that there would be a shortage of rice in the near future (say, due to harvest failures or typhoons), it would import lots of rice to temper its price. If there was no such impending shortage, NFA would not import as much to prevent the price of rice from hitting rock bottom and harming local farmers. The idea is to create a supply buffer and protect ordinary rice consumers (who comprise virtually all Filipinos) from the vagaries of rice prices.

However, the NFA's ability to forecast rice supply and demand has been far from perfect, and has chronically led to over- and under-importation (and, therefore, rice surpluses and shortages) over the years. To the extent that the NFA can stabilize rice prices through its import monopoly, its business model of buying high and selling low is a recipe for economic losses: the NFA has always incurred huge losses and has more often than not been on the brink of bankruptcy. It always had to rely on enormous subsidies from the national government in order to survive. In hindsight, many economists share the sentiment that it was not worth all the trouble it has caused.[12]

Chronic rice shortages were, in fact, a thing during martial law, and these persisted several months after the disastrous floods of 1972, primarily due to a long, drawn-out drought. There were "block long double lines of people" emanating from guarded government trucks that rationed rice. Marcos ordered the military to control rice and corn stocks, and the government was also ordered to stop selling pure rice and instead sell a mix of rice and corn.[13] On media, Filipinos were being told to consume this mix, lest rice supplies dwindled too quickly. On radio and TV, government propaganda blared that even celebrities were doing their part for the New Society, implying the rest of the population should follow suit. One ad said: "The Philippines' top basketball stars eat corn grits. Former world lightweight boxing champ Flash Elorde and popular songstress Pilita Corrales also like the cereal."[14]

Unsurprisingly, there have since been many calls to abolish the monopoly of the NFA—having failed to serve its purpose—and instead convert into tariffs (that is, to "tariffy") its import quotas. When the Philippines joined the World Trade Organization in 1995, we committed to such a policy. But the government ended up postponing tariffication multiple times due to intense lobbying from vested interests. It was not until the signing of the Rice Tariffication Act by President Rodrigo Duterte in February 2019 that the NFA's monopoly power was removed, leaving rice imports largely to the free market.[15] As a consequence, rice ceased to be a major contributor to food inflation.

ANOTHER PROBLEM THAT LED TO THE disappointing agriculture record during martial law is that public investments in irrigation fell drastically in the 1980s (figure 3.4)—all thanks to the debt and economic crisis caused by Marcos's mishandling of the economy. This limited any further rise in rice productivity during the period.

Apart from the slowdown in irrigation, other problems riddled Marcos's land reform program, which yielded too few achievements compared to the grand declarations and targets of the regime. For one, its scope was quite limited: Marcos's Presidential Decree No. 27 on agrarian reform covered only about 1.42 million hectares, or less than 15 percent of the 9.7 million hectares of cultivable land across the country. One big reason is that the decree covered only rice and corn lands that were tenanted.[16] In contrast, lands devoted to coconuts, sugar, and bananas, among others—not coincidentally, sectors that were dominated by Marcos's cronies and served as significant dollar earners through exports—were conveniently exempted from land reform. So, even if Marcos appeared to be eroding the market power of huge rice and corn players, he was, at the same time, propping up even larger monopolies in other crops.

Another reason was that PD 27 stipulated that landowners shall retain seven hectares of their land[17] (this retention limit was deemed a "lucky number" and Marcos was then on his seventh year as president). Meanwhile, farmers could own no more than three or five hectares (if irrigated or non-irrigated, respectively). This retention limit was meant to avoid the awkward situation where tenants end up with more land than their previous landowners. For example—and this was the actual example used in a memo to Marcos dated 17 October 1972[18]—if a tenant is

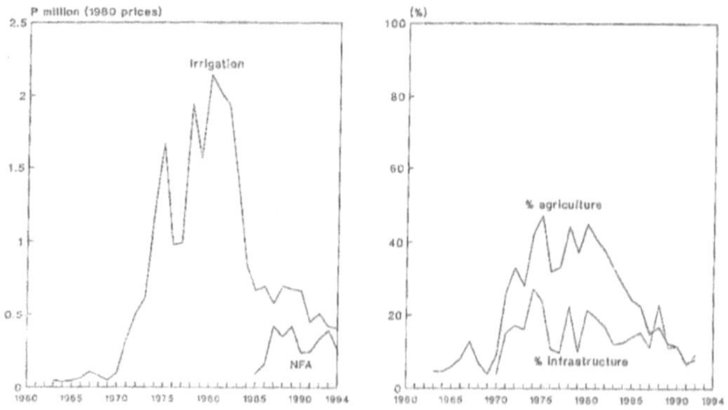

FIGURE 3.4 Irrigation investments (in million PHP) and percent share of irrigation in total infrastructure and agriculture budgets, 1963–1994 (Reprinted from Cristina C. David and Arsenio M. Balisacan, "Philippine Rice Supply Demand: Prospects and Policy Implications," Philippine Institute for Development Studies Discussion Paper Series, no. 95-28, October 1995, 26.)

cultivating 17 hectares, and if one relied solely on the seven-hectare retention limit, the tenant farmers could end up with 10 hectares. But the retention limit—which basically excluded all lands no larger than seven hectares from land reform—meant that more than half (55 percent) of farmers were denied any right to land reform—"condemning them, at best, to a permanent leasehold system."[19] Later, in 1973, Marcos would even increase the retention limit to 24 hectares to curry favor among "the economic middle class, which we are trying to build and therefore deserve as much consideration as the tenants themselves."[20] This further weakened Marcos's agrarian reform program.

Finally, agrarian reform was not so viable given failures in other aspects of agricultural support—including the slow adoption of technologies, declining infrastructure, and failures in supervised agricultural credit. Indeed, it is hard to imagine the rice production boom had IRRI not developed its “miracle rice” and other high-yielding varieties. This development reduced any impetus on the part of government to beef up research into high-yield rice varieties and eventually led to a decline of rice research in the Philippines.[21] The Marcos government focused its research instead on other crops, and rather than improve rice research, it focused on access to high-yielding varieties and low-cost pesticides, mainly by way of the credit program called Masagana 99.

FAST-FORWARD TO THE PRESENT, IMEE MARCOS claims that her father’s Masagana 99 was a “success.” During one Senate hearing she presided in May 2020—concerning the Duterte government’s planned aid or stimulus package for businesses felled by the COVID-19 pandemic—Imee flexed that:

> During Masagana 99 in the early 70s, there was a very effective use of commercial banks, rural banks, and even cooperative banks. And I believe that scheme will truly work, however, perhaps we can consider enlarging the national government stake even in that regard.[22]

But finance secretary Carlos “Sonny” Dominguez III quickly rebutted her by saying that during his stint as agriculture secretary in the first Aquino administration, he “cleaned up the mess of Masagana 99,” which he claimed led to the bankruptcy of 800 rural banks which then had to be rescued by government. (It is hard to gauge Dominguez’s accuracy, though: when Imee answered that, at the least, Masagana 99 led to the country's exportation of rice, Dominguez said, "Ma'am, no, we never exported rice" [in fact, in some years we did].)[23]

Research shows that far from being a rousing success all throughout, Masagana 99 had an early success but eventually proved to be unsustainable. (It died a quiet death in the 1980s.)

Where did Masagana 99 come from anyway?

Despite the initial spurt of rice production from 1968 to 1970 (which resulted in a few rare years when we exported, rather than imported, rice), the Philippines suffered a string of deadly typhoons in the early 1970s as well as severe pest infestations in 1972. In a bid to recover lost productivity, in May 1973—not even a year since martial law was declared—the Marcos regime launched Masagana 99. Although ostensibly a way to boost rice productivity and achieve self-sufficiency among farmers, Masagana 99 was "essentially a credit program" according to economist Emmanuel Esguerra of the UP School of Economics.[24] The government provided loans to farmers to enable them to access a "package of technology" to farmers, consisting not just of seeds of high-yielding rice varieties, but also pesticides, herbicides, and other supplies. Well-meaning as it was, Masagana 99 turned out to be unsustainable chiefly because of the farmer-beneficiaries' inability to repay their loans. From a repayment rate of more than 93 percent in May–October 1973, it went down to as low as 45.8 percent in November–April 1979. According to one report, as much as 80 percent of the loans were never recovered and Masagana 99 inadvertently transformed from an agricultural credit program to a dole-out (actually, many farmers perceived it as such).[25]

There were many possible reasons for the huge non-repayment of loans.[26] The more obvious ones would include natural disasters, insufficient use of the inputs, lack of post-harvest storage facilities, or even misuse of the borrowed money. But there are even bigger problems. First, the lack of serious land reform capped the productivity spike that any small farmer could achieve with their borrowed money: farmers could not repay well if they were beholden and obligated to turnover their harvests to their landlords. Second, a vicious cycle was at play: non-payment of farmers disqualified them from future loans, and, in turn, rural banks facing high delinquency rates could not get help from the Central Bank. Third, there was an element of corruption as well: National Scientist Gelia Castillo documented anecdotes of rural banks coming up with "fake" or "ghost" borrowers in a bid to swindle money from the project. Fourth, the heavy reliance on pesticides ironically led to outbreaks of new pests—defeating the purpose of killing them in the first place.[27] In short, Masagana 99 was plagued with unintended consequences.

BEFORE WE CLOSE THIS CHAPTER, ONE MORE quick fact-check: Marcos did not introduce the tilapia to the Philippines. Instead, biologist Deogracias Villadolid did in 1950 (specifically, the variety introduced was the Mozambique tilapia or *Oreochromis mossambicus*[28])—in his capacity as former director of the Bureau of Fisheries. Marcos became president in 1965, or 15 years after the tilapia's introduction.

To recap, Marcos did not establish the IRRI, we were not the world's top exporter of rice during his time, we were more often an importer of rice than an exporter, Masagana

99 was not an unmitigated success, and Marcos did not introduce the tilapia to the country. Sure, there were initial gains in rice production (borne by the spread of high-yielding varieties developed by the IRRI as well as irrigation projects), but such gains were short-lived. In addition, research into new rice varieties slowed down, the regime failed to sustain the spread of irrigation projects, and the lack of serious land reform diminished the effectiveness of other programs like the credit subsidies of Masagana 99.

Fast-forward to 2022, Bongbong Marcos entered the presidency by taking on the position of agriculture secretary, and with a popular campaign promise of bringing down the cost of rice to PHP 20 per kilogram. But economists and agriculture experts say that this is simply impossible and that it can only be achieved through very costly subsidies that will only bring the public coffers to its knees—strained as they already are, with government facing a record debt of nearly PHP 13 trillion in the first half of 2022.[29] Bongbong's promise (which he later called an "aspiration"[30]) also comes at a time when global food costs are skyrocketing.

Meanwhile, on 29 November 2022, and in what seems to be a nod to the agricultural "golden age" myth, Bongbong visited the IRRI for the first time during his presidency and recreated the famous photograph of his father's 1966 IRRI visit alongside then US president Lyndon Johnson.[31] This happened while the Philippines is grappling with a nearly 14-year-high inflation rate, driven primarily by food prices.[32]

To this day, people are working hard to make it appear that Marcos Sr. was a godsend for Philippine agriculture and, currently, are attempting to extend the same title to the son. But in reality, neither is a godsend.

04 Marcos invented the Nutribun? No one went hungry?

CLAIM 1 Marcos invented the Nutribun and it was his project.	**VERDICT** FALSE
CLAIM 2 No one went hungry during the dictatorship.	**VERDICT** FALSE
CLAIM 3 Corazon Aquino sold Marcos's Food Terminal Incorporated after EDSA 1.	**VERDICT** MISSING CONTEXT

IF YOU LISTEN ONLY TO THE LOYALISTS, YOU WOULD think that the Marcos dictatorship was nothing short of a utopia where everything was okay and nobody went hungry. Hence, there exists a plethora of hunger-related myths.

Specifically, many loyalists allege that Marcos himself was responsible for the development of the bread called Nutribun, which supposedly helped eradicate hunger.[1] One absurd myth even went on to say that in December 1969, when the Marcoses were in the US, Ferdinand Sr. handed

Nutribun to a "skinny child begging for food" in a park—and that child would later grow up to be no less than American basketball star Michael Jordan.[2] Amusingly, the myth somehow implies that Marcos had a hand in the growth and later success of Michael Jordan. (However, records show that Marcos was nowhere in the US at that time.)

The fact that many ordinary Filipinos still strongly link the name of Marcos to the Nutribun (and vice versa) may be partly because the Marcoses themselves have propagated the Nutribun myth. In the 2019 campaign trail, for instance, the word "Nutribun" was plastered on the posters of Imee Marcos (who ended up winning a senate seat). And after her brother Bongbong won the presidency, Imee went around Cebu and Davao to give out Nutribuns with her name on it.[3] At a Davao event, Imee claimed:

> No child went hungry then because there was an abundance of Nutribun. You can't even finish it. And when you eat it, it's like cement in your tummy; there's also a bit of Klim milk. The grandmothers and mommies are still fully charged up to now because they're powered by Nutribun.[4]

Indeed, the more general yet extreme myth that is now circulating in social media is that no one went hungry at all during martial law.

TO BEGIN WITH, THE NUTRIBUN WAS NOT MARCOS'S project or invention. Its recipe was developed back in 1967 by nutritionists at the Virginia Polytechnic Institute and State University, at the behest of the US Agency for International Development (USAID). The Nutribun was meant to be a protein- and nutrient-rich bread that was not costly to produce—a "ready-to-eat complete meal." Not only was it packed with nutrients (containing as much as 500 calories and 17 grams of protein apiece), but it was quite hefty, too (about six to seven times the mass of a regular *pandesal*).[5]

Nutribun was introduced in the Philippines in 1970 and quickly became a mainstay of the Marcos regime's relief and anti-hunger programs. For instance, in 1971, Marcos introduced a four-year Food and Nutrition Program with school-based feeding at its center. The USAID, in cooperation with the Philippine government, handed out Nutribuns (which were baked either at schools or at local bakeries) to stunted or malnourished first- to fourth-grade schoolchildren.[6] Similarly, in the aftermath of devastating typhoons that struck the country in 1971 and 1972, the government handed out Nutribuns to communities as part of its disaster relief. At one point, as many as eight million Nutribuns were airdropped to feed a million people affected by the 1972 "Great Flood."[7]

But even if originally a project of the USAID, the Marcoses brazenly took credit for the Nutribun. For instance, a number of reports indicated that during relief drives after devastating typhoons, plastic bags containing Nutribuns bore labels like "Courtesy of Imelda Marcos—Tulungan Project" to make it appear that Imelda had anything to do with Nutribun.[8] Other local politicians followed suit and stamped their names on it, too. (This brings to mind Imee's recent Nutribun sorties.)

Generations of students would grow up being fed Nutribun (sometimes paired with Nestlé's powdered milk called Klim), as it was distributed well into the 1980s. In fact, it was still being distributed in schools as late as 1997. Some of the staunchest defenders of the Nutribun today are those who ate it as kids during the regime, fondly remembering it as a recess snack handed to them by their teachers. But contrary to popular belief, the Nutribun was not always free: elementary students had to pay PHP 0.10 for each piece, with the price more than doubling to PHP 0.25 apiece by the mid-1980s. Over time, its size and nutritional content also dwindled: from 500 calories to just about 250. Part of the reason for this shrinkage is that the original Nutribun was "too much to eat at one time" by small kids: they would usually bring home whatever they have not eaten at school, to be shared later with family members. Even its flavor was variable: the Nutribun's recipe was allowed to vary across regions depending on local supplies and tastes (e.g., sugar was replaced with molasses in Iloilo). But in other instances, students would say it was not tasty at all. Others remember discovering weevils (*bukbok*) in their Nutribuns.[9]

THE ISSUE OF WHETHER THE NUTRIBUN WAS A project of Marcos or not is less important than the claims that Nutribun eradicated hunger in the Philippines and that there was no hunger at all during the dictatorship. The truth is, despite the Nutribun, hunger persisted during the Marcos years. We even experienced at that time what can be considered the country's last famine.

We only need to look at the country's hunger and malnutrition situation in the dying days of martial law. In August 1985, the USAID came out with a report offering recommendations on when and how to phase out its food assistance program in the country through its Food for Peace Program.[10] They concluded that in 1985—the last full year of Marcos Sr. in power—"malnutrition remains a problem in the Philippines." Sure, the researchers found a "significant reduction" in the prevalence of underweight or wasted preschool children from 1978 to 1982. But they also found, based on limited evidence, a "regression in nutritional status" in 1984 due to greater prevalence of underweight children. This coincided with the country's severest economic crisis then.

Meanwhile, in a study by the Philippine Nutritional Surveillance System, also in 1985, 22 percent of preschool children were found to be severely underweight, 14 percent wasted, and 25 percent stunted.[11]

In a separate 1987 study, renowned pediatrician and National Scientist Fe del Mundo and colleagues found that there was "an overall improvement in the health and nutritional status of children 0–19 years in the decade 1973 to 1983" but qualified that this improvement "may not be impressive nor highly significant."[12]

Even in the relatively better year of 1982, the USAID found that one in three Filipino households did not meet the recommended calories, and per capita energy intake was only 89 percent of the recommended allowance. Worse, among children aged 0 to 6, 17 percent were underweight, more than a fifth (20.6 percent) were stunted, and 1.6 percent were severely malnourished. The situation was worse for school-age children (aged 7 to 14): 24.6 percent of them were stunted, while 5.8 percent were severely malnourished. Across the regions, there was a general reduction in the prevalence of undernourished children from 1978 to 1982, except in Ilocos (of all places), Central Luzon, Northern Mindanao, Southern Mindanao, and Metro Manila. But between 1982 to 1984, there was a regression across all the country's 11 regions, except in Eastern Visayas. The USAID report noted, this "may be taken as evidence of regression in nutritional status," and may be "linked to the decline in economic well-being."[13]

Whether it was possible at all for Marcos to eradicate hunger is another issue. After all, even today in the 21st century, hunger remains a big problem in the Philippines: about a third of children under the age of five remain stunted.[14] But it is clear as day that Marcos had miserably failed to eradicate hunger during his time. In fact, in many ways, hunger even worsened, especially at the height of the economic crises that his mismanagement had precipitated.

Interestingly, in the 1970s, high inflation drove high the demand for alternative food sources. This led to the invention and popularity of (admittedly tasty) street food made from discarded animal parts, such as *isaw* (chicken or pig intestines), *betamax* (grilled coagulated pig blood), *walkman* (pig ears), and *adidas* (chicken feet).[15] Meanwhile, as the economic crisis worsened still in the 1980s, the *Manila Bulletin* was even publishing recipes for "earthworm spaghetti," made of actual cultured earthworms—and this was promoted by Imelda herself. (One granduncle-in-law of mine told me that his brother cultivated earthworms around this time, but the business failed because there was no big market for earthworm as food.) Imelda was more successful, though, in promoting TVP or textured vegetable protein as a meat alternative in the government's Kadiwa stores.[16]

Another thing that Imelda introduced in the early 1980s was the golden *kuhol* or apple snail, meant "to augment the protein needs of the population."[17] But soon it turned out to be a major pest that plagued many areas, including Nueva Ecija, the "rice granary of the Philippines," the famous Ifugao Rice Terraces (where locals reported that the golden kuhol resulted in rice yield loss ranging from 41 to 50 percent[18]), and even—ironically enough—Ilocos Norte.[19] In 2000, during his time as Ilocos Norte governor, Marcos Jr. had spent PHP 2 million to combat the golden kuhol infestation in the province's rice fields. Among his supposed strategies was the unleashing of an "army of ducks."[20]

NOWHERE WAS HUNGER DURING THE dictatorship more apparent and acute than during the famine that devastated Negros Island in the 1980s. In 1985, as many as a million people in Negros Occidental went hungry. But the poorest victims of widespread hunger were children: when Oxfam America started a feeding program there, they found that about 100,000 children were malnourished.[21] By 1986, one in five Negrense children was "seriously malnourished," according to a former overseas director of Oxfam America.[22] Meanwhile, in a 1987 report of a US Congress's appropriations committee, it was reported that:

> There are approximately 2.2 million Filipinos living on Negros. An estimated 40 percent of the children under age 14 (nearly 350,000) suffer from malnutrition, according to a 1985 survey conducted by the National Nutrition Council of the Philippines. The Bacolod City Hospital reported an increase of 67 percent in infant deaths in the first four months of 1985 over the same period in 1984. Infant mortality soared to nearly double the national rate, and most of the deaths stem from malnutrition.[23]

Grim statistics are one thing, but grim photos are another. One of the most famous photos to come out of the Negros Island famine was the emaciated profile of Joel Abong, photographed by Kim Komenich on 4 May 1985 at the Corazon Locsin Montelibano Memorial Regional Hospital in Negros Occidental. Joel's father had lost his job as a sugarcane farmer, like so many others at the time. Joel died in the same year.[24] As reported by veteran journalist Inday Espina-Varona, whose mother was the chief of pediatrics at the provincial hospital, where some of these emaciated children were hospitalized:[25]

> Joel had pneumonia and tuberculosis. He was brought in with bones so brittle doctors had to wrap padding around his limbs. Joel's body was the size of a baby. Stringy hair the yellow-brown of severe malnutrition lay limp on a head that seemed grotesquely big. A rattling sound accompanied every breath. His father was one of those who had fled the cane fields. On an island where people joked about shoveling money from the ground, Joel's family had literally starved.[26]

On the opposite page is a photo of a nine-year-old girl from Bacolod who died days after the photo was taken (figure 4.1).[27] Some wonder why only a handful of photos of emaciated children seem to have come from that crisis. But back then media was controlled by the dictatorship, and the handful of photos we see today came from independent observers and aid workers who happened to be there at the time, helping in the relief efforts.

Our househelp, Josephine Tabago, happened to be a preteen at Binalbagan, Negros Occidental—more than 60

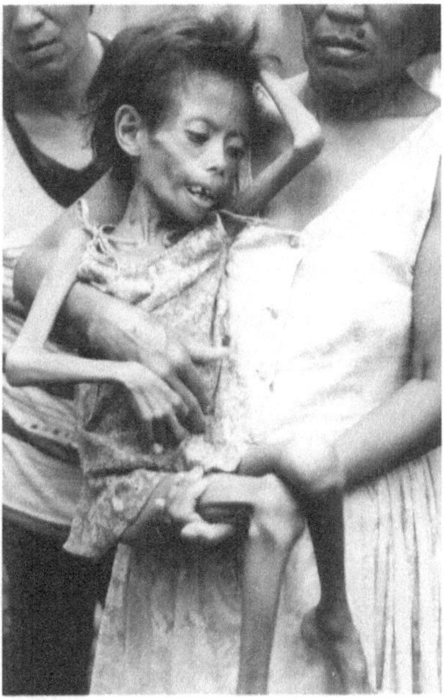

FIGURE 4.1
A victim of the Negros Island famine. Is this the so-called "golden age"? (Photo reprinted with permission from John Silva)

kilometers away from the capital Bacolod City—during the early 1980s. She vividly remembers how hard life was back then. What struck her the most was the abject hunger. For one thing, as she recounts, the government-subsidized NFA rice was extremely foul-smelling when cooked, although it looked nice on the outside. When cooking the rice, it was as if the vapors could induce an asthma attack. No one in their family, including her siblings, wanted to eat NFA rice. So they all had to resort to alternatives such as yellow corn (which was good for some time, but is not a long-term substitute for rice), sorghum (which they made into porridge, although it had a thick husk that was difficult to eat), camote, and even sugarcane (toting small knives, she and her friends would go into the fields and cut sugarcane, peel the outer layer, and snack on it). Luckily, Josephine and her family dodged the worst effects of the Negros famine. But she remembers being exceptionally thin then. Looking back, she could not pinpoint how things had regressed to that point. She also does not recall ever asking her parents how come they were so hungry then and why it was so hard to eat decent rice—let alone a full meal.

Rife hunger in Negros (and other parts of the country) was said to have contributed to the rise of insurgency in the provinces. In Negros alone, there were about 30 to 50 armed members of the New People's Army (NPA) in 1982. But in 1985, their ranks were said to have swelled to about a thousand.[28] Of course, another big reason was the pushback against the increasingly abusive military, which often struck fear in the hearts of local communities.[29] Nationwide, the ranks of the NPA undoubtedly swelled: from about 7,900 members in 1972—as specifically mentioned in Marcos's martial law declaration—to about 20,000 or 24,000 by the mid-1980s.[30] In this sense, it is often quipped that Marcos was in fact the best or greatest recruiter of the NPA.

It is also interesting to note that the annual MassKara Festival in Bacolod City was borne out of the tragedies experienced by the Negrenses in the 1980s. First, on 22 April 1980, there was the famous MV *Don Juan* tragedy, where almost 200 people died when the passenger ship (which departed from Bacolod) collided with an oil tanker off Mindoro.[31] Then there were the sugar prices that dropped precipitously in the years before 1980, which spelled a huge loss of income for most Negrenses. During the MassKara Festival, Negrenses participate in parades wearing masks of all sorts of designs and colors—symbolizing how they "mask" the intense grief that they had to endure decades ago.

This is precisely why some people protested when President Marcos Jr. was made the guest of honor at the 2022 MassKara Festival. The president even said in his speech: "The MassKara Festival was born of a very sad period in the history of Bacolod. The MassKara Festival was born in the eighties when world sugar prices crashed and with the attendant effect to the businesses and the income to all of those here in the sugar-producing lands."[32] Didn't his father have anything to do about that "very sad period"?

FAMINES ARE SUCH A RARE EVENT THESE DAYS—even in developing countries like the Philippines—that it is difficult to imagine how one could arise in the first place. But what happened in Negros is that over the span of decades, all the eggs were put in one basket: sugar.

From a bustling economy with diversified trade, Negros during the latter years of the Spanish colonial period pivoted increasingly toward the production of just one crop—sugar.[33] There was great demand for it abroad, especially in Europe, and Negros evolved to be one of the world's major sugar producers. But sugar production there has long been concentrated in the hands of few families, who owned huge tracts of land called *haciendas* and employed scores of sugarcane farmers called *sakada*.[34] Therefore, while sugar was a booming industry in the island, its gains went primarily to the rich landowning families—and not the working population.[35] The flourishing of sugar in Negros carried over during the American colonial period, especially since the Bell Trade Act and the Laurel-Langley Agreement ensured that the Philippines regularly exported huge quantities of sugar to the US. The US also paid much higher prices for our sugar vis-à-vis the rest of the world.[36]

Negros's sugar industry thrived well after independence. The 1960s was a particularly auspicious time for the industry, partly owing to the partial devaluation or weakening of the peso—thanks to the policies of Diosdado Macapagal—which boosted our export earnings (that is, our exports became relatively cheaper in the world market). And when the US stopped importing sugar from Cuba due to an embargo, it came to rely on other sugar-exporting countries like the Philippines. As a result, sugarcane farms in the Philippines grew by 80 percent from 1960 to 1972, while the number of sugar mills increased by 40 percent from 1967 to 1974—partly financed by loans from the country's largest bank then, the Philippine National Bank (PNB).[37]

But the thriving of the sugar industry came at a price: our high dependence on sugar exports (chiefly from Negros) meant that we also came to rely more on the world sugar market. This meant that the fortunes of all those in the sugar industry in the Philippines and especially Negros (from the *hacienderos* to the sakadas) were also inextricably tied to the rise and fall of sugar prices worldwide.

Luckily, in the early 1970s, the world sugar price grew by more than fourfold (figure 4.2). But with the expiry in 1974 of both the US Sugar Act of 1948 and the Laurel-Langley Agreement, the Philippines' sugar exports to the US plummeted from 1.2 million tons a year to only about 330,000 tons. This lower US demand meant a precipitous drop in world sugar prices in 1975 and 1976, and, therefore, a commensurate plummeting of our export earnings.[38]

In 1981, sugar prices bounced back again and peaked, auguring well for the sugar industry once more. From 1981 to 1984, the government, through the sugar trading agency called National Sugar Trading Company (NASUTRA) was

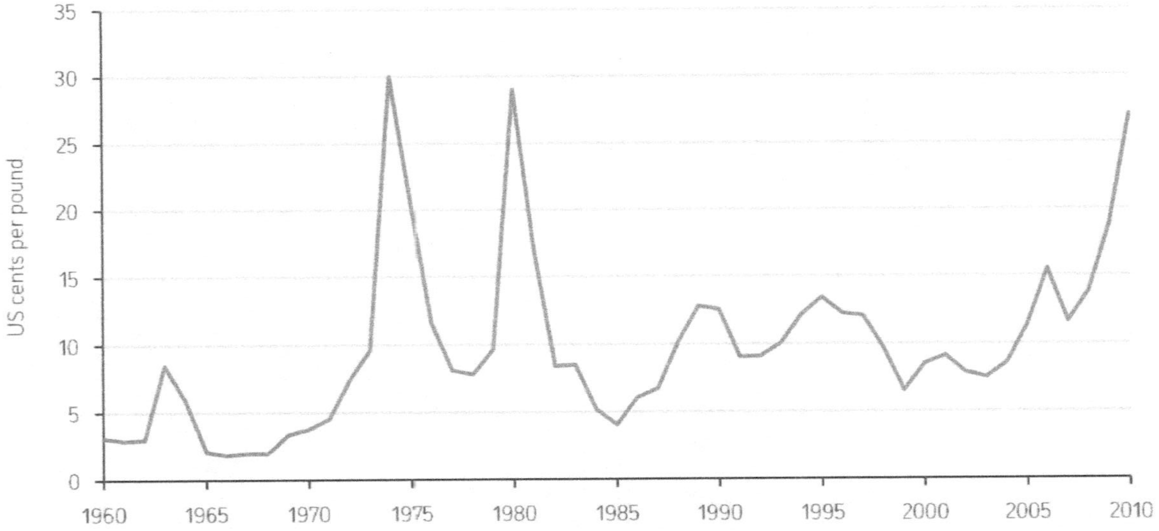

FIGURE 4.2 World raw sugar prices, 1960–2010 (Source of data: United States Department of Agriculture)

able to secure contracts to export 565,000 tons of sugar at the elevated prices. At the same time, the US imported sugar again from the Philippines, with a quota of 342,000 tons (although this quota would shrink eventually).

Alas, this happy episode was not to last. In 1983, Negros produced a mere eight percent of the country's sugar output, way below than about 50 percent during its height. And in 1984, the world price tumbled dramatically. As a result, sugar production dropped by 16 percent. By 1985, NASUTRA could no longer pay sugarcane farmers and maintain a low price for consumers. This would take a heavy toll on Negros: an estimated 190,000 sakadas lost their jobs.[39] The island's local economy had tanked, leading to severe economic misery and hunger. This was the proximate reason for the Negros famine.

But beyond bad luck, the Negros famine was also very much the product of economic mismanagement by the Marcos dictatorship.[40]

Seeing the sugar industry's vast earnings and profitability in the 1970s, the government increasingly intervened in it. For instance, the government imposed new taxes on sugar during the 1970 peso devaluation (which made exports more profitable) as well as during the 1974 rise in world sugar prices.

More importantly, sugar came to be dominated by one of Marcos's top cronies—Roberto Benedicto (also known as the "Sugar King"). Benedicto was born in La Carlota, Negros Occidental in 1917—the same year as Marcos, making him a contemporary of the dictator. They met at the UP College of Law, where Benedicto became a fraternity brother of Marcos in the Upsilon Sigma Phi.

During martial law, Benedicto controlled the Philippine Exchange Company (PHILEX), which monopolized the export of all sugar from the Philippines. At the time, the government suspected that a lot of middlemen and traders were hoarding sugar—wishing to sell their supplies once prices become even higher. So, the government put the PHILEX, a subsidiary of the PNB, in charge of all sugar exports. PHILEX made colossal profits from buying sugar from planters at low prices and selling it at sky-high prices. The profit margins were substantial: at one time, PHILEX (along with the PNB) would buy sugar at a measly USD 19.75 per picul (one picul is about 133.3 pounds) and then sell it at USD 69.35—a 251-percent profit margin that would instantly translate to profits totaling USD 700 million.[41] PHILEX's operations peaked in 1974, just as world sugar prices skyrocketed.

But PHILEX itself committed what it had set out to prevent. The gap between the price they paid to sugarcane farmers and the price they were able to sell abroad represented a huge, irresistible profit. Encouraged by such windfalls and anticipating further price increases, PHILEX hoarded too much sugar themselves. But when sugar prices dropped like a rock in 1977, they sold their stocks at a massive loss. And since they were obligated to sell sugar to Filipinos at a low price, they had to borrow significant sums to cover their losses.

Even with the demise of PHILEX, Benedicto's rule over sugar did not end. Marcos transferred sugar trading from PHILEX to a new agency called the Philippine Sugar Commission (PHILSUCOM), tasked to "act as the single agency engaged in the buying and selling of sugar."[42] In turn, PHILSUCOM had NASUTRA (established through Presidential Decree No. 1192, s. 1977) as its trading arm. Both entities were headed by Benedicto, and PHILSUCOM was financed primarily by Republic Planters Bank (which was also led by Benedicto).[43] Hence, just like PHILEX before it, PHILSUCOM was just another monopoly. Sugar producers in fact earned even lower prices relative to the world price of sugar. But there was an added layer to their modus operandi. While both PHILSUCOM and NASUTRA sold sugar domestically at government-set prices, they sold sugar at low prices to international sugar trading companies owned by Marcos cronies—which in turn sold such sugar to the world market at the usual steep prices. Hence, PHILSUCOM and NASUTRA effectively *monopsonized* (not monopolized) sugar, meaning they were the single buyer of sugar to be traded abroad. Talk about industry capture!

In the 1960s, Filipino sugarcane farmers were earning lots from their exports; by the 1970s to the early 1980s, they were suffering massive losses. Both PHILSUCOM and NASUTRA set up new sugar mills, refineries, and centrals. But these were often overpriced, ridden with kickbacks, and operated by Marcos's cronies—including Benedicto himself. These businesses also got loans guaranteed by the PNB, which, at that time, was also headed by Benedicto. This strategy by the government did not do the sugar industry any favor. Rather than increase efficiency and productivity (as measured by yield per hectare), much of the growth that the sugar industry experienced during the 1960s and 1970s came from the expansion of the hectarage of sugar farms and the introduction of new sugar mills. Rather than promote crop diversification, the Marcos dictatorship propped up the sugar industry. In the process of intervening heavily, the regime gained massive economic benefits through price speculation, taxes, rents, and corruption—to say nothing of the political influence that went along with it. In March 1986, an investigation conducted by the Corazon Aquino government had estimated that the plethora of "anomalies" in the sugar sector from 1975 to 1984 had generated no less than USD 1.15 billion in industry losses.[44] All these, at the expense of ordinary Filipinos, especially in Negros Island, whose hardships are now being belittled—and even denied altogether—for the sake of malicious historical distortion.

TO CLOSE THIS CHAPTER ON MARCOSIAN HUNGER, let us address one last claim: that former president Corazon Aquino sold the Food Terminal Incorporated (FTI), touted as another innovative brainchild of Marcos. The FTI was meant to strengthen agriculture and address hunger by serving as a hub for food trading and processing.[45] By selling it, loyalists claim that Aquino had needlessly killed such a well-intentioned Marcosian project, and even profited a lot from it.

Although primarily engaged in the wholesale of commodities, the FTI was also responsible for the famous Kadiwa centers of old, where the government sold to the public cheap (subsidized) basic food items—like fresh vegetables, fish, sugar, and fruits—in various sites and even in mobile or "rolling" stores.[46] Perhaps the association with Kadiwa is one of the reasons loyalists today are harping on what had happened to FTI.

FTI was indeed part of Aquino's privatization plan in December 1986, when she cited the need for government to let go of government assets and corporations that overly burdened the national coffers. (Remember that, at the time she took office, the economy was still reeling from the economic crisis wrought by Marcos.)

But in fact, in early February 1986, right before he was kicked out of Malacañang, Marcos signed Presidential

Decree No. 2030 that authorized the disposal of government institutions' assets that "adversely affect their financial viability and liquidity."[47] In other words, back then, Marcos had already realized that the boat that was the Philippine economy was sinking, and a quick way to keep it afloat (in his words, to get "immediate substantial cash returns to the national government") was to get rid of government assets and corporations that his regime had previously amassed over the dictatorship. One of those needless assets was the FTI. Fast-forward to November 2012, the FTI assets in Taguig were sold to Ayala Land (a part of these assets is the current location of Arca South).

To be fair, FTI's Kadiwa had good intentions, and there was no inherent reason for it to fail. One study that surveyed similar food terminals and commodity exchanges in other Asian countries saw many examples of success. But in their international comparison, only Marcos's FTI failed. They cited FTI's "unclear vision and mission, its overdesign given the lack of provincial linkages (e.g., packing houses), bureaucratic constraints to its operations, politically motivated entry into retail operations (in the case of the Kadiwa program), and fast turnover of management."[48] In other words, while the core idea behind FTI and Kadiwa was generally good, it ultimately fell victim to Marcos's bad execution. Kadiwa also died during the crisis in the early 1980s brought about by Marcos's economic mismanagement. Economist Ramon Clarete writes,

> Because of the economic crisis, the government was open to ideas that would get the economy out of depression. In 1985, in need of foreign exchange to manage its foreign debt, the government agreed with the Asian Development Bank to

> end both the Kadiwa program and the wheat import monopoly of NFA. Political support for the program weakened as the Marcos government became increasingly isolated.[49]

Occasionally, there have been proposals to revive Kadiwa. But in a way, the Kadiwa program never really went away: the National Food Authority simply renamed the government's rolling stores in succeeding administrations, transforming it into ERAP (Enhanced Retail Access Program) and then to GMA (Greater Market Access).[50] Succeeding governments pursued several other food and commodity exchanges. But somehow, the name of Kadiwa keeps cropping up: for instance, it was relentlessly mentioned by Imee Marcos during her 2019 senatorial bid.[51] Clearly, what is being revived in recent years is not so much the idea of food hubs, but the false idea that Kadiwa was another rousing success of Marcos—thus putting it in the same league as the Nutribun. In 2022, President Marcos Jr. actively revived Kadiwa and is touting it as a way to abate agricultural shortages and bring down the price of rice to PHP 20 per kilogram—his most prominent campaign promise. However, his Kadiwa stores are limited to select areas, and average rice prices nationwide are, as of writing, still twice the level he is "aspiring" for.[52]

IN SUM, IT WAS NOT AT ALL TRUE THAT THE Marcos dictatorship had a cornucopia of food or it was a hunger-free utopia. The idea that Marcos eradicated hunger through programs like the Nutribun and the Kadiwa centers is totally false. If there is any more doubt, just remember Joel Abong and the countless other children who perished in the country's last famine, a famine that Marcos not only allowed to happen but also—through his actions and policies—directly brought about.

05 No public funds were spent for Imelda's hospitals?

CLAIM 1 No public funds were spent for Imelda's pet projects, such as her designer hospitals.	**VERDICT** FALSE
CLAIM 2 Filipinos became a lot healthier during martial law.	**VERDICT** FALSE

ON 3 JULY 2019, A DAY AFTER IMELDA MARCOS'S 90th birthday, loyalists organized a grand birthday party for her at the Ynares Sports Complex in Pasig City.[1] About 2,500 people, mostly clad in red (the Marcoses' signature political color) came to the event. Imelda was presented cakes and bouquets of flowers onstage. For lunch, guests were served rice, chicken adobo, and boiled egg. But in the middle of the proceedings, at around 2:00 p.m., several people—women, men, and even children—experienced dizziness and vomiting. Soon, ambulances started coming in and rushed to nearby hospitals dozens of people suspected to have experienced food poisoning. In a presser, the secretary of

the Department of Health announced that the people who were food poisoned and hospitalized numbered 261. Imee Marcos, who had just sworn an oath as a first-time senator that week, tried to distance their family to the accident by saying they did not organize the party. But even as nearly a tenth of the guests were being rushed to hospitals, the birthday celebration went on. And Imee was later quoted saying, "The food may have been spoiled, but we remain solid."[2] (This calls to mind the similar food poisoning incident that was said to have happened during Irene Marcos and Gregorio Araneta's "wedding of the century" at Sarrat, Ilocos Norte in 1983.)[3]

The blasé attitude by which the Marcoses responded to the food poisoning of their supporters is emblematic of the way the Marcos dictatorship treated Filipinos' health.

Today, loyalists like to point as "solid" proof of Marcos's exemplary focus on health the designer hospitals built in Quezon City, near the Quezon Memorial Circle: the Philippine Heart Center (previously known as the Philippine Heart Center for Asia), the Lung Center of the Philippines, the National Kidney and Transplant Institute (then called the Kidney Foundation), and the Philippine Children's Hospital.[4] Some people even claim that these structures—along with others like the Philippine International Convention Center and the Cultural Center of the Philippines (CCP) in Pasay City—were not built using public funds. Imelda herself was once quoted as saying in one interview, "I did not use government money in building any one of these [buildings]."[5] (The claim is weird off the bat: if they are so proud of Marcos's involvement in the hospitals, why even distance such projects from public spending?) To this day, the Heart Center continues to be a focal point in Marcosian disinformation. In 2021, the Heart Center denied that it was behind or had any links with a legitimate-looking Heart Center Facebook page (with more than 21,000 followers) that was found out to be spewing viral Marcos propaganda.[6]

RECORDS EASILY BELIE THE CLAIM THAT THE Marcoses did not spend any public money on Imelda's hospitals.[7] In the Batasang Pambansa's question hour on 23 May 1985, former health minister Jesus Azurin answered questions surrounding the finances of Imelda's designer hospitals. Azurin admitted that, in the case of the Heart Center, PHP 306 million of public funds were advanced by the Government Service Insurance System (GSIS) and spent for the hospital's construction. A similar amount of PHP 306.5 million, financed by the Philippine Charity Sweepstakes Office (PCSO), was used to build the Lung Center. And PHP 363 million were "taken from the proceeds" of the Philippine Games and Amusement Corporation (PAGCOR) for the construction of the Kidney Foundation. Aside from construction, Azurin admitted too that public funds were allocated for the annual operations of these hospitals: in 1985 alone, PHP 13 million was spent for the Heart Center, PHP 10 million for the Lung Center, and PHP 20 million for the Kidney Foundation.

So, evidently, public funds were used for the construction and maintenance of these hospitals. This fact should not come as a surprise: the Heart Center and the Lung Center were both attached agencies to the Ministry of Human Settlements headed by Imelda herself, while the Kidney Foundation was attached to the Office of the President. Note that the involvement of government corporations like PAGCOR and PCSO in the construction of the designer hospitals was a manifestation of the regime's increasing preference for using government institutions to funnel public funds for the construction of its infrastructure projects, among other investments.[8]

THERE ARE MORE THINGS TO BE SAID ABOUT these designer hospitals, sometimes called "*bopis* hospitals" after the famous Filipino dish made of minced pig heart and lungs.

First, the designer hospitals were expensive vanity projects of Imelda that were, in the words of de Dios, Gochoco-Bautista, and Punongbayan, "motivated more by prestige and image"[9] than a genuine desire to take care of Filipinos' health. Constructed by architect Jorge Ramos with a brutalist design (which was used as well in many other Marcos edifices like those at the CCP Complex), the Heart Center was "rushed" by Imelda in time for a Valentine's Day inauguration in 1975.[10] Footage of the inauguration shows several children singing and parading while wearing shirts emblazoned with the Heart Center logo, and they were waving flags bearing the same logo. Helicopters flew overhead, and Imelda was said to have "persuaded every corporation doing business in the Philippines to have its aircraft join in a heart-shaped formation that showered the facility with pink confetti."[11] There was also a parade of spanking new mobile hospitals bearing on their sides a quote by Imelda: "Be there but one Filipino sick and uncared for, our mission is not done." To this day, there stands a commissioned mural in the Heart Center's lobby—painted by National Artist Vicente Manansala and titled *Inang Bayan*—featuring a young Imelda, hands outstretched for the poor in front of her, with doctors and nurses behind her.

If Imelda really wanted to help the poor, why does her face have to be painted all over her hospitals?

Second, that Marcoses had built the designer hospitals concentrated in Quezon City, instead of constructing quality hospitals all throughout the Philippines. As one might expect, this made it quite difficult for these hospitals to cater to the health needs of Filipinos in the provinces. Patients in need of specialized care but living in the provinces had to be transported all the way to the Quezon City hospitals, admission to which was also expensive and out of reach for most Filipinos. It is said that admission to these hospitals also required "consent or permission [from] Malacañang"—although this was denied by health minister Azurin.[12] According to one UNICEF report, all the designer hospitals "cater[ed] to upper income families."[13] The inequality of it all was also reflected in the Marcos dictatorship's budget priorities: in 1984 and 1985, the Marcos government subsidized the three major hospitals (i.e., Heart Center, Kidney Foundation, and Lung Center) with a total sum of USD 229 million, which was as much as five times the total government budget for primary health care.[14] While the well-to-do enjoyed world class facilities, most ordinary Filipinos in the rural areas were left to fend for themselves and resort to the local *albularyo* or herbalist.

Third, despite the huge sums of money poured for Imelda's grand hospitals, Filipinos' health did not improve commensurately. Doherty pointed out that the Marcoses' "investments in curing the few diseases the majority of Filipinos do not live long enough to contract are much more important to them than preventing those diseases that would keep the nation healthy."[15] He pointed out that, even with the designer hospitals, the Philippines "[held] the world records for the highest incidence of whooping coughs, rabies, leprosy, schistosomatosis and polio."[16]

And across a slew of health statistics—infant mortality, malnutrition, protein deficiency, and average calorie consumption—the Philippines lagged behind other developing countries. De Dios et al. noted that in just two years, from 1975 to 1977, infant mortality rose from about 76 to 78 in a thousand live births.[17] World Bank data also show that infant mortality rose in urban areas from 45 to 55 per thousand live births from 1970 to 1983, while it rose from 54 to 59 per thousand live births in rural areas.[18] Meanwhile, in a 1987 paper, pioneering pediatrician Dr. Fe del Mundo and her co-authors noted that while there were some improvements in health indicators from 1973 to 1983, "these are still far from significant or satisfactory, even as compared to countries around the Philippines."[19] One problem is that data are not altogether consistent, owing to methodological differences across studies. At any rate, the "negative impact on health" of the economic crisis in the 1980s was deemed "all too transparent."[20]

Indeed, figure 5.1 shows that in the late 1970s and early 1980s, the Philippines—vis-à-vis Thailand—had a noticeable slowdown not just in the decline of infant mortality but also in the rise of life expectancy. Before this period, Thailand fared worse in both health statistics, but their health outcomes steadily improved and, eventually, they overtook us. Although more research is needed to determine exactly how the Marcos regime let this happen, the slowdown of our health improvement challenges the notion that Filipinos were a lot more healthier during martial law. In fact, to the extent that there were any improvements, martial law measurably slowed them down.

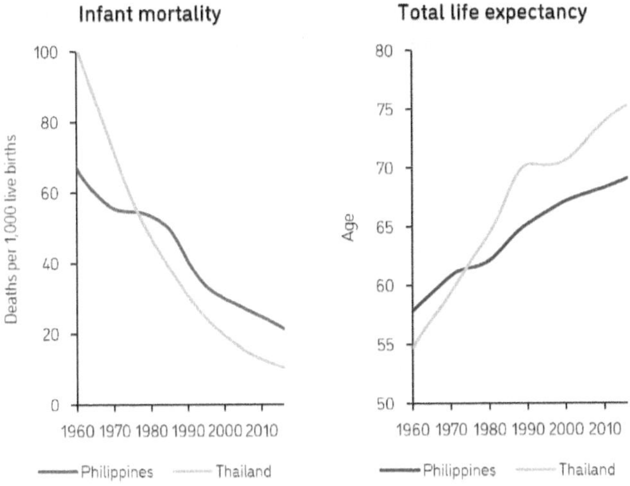

FIGURE 5.1 Health outcomes in the Philippines and Thailand, 1960–2016 (Source of data: World Development Indicators)

Fourth, the designer hospitals were self-serving: although ostensibly built for the masses, the Marcoses were keen to build them in order to support the Marcoses' own health and maintain a coterie of physicians that will safeguard Marcos Sr.'s own health—and keep it secret from the public for as long as possible, for they wanted to maintain Ferdinand Sr.'s image as a virile strongman.

As early as 1979, there were rumors that Ferdinand had acquired systemic lupus erythematosus, an "autoimmune disease in which the immune system attacks its own tissues, causing widespread inflammation and tissue damage in the affected organs."[21] Marcos's lupus was further complicated by diabetes. Then in 1982, rumors regarding Ferdinand's kidney problems spread. But because of a news blackout around his health, it was not until 1984 that Blas Ople, then labor minister, confirmed Ferdinand's illnesses. Later, it was divulged that Marcos had received two transplants in his very own Kidney Foundation: the first in August 1983, but with the kidney being rejected, there had to be a second transplant, which was done in November 1984.[22] Until the very end of the regime, the Marcoses tried to hide Ferdinand Sr.'s increasing frailty and infirmity. Right after their ouster from Malacañang, a number of people were able to look at Marcos's bedroom. One Associated Press report said that inside, "the smell of medicine hung in the air," with an "unmade hospital bed," "a man's pajama top tossed over the footboard," and "a box of disposable syringes [which] sat on a bedside table." All in all, Marcos's Malacañang bedroom "appeared to be the refuge of a very sick man."[23]

THIS IS NOT TO SAY THAT THERE WERE ZERO improvements in the health of Filipinos during martial law. If there was one health improvement program that Marcos deserves credit for, it would be his population program.

Back in December 1967, Marcos signed the United Nations Declaration of Population that underscored the importance of population measures for development. In 1970, amid much opposition from the Catholic Church, Marcos established the first family planning program of government, and in 1971, he established the Commission on Population (POPCOM; now the Commission on Population and Development) in order to implement the program.[24] Since then, such plans were incorporated in the government's development plans and even in the 1973 Constitution.

Contraceptive use soon became widespread: from about 15 percent in 1968, it more than doubled to 35 percent in 1978 and further increased to 40 percent by 1986—after the ouster. But even with a "strong commitment to reduce fertility and population growth," the implementation of Marcos's family planning program "shifted from vigorous to benign neglect depending on who was the head of the Popcom Board."[25]

In any case, the gains in population policy and control were offset by a deterioration of many other aspects of the health system, including the slowdown of the decline of infant mortality, the slowdown of the rise of life expectancy, as well as the prevalence of hunger and malnutrition and poverty.[26] These outcomes were not prevented by the construction of Imelda's extravagant and designer hospitals, which were definitely built using public money but inaccessible to most Filipinos then—even until now.

06 Nobody was poor?

CLAIM 1 Nobody was poor during the Marcos regime.	**VERDICT** FALSE
CLAIM 2 Poverty went down across the entire country.	**VERDICT** FALSE
CLAIM 3 Poverty was much higher after the Marcos regime.	**VERDICT** FALSE

CLOSELY RELATED TO THE MYTH THAT NOBODY went hungry and that Filipinos' health was taken care of during the Marcos dictatorship is the idea that nobody was poor. It is also claimed that poverty went down across the country during that time. But a quick look at the statistical record obliterates this myth.

When Marcos first took office in 1965, there were only about 3.4 million poor families in the country. But that rose to 3.9 million in 1971 (or in just 6 years) and rose by more

TABLE 6.1 Number of poor families and poverty incidence, 1961–1985

	Families (in thousands)	Poor families (in thousands)	Poverty rate (%)
1961	4,426	3,320	75.01
1965	5,127	3,439	67.08
1971	6,348	3,912	61.63
1985	9,847	5,874	59.65
1988	10,533	5,814	55.20

Source: Emmanuel de Dios, "Poverty, Growth, and the Fiscal Crisis," in *Poverty, Growth and the Fiscal Crisis*, ed. Emmanuel de Dios (Makati City: Philippine Institute for Development Studies, 1993), using data from Arsenio M. Balisacan, "Rural Poverty in the Philippines: Incidence, Determinants, and Policies," *Asian Development Review* 10, no. 1 (1992), 125-63.

than 50 percent to 5.87 million by 1985, at the height of the country's economic crisis (table 6.1).

While the number of poor people increased, the *proportion* of poor families kept declining during the Marcos years: from 67 percent in 1965 to a little under 60 percent in 1985, or two decades later. This, however, only means that the number of families then grew at a faster rate than the ranks of the poor. There was another set of estimates by Tan and Holazo showing that the proportion of poor Filipinos went up from 41 percent in 1965 to 43.8 percent in 1971 and then to 51.5 percent in 1975.[1] Methodological differences in computing poverty rates prevent us from linking these numbers to later estimates.

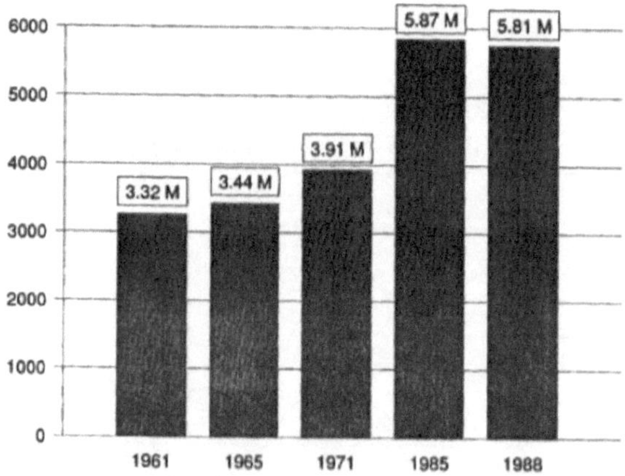

FIGURE 6.1 Number of poor families (in thousands), 1961–1988 (Reprinted from Arsenio M. Balisacan, "The Human Face of Poverty During a Period of Macroeconomic Adjustment," in *Perspectives on Philippine Poverty*, ed. Arsenio M. Balisacan et al. [Quezon City: University of the Philippines Press and Yale University Council on Southeast Asian Studies, 1993].)

At any rate, the data clearly show that poverty did not go away during martial law and, at all times, more than half of Filipino families were considered poor. Also, notice from figure 6.1 that it was not until after 1985 that the number of poor families started to go down, albeit slowly. This instantly belies the second myth that poverty was much higher post-EDSA.

THE EAGLE-EYED READER MIGHT NOTICE THE HUGE gap in official poverty records between 1971 to 1985.[2] Although government surveys,[3] which have long been the basis of poverty statistics (until today), were conducted in both 1975 and 1979, these "were not published due to some technical problems, one of which was the implausibility of the data generated arising from substantial underrepresentation of certain groups of households (e.g., wealthy households in plush subdivisions)."[4] This gap is unfortunate because we do not have a clear picture of the extent of poverty through the intervening years, which was the bulk of the dictatorship.

Yet the absence of official records had not prevented economists from learning about those gap years.

The economist Nobuhiko Fuwa used data from another survey, the Labor Force Survey, to estimate poverty from 1972 to 1984.[5] He found that although poverty—at least in rural areas—went down from 1971 to 1978 (reaching 48.6 percent), that number climbed again to reach as much as 57.1 percent in 1982 and 60.6 percent by 1983 (figure 6.2). This rather corroborates reports saying that poverty probably reached as much as 70 percent at that time.[6] Hence, as the economy deteriorated, poverty invariably rose, and we see this in the data. Fuwa added, "the level of rural poverty incidence in the mid-1980s was not too much lower than the level in the early 1970s." But by his own data, the incidence of poverty in 1983 was higher than at any point in the 1970s. According to him, the glaring lack of progress in poverty reduction may either be due to a weak response of poverty to the heady growth rates of the economy (including agriculture) in the 1970s, or because what little poverty reduction was experienced in the 1970s was "completely wiped out" by the economic crisis by the early and mid-1980s.

Although the poverty rate of the Philippines went down from 1965 to 1985, it did so marginally. Poverty dropped a lot faster in neighboring countries in the ASEAN. From 1971 to 1988, our poverty rate fell by a measly average of

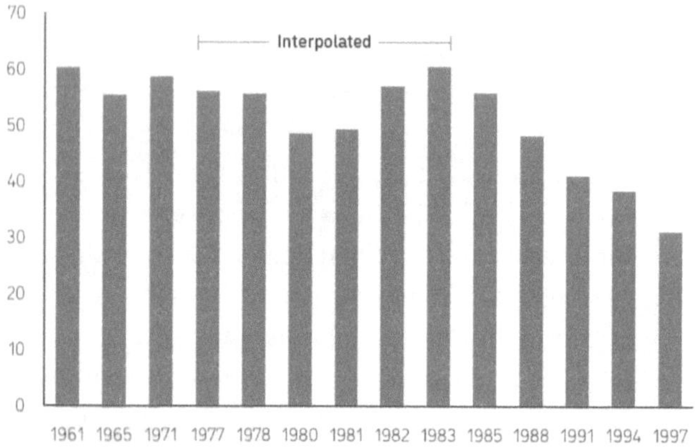

FIGURE 6.2 Rural poverty incidence (in percent), 1961–1997 (Source of data: Nobuhiko Fuwa, "Evolution of Rural Poverty in Indonesia, the Philippines and Thailand" [unpublished manuscript, 2002].)

0.38 percent each year. In contrast, it went down by 2.34 percent a year in Indonesia (from 1970 to 1984), 1.66 percent a year in Malaysia (from 1973 to 1987), 1.40 percent a year in Thailand (from 1962 to 1986), and 1.04 percent a year in India (from 1972 to 1983).[7] This, despite some years of good—if not impressive—growth recorded in the 1970s, as boasted by the Marcos regime itself.

Indeed, it is curious how poverty worsened during the dictatorship despite some years of growth, especially in the 1970s. This was called by Boyce as "immiserizing growth,"[8] which one can take to mean "not only to describe a situation in which the poor became poorer even as income per person grows, but also in a stronger, casual sense to mean that growth itself is a cause of impoverishment."[9] Although growth happened, it did not uplift the poor. Traditionally, growth and equity have been regarded as at odds with one another: you cannot pursue one without sacrificing the other. But as Boyce elaborated:

> Equity was not "traded off" for growth in the Philippines. Rather, both were sacrificed to a technocratic development strategy wedded to an unjust political and economic order.[10]

He was referring to the economic mismanagement of the Marcos dictatorship and the policies that it came up with. Boyce went on to say that "the country could have achieved more rapid growth under alternative policies."[11] This calls to mind a quote from National Scientist Raul V. Fabella: "The annals of underdevelopment are filled with chapters on failures due to wasted opportunities, with hardly any account of failure due to scarcity of resources."[12]

THAT WAS THE NATIONAL SITUATION ON POVERTY. But what about the regions? It is also not true that poverty went down across the entire country. Figure 6.3 shows that poverty was significantly higher in 1985 than in 1965—with the exception of the Ilocos Region and the Cagayan Valley. But this makes sense: Marcos took special care of the northern provinces while he brought the rest of the regions down to the ground. Notice, however, that even the decline in poverty incidence in these two northern regions were not that steep in those two decades. And the decline for the Cagayan Valley was even larger than for the Ilocos Region.

Even today, one might go to a road trip up north and validly raise the question: how come the Marcoses' bailiwicks are not as prosperous as one might expect, given that Marcos Sr. himself hailed from Ilocos Norte? In fact, today

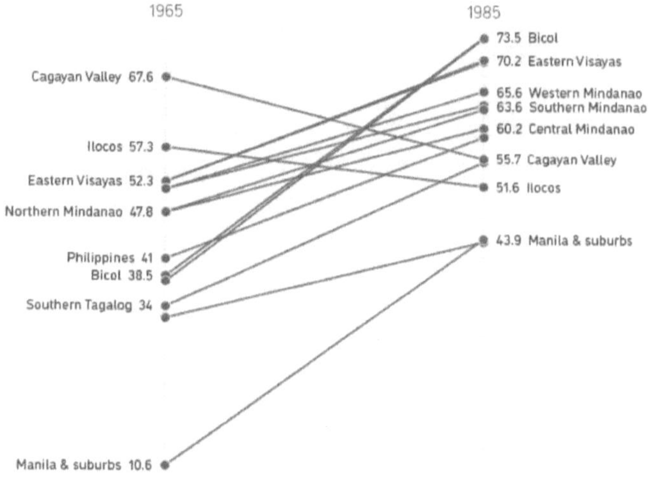

FIGURE 6.3 Regional poverty incidence (in percent), 1965 and 1985 (Source of data: James K. Boyce, *The Philippines: The Political Economy of Growth and Impoverishment in the Marcos Era* [Hampshire: The Macmillan Press Ltd., 1993]; Note: Data for 1965 is from Edita A. Tan and Virginia Holazo, "Measuring Poverty Incidence in a Segmented Market: The Philippine Case," *Philippine Economic Journal* 18, no. 4 (1979): 450–90. Meanwhile, data for 1985 is from the National Economic and Development Authority Technical Working Group on Poverty, *A Monograph for the Estimation of the 1985 Poverty and Subsistence Thresholds and Indices* [Manila: National Economic and Development Authority, 1988].)

in the twenty-first century, many cities and municipalities in the Ilocos Region are not "first class," a classification based on average annual revenues. As of writing, Sarrat (the birthplace of Marcos Sr.) is a fourth-class municipality, Bangui (site of the famous windmills) a fourth-class municipality, Batac (site of Marcos Sr.'s former mausoleum) a fifth-class component city, and Laoag (the seat of power in Ilocos Norte) a third-class city. Perhaps most tellingly, a town called Marcos is a fourth-class municipality.[13]

Of course, there is only so much that can be inferred from a local government unit's average annual revenues; it is not the be-all and end-all of development. But while Ilocos Norte only has one first-class municipality (Vintar), other provinces in the Ilocos Region have more: Ilocos Sur has two, La Union six, Cagayan eight, Isabela 16, and Pangasinan 19.[14]

Even after several decades in power and in command of a "fat dynasty"[15] spanning local and national electoral posts, the Marcoses have failed to transform their home province into a shining beacon of economic activity and growth. What have they done—or better yet, *not* done—to end up in this situation?

BEYOND STATISTICS, PLENTY OF STORIES OF poverty during martial law abound. For example, in February 1981, when Pope John Paul II visited the Philippines, he was scheduled to have an "encounter" with the poor of Tondo, Manila. But in preparation for this, Imelda—then governor of Metro Manila and minister for human settlements—supposedly "beautified" the slums of Tondo by erecting a stage in the middle of a "pleasant lawn" surrounded by trees, bushes, painted houses, and posters bearing the faces of the pope and Ferdinand and Imelda.[16] Despite the cover-up, the Pope supposedly "expressed alarm at the large numbers of the poor."

In the following year, the number of informal settlers would rise by 38 percent, with a whopping third of it coming from Metro Manila.[17] But rampant poverty was hardly confined in the metropolis. Life in the barrios was even harder, and there is perhaps no better illustration of it than the Negros famine in the mid-1980s.[18]

In summary, as Boyce had put it: "If the central aim of economic development is the reduction of poverty, then the Philippine development strategy in the Marcos era was an abysmal failure."[19]

Fast-forward to 2018, only 12.1 percent of families were considered poor, translating to three million families.[20] This is impressive considering that there were 24.8 million families at the time, and three million poor families is fewer than the number of poor families when Marcos first took office in 1965.[21] So to say that poverty became a lot worse after Marcos is beyond disingenuous: it is a big, fat lie.

07 Most literate country in Asia?

CLAIM 1 The Philippines' literacy rate was more than 90 percent during the Marcos years.	**VERDICT** TRUE (but only if we are referring to *youth* literacy)
CLAIM 2 The Philippines' literacy rate dropped since Ferdinand Marcos was "changed" in 1986.	**VERDICT** FALSE
CLAIM 3 The Philippines was the most literate country in Asia during the Marcos years.	**VERDICT** FALSE

AKIN TO THE MYTH THAT THE PHILIPPINES WAS the "richest country in Asia," Marcos loyalists also like to claim that the country was the "most literate country in Asia." Imelda herself made such a claim in 2015, when she defended before the press Bongbong's vice presidential bid.[1] Later, in the 2016 campaign trail, Bongbong reaffirmed this by saying that the Philippines had one of the highest literacy rates in Asia during his father's reign.[2]

At face value, if one believes the first statement (that the Philippines was the richest country in Asia), then it should not be difficult to believe the second (that we were the most literate country in the continent). Prosperity is associated with literacy and a correlation between the two intuitively makes sense. But a deeper examination of viral social media posts hints at the true purpose of this education myth. One post seems to make the following perverse chain of reasoning: during Marcos's time, the Filipino youth were smart (this is not surprising, since Marcos himself was smart); smart people will only vote for smart leaders, while stupid people will vote for stupid leaders; hence, you should vote for Marcos—if you are smart.[3]

This claim is fallacious all the way down. Smart people are just as susceptible to lies and deception as stupid people. And just because Marcos himself was smart does not at all imply that Filipinos in general during his time were just as smart, or that the literacy rate then was high—let alone the "highest" in Asia.

DID WE REALLY HAVE A LITERACY RATE OF MORE than 90 percent during the Marcos years? First, it depends on which literacy rate we are referring to. There are some social media posts citing a 91.79-percent literacy rate based on data from the United Nations Educational, Scientific and Cultural Organization (UNESCO). This is actually true; however, it refers to the *youth* literacy rate (among those aged 15 to 24) and not the simple literacy rate. (Although seemingly impressive, our 91.79-percent youth literacy rate was beaten by Thailand and even Vietnam by 1980.)

What about the more commonly cited *simple* literacy rate—that is, literacy among those aged 10 and above? As far as the official government statistics tell us, we did not achieve a simple literacy rate greater than 90 percent until *after* martial law. The last official simple literacy rate during the Marcos regime was recorded in 1980—at 82.72 percent—while the literacy rate for those aged 15 and above was 83.32 percent. (Interestingly, in his 1980 State of the Nation Address, Marcos himself boasted that the simple literacy rate was at 88.9 percent, a lot higher than a decade ago.[4] But this does not jive with the official data.)

It should also be readily apparent in figure 7.1 that the simple literacy rate did not deteriorate after Marcos was ousted. In fact, there was a significant jump (of 7 percentage points) of the simple literacy rate from 1980 to 1989, and an even greater jump (of 10.25 percentage points) of the literacy rate among those aged 15 and above from 1980 to 1990. Fast-forward to 2010, the simple literacy rate was at 97.13 percent, while the literacy rate for people aged 15 and above was 98.18 in 2015. Simply put, literacy rates have been on the rise since the Marcoses fled to Hawai‘i.

If we look closely at the official data, there was in fact a slight *deterioration* of the simple literacy rate from 1970 to 1980, years falling squarely within Marcos's years in power. In 1970, the literacy rate was at 83.37 percent, but by 1980, it had fallen to 82.72 percent, a 0.65-percentage point decline. (The only other recorded decline of the literacy rate in the entire series occurred in 1994 to 2000, but that was an even larger decline: 1.62 percentage points.)

What accounted for the decline of simple literacy during martial law? And why do Marcos loyalists fail to mention this?

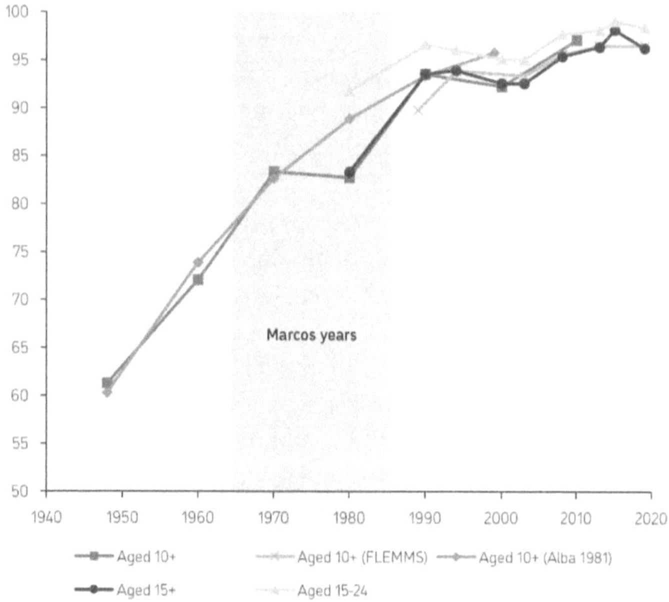

FIGURE 7.1 Literacy rates in the Philippines (in percent), 1940–2020 (Sources of data: For aged 10+, 1948–1970 data from *Philippine Statistical Yearbook 1978* [Manila: National Census and Statistics Office]; *Functional Literacy, Education and Mass Media Surveys 1989, 1994, 2003, 2008, 2013, 2019* [Manila/Quezon City: National Statistics Office/Philippine Statistics Authority]; and *Census of Population and Housing 1980, 1990, 2000, 2010* [Manila/Quezon City: National Statistics Office/Philippine Statistics Authority]. For aged 15+, "Literacy rate, adult total [% of people ages 15 and above]," World Development Indicators, World Bank/UNESCO Institute for Statistics, https://data.worldbank.org/indicator/SE.ADT.LITR.ZS. For aged 15–24, "Literacy rate, youth total [% of people ages 15–24]," World Bank/UNESCO Institute for Statistics, https://data.worldbank.org/indicator/SE.ADT.1524.LT.ZS; and Michael Alba, "Estimating Literacy Rate: A Study Relating Literacy Rate with Combined Gross Elementary and Secondary Schools Enrollment Rate," *Philippine Journal of Development* 8, no. 1 [1981]: 71–87.)

AT THIS POINT, WE SHOULD NOTE THAT ONE difficulty when it comes to historical datasets on literacy is that they are few and far in between. There are several huge gaps in the data, as made apparent in figure 7.1.

To address these gaps, in 1981, the economist Michael Alba (presently the president of the Far Eastern University) estimated the literacy rates in the years when official data are unavailable. Based on existing data, and assuming the increase of literacy rate follows a logistic model (imagine a curve that rises over time, but at a very slow pace), Alba estimated that we *might* have achieved a simple literacy rate of 90.33 percent in 1983, which further increased over time.[5] But this interpolation of the data depends on certain strict assumptions.

Given the huge data gaps in literacy rates, an even harder question to answer is whether our literacy rates during martial law were the highest in Asia, as claimed by many loyalists.

In 1960, data from the UNESCO showed that the adult literacy rate of the Philippines was 71.9 percent, higher than in Thailand (68 percent) and Indonesia (39 percent). But in the absence of comparable data from other Asian countries, it is really quite hard to say if our literacy rate then was indeed the highest in Asia. Meanwhile, by 1970, our simple literacy rate of 83.4 percent[6] was higher than in Thailand (78.6 percent) and Indonesia (56.6 percent).[7] Again, we need data from other countries to say with any accuracy that we had Asia's highest literacy rate. But these data somehow indicate that, at least in 1960 and 1970, we seemed to have had a head start vis-à-vis some of our neighbors (we will get back to this point later).

The earliest internationally comparable literacy data that we have for a greater set of Asian countries comes from

TABLE 7.1 Asian countries with higher literacy rates than the Philippines, 1980

Youth and adults (15+ years, both sexes)	Thailand Vietnam (1979 data)
Youth (15–24 years, both sexes)	Thailand Singapore Vietnam (1979 data)
Adults (25–64 years, both sexes)	Thailand

Sources: World Bank, UNESCO

the World Bank and UNESCO.[8] In their databases, which can be downloaded from their websites, the earliest year on record for the Philippines was 1980, Marcos's fifteenth year as president. This is fine: if Marcos had done a good job in improving children's education, and assuming that this literacy rate should be increasing over time, then we should expect that the Philippines by 1980 should have ended up with a very high literacy rate—indeed Asia's "highest," as his loyalists claim.

But a quick look at the data reveals that the Philippines did *not* have the highest literacy rate then (table 7.1). Across a number of literacy rate definitions, we were beaten by Thailand, Vietnam, and Singapore. Likewise, other countries were not far behind us. In terms of adult literacy (among those aged 25 to 64), although we beat Singapore and Vietnam, they were close behind us. And when it comes to youth literacy (among those aged 15 and above), we beat Malaysia and Indonesia but they, too, did not fall behind so much. In any case, we certainly did not have the highest literacy rate in Asia in 1980.

IN SUM, THE PHILIPPINES HAD A LITERACY RATE of above 90 percent by 1980, but only among the youth—and such a rate was actually dwarfed by the comparable literacy rate of neighboring countries. In addition, there was a deterioration of the literacy rate during Marcos's time, while there was a continual increase of the literacy rate after he was ousted. Near the end of the regime, when Marcos supposedly did wonders to the education system, we did not have Asia's highest literacy rate—no matter which definition of literacy is used.

On one level, the poor education performance during Marcos's regime is somewhat surprising. First, as noted by economist Ernesto Pernia back in 1990, we seemed to have had a head start vis-à-vis some neighboring countries like Thailand and Indonesia in the postwar years, not just in terms of literacy rate but also in gross enrollment rates from primary to tertiary education.[9] This head start in education was what propelled our economic growth in the postwar years, argued Pernia.

Second, the Marcos regime is known for pouring massive investments in the construction of prefabricated school buildings (known as "Marcos-type" buildings) all over the country. In 2001, when I entered Quezon City Science High School (QueSci), I distinctly remember there was still one of these airy prefab buildings standing and, at the time, it housed the QueSci's cafeteria, a photocopy shop, and a music room.

But beyond these investments, it is safe to say that Marcos neglected the country's education system.

First, the regime was too fixated on the construction of school buildings as part of the "golden age of infrastructure" and not on other crucial education inputs such as textbooks and teachers. A lot of buildings were built using foreign assistance but, as recounted by a former head of the US Agency for International Development (USAID): "It was a public works project . . . . We offered many times to use the [aid money] to buy textbooks, but the government always refused."[10]

Second, upon his declaration of martial law, Marcos slashed the government's education budget and diverted it to other things such as his infrastructure spending spree as well as the military. Teacher's salaries went down while military pay went up, and "the teachers were being treated shabbily, and they lost their sense of mission," said one former education undersecretary.[11] As another former education undersecretary puts it, "Marcos single-handedly destroyed education in this country," and in the process Marcos "raped its budget, and he ruined its teachers."[12] This coincides with the finding of UP economists in 1984 that during martial law, an ever increasing share of the budget went to economic services and the military, away from social services like health and education.[13] Marcos's misplaced budget priorities came at a heavy toll: by failing to continuously invest in education throughout the dictatorship, the Philippines lost the educational (and therefore economic) advantage it used to enjoy during the postwar years.[14] Meager educational investments would be compromised further with the onset of the severe economic crisis in the early to mid-1980s.

Third, and no less important, the education sector during the Marcos years neither fostered an environment of free thinking and speech nor promoted critical thinking. Said eerily by one teachers' union leader,

> It was not just a cult of personality; it was a cult of fear and of mindlessness . . . . You were not supposed to think. You were not supposed to

> contest. You were not supposed to question. You were supposed to follow, to implement and to obey.[15]

Apart from the several volumes that Marcos himself ostensibly wrote (but would later turn out to be written by a cadre of academics-cum-ghostwriters[16]), textbooks were filled with government propaganda and proved to be quite important in Marcosian myth-building. Soon after Marcos declared martial law, his regime "tried to take over the functions of the Department of Public Information, the Bureau of Posts and the Textbook Board in a bid to become the supreme authority on anything remotely related to mass media."[17] Later, textbooks—even those meant for the elementary students—would overtly praise and glorify the Marcoses. For instance,

> A 1980 Grade 4 Communication Arts (Filipino) textbook . . . featured Imelda Marcos as *huwarang Filipino* (model Filipino) and portrayed her as *Ina ng Bayan* (Mother of the Nation), also mandating the study of a poem (*tula*) where she is further compared to the mythical Queen Esther of Persia.[18]

College-level textbooks were not spared. One of the most popular textbooks on Philippine history—*History of the Filipino People* by Teodoro A. Agoncillo—was famously censored by the Marcos regime soon after martial law started. Specifically, the Mass Media Council at the time commanded Agoncillo to "delete or rewrite objectionable portions" of a chapter titled "The Continuing Crisis," which was first added in the book's 1967 edition and centered on controversial events during Marcos's first term as president.

Agoncillo essentially acquiesced: he was allegedly quite friendly to Marcos, but rather than make the revisions he just decided to write a new edition of the textbook with a new co-author (having had bitter conflicts with the previous co-author) and excised the controversial chapter.[19] Several future editions of the same textbook whitewashed and omitted key aspects of the dictatorship, including corruption, police brutality, and the economic crisis.[20] Unfortunately, generations of Filipinos (including my own) encountered this book. We even had it on our bookshelf at home as early as my elementary years (my foster mom and dad being history and social science teachers themselves) and, later, the book was required reading in our high school.

In retrospect, with the extent of propaganda and historical denialism in textbooks, it is no wonder that many of today's adults know little about the horrifying aspects of martial law. And no wonder there is so much disinformation about martial law in and out of social media today. The poor and flagging literacy rates during martial law were at the surface of the education crisis that Marcos had wrought in Philippine society—a crisis that plagues us until today.

08 "Golden age" of infrastructure?

CLAIM	VERDICT
CLAIM 1 There was a "golden age of infrastructure" during the dictatorship.	**VERDICT** MISLEADING
CLAIM 2 Marcos built 50,000 bridges.	**VERDICT** FALSE
CLAIM 3 Marcos was great because of all the infrastructure projects that he had built.	**VERDICT** FALSE and MISLEADING
CLAIM 4 No mass transit systems were built after martial law.	**VERDICT** FALSE
CLAIM 5 Former president Benigno Aquino III ordered the demolition of Marcos's bust at Tuba, Benguet.	**VERDICT** FALSE

FOR THE LOYALISTS, PERHAPS THERE IS NO better proof of Marcos's genius and greatness than the grand infrastructure projects he had built during his reign. And for the uninitiated, it is easy to be convinced: many of those iconic projects have stood the test of time for everyone to see.

Nearly 60 years since Marcos first took office, such infrastructure projects continue to be heavily associated with his name. For instance, before Imelda Marcos's ninetieth birthday in 2019, an advance celebration was held at Paoay, Ilocos Norte, specifically at the so-called Malacañang of the North. One of the party's highlights was the presentation to Imelda of several cakes shaped in the form of infrastructure projects commonly associated with the Marcoses,[1] such as the Cultural Center of the Philippines (CCP), the Philippine International Convention Center (PICC), the Manila Film Center, the "designer" hospitals in Quezon City (namely the Philippine Heart Center, which was inaugurated on Valentine's Day in 1975 at Imelda's request, the Lung Center of the Philippines, and the National Kidney Institute), the Golden Mosque at Quiapo, and the Meralco Building (completed in the late 1960s).[2] By the way, the venue of the party itself, the Malacañang of the North, was built by the Philippine Tourism Authority in 1977 in time for Ferdinand Marcos Sr.'s sixtieth birthday.

The cakes were just a sampling of the grand infrastructure projects of Ferdinand Sr. and Imelda (although contrary to popular belief, the Golden Mosque and the Meralco Building were not really Marcosian projects). A lot more can be found in the reclaimed land in a portion of Manila Bay known as the CCP Complex: apart from the CCP, PICC, and Manila Film Center, one can find there the Coconut Palace, the Folk Arts Theater,

and the Philippine Plaza Hotel (presently known as Sofitel Philippine Plaza Manila). The very reclaimed land on which all these projects stand was also initiated by Marcos, with the help of construction magnate and crony Rodolfo Cuenca. In neighboring Pasay City, there is the Terminal 1 of the Manila International Airport (MIA), the Nayong Pilipino (located near the airport, it was in its heyday a sampler of major tourist spots around the country), and the Coastal Road leading to Cavite.

Farther south of Metro Manila, there is the National Arts Center (formerly the Makiling Center for the Arts) in Los Baños, Laguna, and the Palace in the Sky in Tagaytay City. In Samar and Leyte, there is the San Juanico Bridge—also called the "Bridge of Love" because it was supposedly Marcos's birthday gift to Imelda, who hails from Tacloban City.[3] In Tacloban, Imelda also built the Sto. Niño Shrine at the site of her alleged childhood home.

North of Metro Manila, there is the abortive Bataan Nuclear Power Plant (BNPP) in Morong, Bataan, as well as several dams like the Angat, Magat, and the Chico River Project.

Connecting the north and south of Metro Manila, Marcos also oversaw the building of the Manila North Expressway and Manila South Expressway—precursors of today's North Luzon and South Luzon Expressways. According to one specific myth, former South Korean president Park Chung-hee visited the Philippines in the 1960s and was awestruck by Radial Road 8, which would become the North Luzon Expressway. Park was so impressed by the road that he "literally cried on Mr. Marcos's shoulder saying 'I wish my country would be just like the Philippines.'"[4] There is no record that this exchange ever happened during Park's only visit as president of South Korea in October

1966. And by the way, the Manila North Expressway opened in 1968.

Other notable infrastructure projects under the regime include the Philippine Children's Hospital in Quezon City, the University of Life building in Pasig City (today the Department of Education Central Office), and the Tondo Urban Renewal Project funded by the World Bank. Up and down the country, there was also the housing project called the BLISS (Bagong Lipunan Improvement of Sites and Services). On a smaller scale, the Marcos dictatorship was also known for its expansive investments in irrigation (which indeed benefited farmers[5]) as well as prefabricated public schoolhouses (bungalows known across the nation as "Marcos-type" school buildings). Marcos has also been credited on social media for supposedly creating 50,000 bridges during his years in power.[6] At his inauguration on 30 June 2022, President Marcos Jr. also boasted that his father had "built more and better roads . . . than all administrations before his."[7]

Note that Marcos's infrastructure spending started as early as his first term as president, from 1965 to 1969. And it continued well into the dictatorship until the early 1980s.

PERHAPS THE FIRST THING TO SAY IS THAT MANY of the infrastructure-related claims made by Marcos supporters on social media are prone to exaggeration. For instance, data from the *Philippine Statistical Yearbook* show that in 1985, the country only had a total of 19,738 national and local bridges—well below the 50,000-figure claimed by loyalists.[8] Meanwhile, though the regime did build a lot more roads, most of these were local roads. By 1984, there were 3.3 times more local roads than in 1964–1965; in contrast, the number of national roads grew by just 1.6 times more.[9] Although the expansion of roads seems impressive, this only served to entrench a car-centric culture that accounts for the severe traffic congestion problems that have spilled over into the twenty-first century (more on this later). Some people also claim that Marcos Sr. built the Manila International Airport—when, in fact, it was first built in 1953, well before Marcos became president in 1965.[10]

Every administration is expected to build roads, bridges, airports, ports, and other infrastructure. But the Marcos regime was infamous for constructing needlessly grandiose and expensive buildings that were the brainchild of Ferdinand Sr. and Imelda themselves—but chiefly of Imelda. Her penchant to build grand structures has been pejoratively called "edifice complex," a play on Oedipus complex.[11] Imelda saw herself as a patroness not only of architecture, but more broadly, of arts and culture. Unsurprisingly, she tapped National Artists not only in building these structures but also to fill them with notable works of art (such as paintings, sculptures, and furniture). For instance, Imelda recruited National Artist Leandro V. Locsin to design many iconic edifices, including the CCP, the PICC, the Folk Arts Theater, and the National Arts Center—most of which were dominated by an aesthetic called "brutalist" architecture.[12] Meanwhile, National Artist Francisco Mañosa designed the Coconut Palace. So aside from a "golden age of infrastructure," some say that there was a "golden age of architecture" as well. At any rate, all of this stems from Imelda's insatiable desire "to show the world that . . . we have a pretty face."[13] Imelda's involvement in numerous infrastructure projects came to a point of what one might consider a feverish obsession:

> In those days Imelda hardly slept, and people who worked closely with her recall how she would sometimes call them in the middle of the night to check on the progress of construction. Sometimes she would even make pre-dawn visits to the sites.[14]

It is not hard to grasp that the Marcosian edifices had something to do with the Marcoses' political ambitions and goals. Even today, politicians love to plaster their names (or at least their initials) or even their faces on highly visible infrastructure projects, including school facades, multipurpose buildings, and waiting sheds (and even ambulances!). Their objective is to boost visibility and improve name recall come election time. Likewise, the Marcoses were motivated by the same underlying incentive, but in their case, they went farther than anyone else in cementing their name in the national psyche—and for the long haul. Indeed, Marcos Sr. used the following slogan in his reelection bid in 1969: "Rice, Roads, Schoolhouses." And in the 11 November 1969 elections, he won on a landslide: 61.5 percent of votes, versus just 38.5 percent for his opponent, Sergio Osmeña Jr., former Cebu City mayor.[15] Marcos's 61.5 percent was almost 10 percentage points higher than what he got when he first won the presidency in 1965.[16]

One good example of a politically motivated project was the Cultural Center of the Philippines. Ostensibly, it served Imelda's purpose of showcasing to the world Philippine culture and arts as well as a gateway for Filipino audiences to enjoy the performances of international artists. Indeed, in its heyday, the CCP would feature performances from renowned international artists, such as pianist Van Cliburn (with whom Imelda formed a close personal relationship[17]), opera singer Plácido Domingo, French mime Marcel Marceau, The Royal Ballet, the Bolshoi Ballet, and the New York Philharmonic Orchestra.[18] But at the same time, the CCP was built in the late stages of Ferdinand's first term as president and its construction was a way to anchor the Marcos name as he sought reelection in 1969.

Meanwhile, many other projects were built to show the world—specifically visiting world leaders—the purported prosperity of the Philippines under Marcos's New Society. The Philippine Plaza Hotel, for instance, was built in time for the 1976 Annual Meetings of the World Bank and the International Monetary Fund[19] (Marcos himself was quite close to Robert McNamara, the president of the World Bank, who propped up the dictatorship with significant loans). Aside from the Philippine Plaza Hotel, many other luxury hotels were built for those 1976 meetings, and about 14 hotels received loans amounting to USD 500 million—about 30 to 40 times as large as the regime's spending on public housing.[20] Meanwhile, the Coconut Palace was built to be the guest house of Pope John Paul II during his 1981 visit. However, the Pope ultimately chose to stay at the humble abode of the Papal Nuncio because he reportedly could not stand the Coconut Palace's opulence.[21] The Palace in the Sky was also meant to be US president Ronald Reagan's guest house for his planned visit in 1983. Construction started in 1981, but the Palace in the Sky was not completed because Reagan's trip was cancelled, and the Marcoses "couldn't be bothered with finishing it."[22] At that point, however, the project—featuring a "sweeping spiral staircase," a "sweeping veranda," and endless rooms—had already cost USD 10 million. During the Corazon Aquino administration, visitors were allowed to enter the Palace in the Sky for the first time, and guests were said to have been equally amazed and outraged by its opulence.

Indeed, the Marcoses went to ridiculous lengths to rush infrastructure projects and showcase them to visiting world leaders or celebrities. This obsession is perhaps best exemplified by the hasty and haphazard construction of the Manila Film Center. Modeled after the Parthenon in Greece, and costing about USD 25 million[23]—a significant sum then, especially considering that the economy was already deteriorating—Imelda commanded that it be built within ten months. But on 17 November 1981, about two months before the slated opening (in time for the Manila International Film Festival), the upper scaffolding at the sixth floor collapsed—killing 26, injuring about 41, and allegedly burying alive "at least 30" more people under quick-drying cement.[24] Later counts put the number of people buried at 168 or 169.[25] As recounted by acclaimed director Lino Brocka in a video that went viral on social media:

> It was a choice between going through with the building, and burying those people, or stopping the construction, in which case it would not have been ready for the festival then. And so [Imelda] made a very controversial decision, she says 'Go ahead and bury them.' So some of those workers were buried here, and right away there was a news blackout, but some pictures came out . . . . [Some workers] were just cut into pieces, and some of them were still I think alive, but then it was not possible to get them out, because the cement by then hardened already . . . [26]

So rushed was the Manila Film Center that during its inauguration, the fountain in front was not working and firetrucks had to be brought in to fill it with water (the firetrucks were hidden beneath coconut leaves, but reportedly, no one was fooled by this disguise). Also, rather symbolically, at the opening night of the Manila International Film Festival, Imelda was said to have swatted an "enormous cloud" of huge flies (or *bangaw* in Filipino)—presumably attracted by the stench left by the corpses buried below.[27]

Meanwhile, the Tondo Urban Renewal Project was funded by the World Bank with a USD 32-million loan in 1976 to develop the area and resettle informal settlers to Dagat-Dagatan in Caloocan.[28] But since the project started late, not much progress could be seen in time for the 1976 Annual Meetings of the World Bank and IMF held in Manila. To make up for its embarrassing lack of progress, Imelda—as governor of Metro Manila—ordered the hasty eviction of hundreds of families in Tondo and the demolition of their houses.[29] Another account says that about 60,000 shanties were removed "so as not to offend [Imelda's] banker guests," and that Imelda bulldozed the houses of informal settlers along Del Pan Bridge, which she considered an "eyesore."[30] According to a *New York Times* report, "most of those displaced were carted, many in garbage trucks and with armed police at hand, to remote sites as far as 20 miles outside the city where they put up shanties no better than what they had left."[31] These evictions proved "embarrassing" for the World Bank. Similar mass evictions were made to pave the way (literally) for Pope John Paul II's 1981 visit.[32]

Other structures were deeply personal for the Marcoses. Take for instance the Sto. Niño Shrine in Tacloban, a mansion that was ostensibly the ancestral home of Imelda's family, the Romualdezes. Imelda's brother Bejo once claimed that the Romualdezes "owned" the Sto. Niño Shrine "since 1880." But in fact the shrine was built only in the early 1980s.[33] Evidently, the shrine, too, is part and parcel of Marcosian myth-making.

In 2016, I was able to visit the Sto. Niño Shrine—now sequestered and maintained by the PCGG—while being toured around Tacloban City by an economist friend teaching at the local UP campus there. After paying a small entrance fee, we made our way inside the shrine and I was immediately struck by how palatial it was. There were two floors: at the center of the ground floor was a chapel surrounded by 13 display bedrooms of different motifs or themes, named after different regions of the Philippines (Palawan, Bicolnon, etc.) and indigenous materials (*banig*, *capiz* shells, etc.). There was a grand staircase (Imelda was fond of these) that led to the second floor where you can find the Marcoses' personal living room and bedrooms (Imelda supposedly stayed here on just one occasion). The shrine was adorned with grand paintings, furniture, chandeliers, and other artifacts. Even though much of the rooms were dusty and had an air of neglect about them, one could still detect the needless opulence of it all. Here is what I wrote about it on Facebook shortly after my visit:

> Nothing could've prepared me for the degree of opulence inside. Two paintings in particular left an indelible mark [on] me. The first was a big portrait of Imelda's family tree, which can be found at the grand staircase. Second was a huge portrait of Imelda behind what seem to be thrones flanked by two antelopes. Upon closer inspection of the

FIGURE 8.1 Inside the Sto. Niño Shrine in Tacloban, 2016 (Photo by the author)

> portrait, Imelda seems to be clutching a huge shell which contains smaller shells bearing the faces of her children (including that of Bongbong). What's more, a ghostlike image of [Marcos Sr.] was hovering in Imelda's background.

I left the place thinking: was it a shrine in honor of the Sto. Niño or of Imelda?

AMBITIOUS AND GRAND AS THE MARCOS infrastructure projects were, these came at a colossal cost to Philippine society and do not rightly deserve adulation from Filipinos. The reason is threefold.

First, a vast majority of these infrastructure projects were financed on the back of huge external loans that buried the country deep in debt by the 1980s. A common theme throughout the dictatorship was an increasing role of the government in markets and daily life. This is manifested not just in the tremendous sums of money spent by the government but also in the changing *structure* of its spending. De Dios et al. noted that the Marcos regime spent an increasing share of its money on "economic services" (i.e., roads, construction, mining, manufacturing, agriculture, fishing, forestry, etc.), defense, and public administration.[34] Construction spending in particular grew by more than 65 percent during Marcos's first term (compared to the term of Diosdado Macapagal) and further ballooned since then (figure 8.2). By 1982, the Marcos regime was spending PHP 5.4 billion on construction—more than five times when martial law was declared a decade earlier.

In contrast, the share to total spending of social services, such as education and health, dwindled.

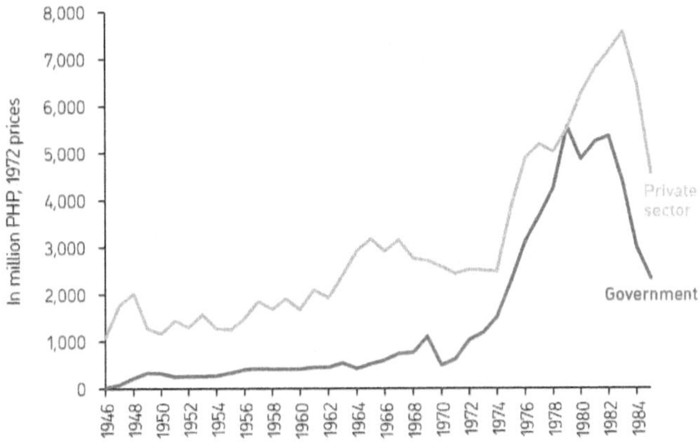

FIGURE 8.2 Government and private construction spending, 1946–1985 (Sources of data: *Philippine Statistical Yearbook*, various years)

Infrastructure spending per se is not bad; in fact, it is good—at face value. However, while Marcos was spending profligately on projects left and right—in fact a lot more than his predecessors—his government was not earning so much money. Revenues grew, but at a much more muted pace than spending. When the government spends more than it earns, it incurs a *budget deficit*. Expectedly, the budget deficit skyrocketed during martial law, especially in the mid-1970s until the early 1980s. Simply put, Marcos spent well beyond his means. At the same time, remember that the government continually ran out of dollars due to prevailing trade and industrial policies. This led the Marcos regime to borrow significant sums of dollars from abroad, and this snowballed into the full-fledged debt and economic crisis that Filipinos endured in the early 1980s.[35]

Second, many of the infrastructure projects proved needless or inefficient. We know from everyday experience that borrowing per se is not bad—so long as we spend the money we borrow wisely and on items with good returns on investment. However, this was not at all the case with Marcos's infrastructure projects. De Dios et al. could not have said it plainer: "the bulk of construction and other capital outlays in both the private and public sectors were not very productive and many were outright wasteful."[36]

A perfect example of the inefficiency of Marcos's big infrastructure projects is the white elephant that is the Bataan Nuclear Power Plant (BNPP)—which some people erroneously claim was copied by South Korea to build their own Hanul Nuclear Power Plant.[37] The BNPP cost USD 2.3 billion,[38] took about a decade to build, and took about three decades for Filipinos to pay in full (the payments ended only in April 2007, or 21 years after EDSA 1). Despite its colossal cost, the BNPP did not produce a single kilowatt of electricity to prevent or abate the energy crisis that it was supposed to address in the first place. (We have more to say about this project later.)

Many of the Marcos projects were also "overdesigned," including the designer (or *bopis*) hospitals in Quezon City. Apart from being overdesigned, such hospitals were criticized for being not at all equitable: they were located around Quezon City, within a kilometer of one another; what about patients in dire need of medical care from areas outside of Luzon, let alone in the Visayas and Mindanao?[39]

The large-scale inefficiency of Marcosian projects is captured by a statistic called the *incremental capital-output ratio* (ICOR). Simply, this tells us the amount of capital

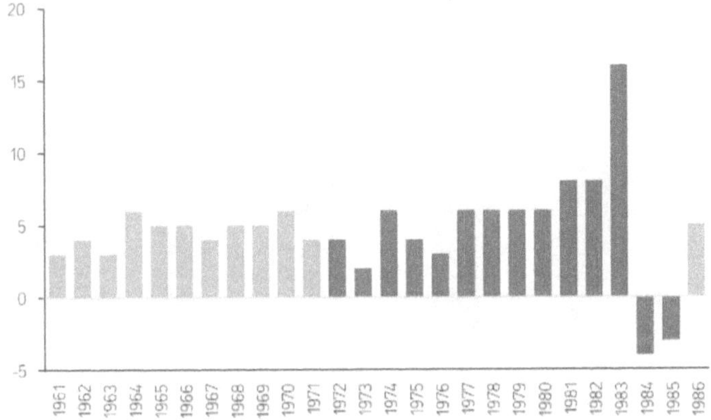

FIGURE 8.3 Incremental capital-output ratio of infrastructure projects, 1961–1986 (Notes: Higher values mean greater inefficiency, dark gray bars denote martial law years; source of data: Philippine Statistics Authority)

needed to produce a unit of output. A higher value of ICOR means higher inefficiency. Throughout the 1970s, the Philippines' ICOR continually increased until it reached record highs in 1981 to 1983 (figure 8.3). The country's ICOR was also considerably higher than that of neighboring countries like Indonesia, Thailand, and Malaysia from 1974 to 1980 (figure 8.4).[40]

An even simpler way to appreciate this point about infrastructure inefficiency is simply to look at the growth rates of the Philippine economy throughout martial law. Even if we were borrowing significantly larger sums than our neighbors in ASEAN during martial law, such borrowings did not at all translate to faster growth. Although the economy grew from 1972 to 1981—in fact, we would register an amazing annual growth rate of 8.8 percent in both 1973 and 1976, which is still unmatched to this day—

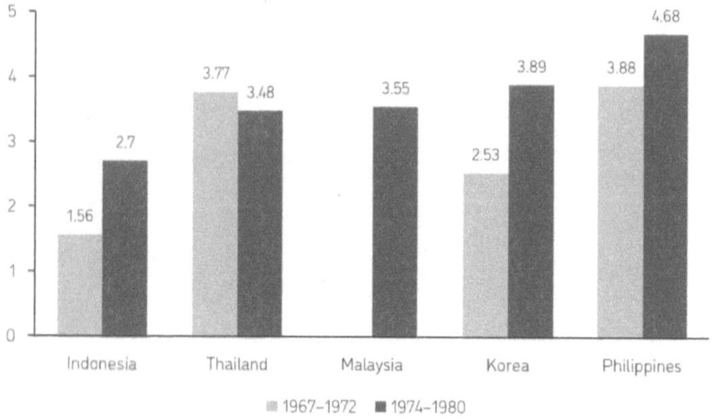

FIGURE 8.4 Incremental capital-output ratio of infrastructure projects in select Asian countries, 1967–1980 (Note: Data for Malaysia [1967–1972] not available; source of data: Robert S. Dohner and Ponciano Intal Jr., "Debt Crisis and Adjustment in the Philippines," in *Developing Country Debt and the World Economy*, ed. Jeffrey Sachs [Chicago: University of Chicago Press, 1989], 169–92.)

our total debt outpaced the growth of our national income by a factor of 3.4 (and outpaced exports by a factor of 2.0). In other words, the recorded peak economic growth rate of 8.8 percent paled in comparison with the growth of debt, which skyrocketed to more than 30 percent by the late 1970s (and even exceeded 40 percent in 1979). Also, as we discussed in chapter 1, the list of countries that became more prosperous than us only became longer from 1965 to 1985, telling us that we undeniably lagged behind. While we experienced economic growth, it was debt-driven—and not impressively high at that.

Nor did the multitude of Marcos's transportation investments alleviate traffic. In fact, things got worse because such investments were decidedly car-centric. Between 1962 and 1985, the number of private cars reportedly grew by a whopping 500 percent, while the number of buses fell by 17 percent. By 1976, cars constituted about two-thirds of traffic in Metro Manila vis-à-vis buses, which constituted just five percent.[41] Moreover, spending on cars amounted to about USD 3.25 billion in the 1970s. All of these mean several things. For instance, the significant debts of the Marcos regime partly went to the imported goods (including cars) for the rich, highlighting the privileges of the rich as well as the inequality prevailing at the time. More importantly, the privileging of cars and the massive investments placed in roads during the time set the trend and planted the seeds of even worse traffic congestion in succeeding decades, representing a penalty on future economic growth. Fast-forward to 2018, Metro Manila traffic cost our economy PHP 3.5 billion daily, according to the Japan International Cooperation Agency (JICA). They said it could go up to as high as PHP 5.4 billion daily by 2035 sans necessary changes in traffic investments and policies.[42]

Third, and perhaps most egregiously, the Marcosian infrastructure projects became vehicles for massive corruption and plunder. Many were "designed to secure a political constituency, to get a commission, or to corner a contract."[43] Perhaps, to make the corruption less obvious, some projects were ostensibly "endowed with some plausible or social justification." But in truth, each project served as an "opportunity to use government activity as a vehicle for private gain, whether pecuniary or political."[44]

Again, the BNPP is a perfect example.[45] In the aftermath of the 1974 oil price hike, many governments—including those in oil-dependent countries like the Philippines—felt the need to ensure energy independence for their citizens.

Hence, the Marcos regime was on the lookout for a project to address an impending energy crisis. At the same time, the American company Westinghouse was looking for a client who might be interested in nuclear power plants, in the face of continuing fears about the technology as well as dwindling demand for it abroad. Seeing a potential client in Marcos, Westinghouse offered to build a nuclear power plant in the country.

But the ensuing deal was riddled with anomalies. First, it is said that Westinghouse secured the deal by just proffering a brochure to Marcos, instead of sending a proper quotation.[46] Second, the initial cost was USD 500 million but ballooned to USD 1.9 billion, with an overprice of no less than USD 75 million according to some reports. Third, Westinghouse got the deal with the help of a broker—Herminio Disini, one of Marcos's cronies. It is said that from the BNPP deal alone, Disini got commissions amounting to USD 43 million to USD 80 million, while Marcos himself profited by no less than USD 30 million.[47] Apart from this, Disini later earned money from various subcontracting projects revolving around the BNPP. So overpriced and riddled with kickbacks was the contract that it was described by one industry secretary as "one reactor for the price of two."[48] Fourth, the BNPP was rushed and built within a 100-mile radius of four active volcanoes, including the still "potentially active" Mt. Natib.[49] This necessitated additional retrofitting and installation of safety equipment that padded the costs further by USD 100 million. Fifth, the US Export-Import Bank agreed to underwrite and finance the project despite all the glaring red flags. Years later, cases were filed against Westinghouse for bribery and overpricing. However, these cases did not prosper. Disini was also charged for his complicity, but it was only in 2021 (35 years after Marcos's ouster) that the Supreme Court concurred with the decision of the Sandiganbayan back in 2012 ordering Disini to pay (from his estate) the government damages totaling PHP 1 billion.[50]

Corruption also prospered thanks to the Marcosian projects erected by crony Rodolfo Cuenca. Cuenca first came into the orbit of Marcos from being a frequent golfing buddy as well as a supporter of Marcos's first bid for the presidency in 1965.[51] Cuenca's social capital paid off when Marcos won. In the same year as Marcos's first victory, Cuenca established the Construction and Development Corporation of the Philippines (CDCP), which in 1967 won the contract for the construction of the Manila North Expressway (amounting to USD 7.4 million) and the Manila South Expressway (for USD 8.7 million). Over time, the CDCP also won the contracts to build the Terminal 1 of MIA, the San Juanico Bridge, and the Light Rail Transit (LRT) in Manila (together with a counterpart Belgian firm).

All of these projects were riddled with problems.[52] For instance, the CDCP won all related contracts for the MIA terminal—except for electro-mechanical work, which was obtained by Tasei, a Japanese company. But Tasei was not granted a permit by the Marcos government, and in the end, the CDCP bagged this final contract as well. There were criticisms, too, that the San Juanico Bridge—the "Bridge of Love"—was quite needless because the small volume of trade between Samar and Leyte did not warrant its construction. Also, studies indicated that, instead of a light rail system, a "street-level transport system" was far less costly and more efficient than the LRT—whose cost blew up from USD 216 million to USD 279 million and which needed colossal subsidies from the government to avoid bankruptcy.

But Cuenca's biggest project was the USD 1-billion reclamation of Manila Bay. Meant to solve the growing problem of parking and traffic in the metro, it involved the addition of 3,000 hectares of land over Manila Bay as well as a new highway going to Cavite (known as the Coastal Road). Soon enough, signs of Imelda's excesses were manifest: aside from the erection of edifices like the CCP, Imelda also ordered the construction of a 240-hectare artificial beach behind CCP to simulate the shores of Cannes, France and impress visitors to the Manila International Film Festival. Several tons of sand from Cavite and Mariveles, Bataan were brought in to satisfy Imelda's luxurious wish.[53]

Cuenca had intended to sell land from the project and estimated that such properties would earn "quick money"—estimated at USD 427 million. Cuenca also banked on the appreciation of such properties, especially with Imelda's edifices built all around it.[54] Although the properties were offered to potential companies in Hong Kong and Singapore, few were really interested. By 1979, when the reclamation project was incurring huge losses, the Marcos regime allowed the CDCP to sell 222 hectares of the reclaimed land. Buried in debt and with little sales to show for, the CDCP incurred losses amounting to USD 158 million by 1978, which blew up to USD 650 million by 1980 or in just two years.

Eventually, Cuenca's businesses had to be taken over and bailed out by government banks such as the DBP and the PNB.[55] In 1981, the government took over Cuenca's hotels, including the Taal Vista Lodge and Hotel Mindanao. Marcos also instructed government financial institutions like PNB and GSIS to take over CDCP. Much of CDCP's debts (amounting to USD 460 million by 1983—or even as large as USD 700 million according to other estimates) were converted as shares of these government financial institutions. That amount was equivalent to about a fifth of the country's total foreign exchange reserves then as well as a fifth of the total money supply in cash. Essentially, the Marcos regime condoned or forgave Cuenca's debts, including interest. Worse, some other companies of Cuenca had easy access to loans even as the CDCP was already in the doldrums. All in all, the Marcos regime bailed out CDCP with PHP 5 billion worth of taxpayers' money, in the form of new loans (PHP 1.1 billion) and old debts converted into equity or shares (PHP 3.9 billion).[56] Another estimate put the total bailout at PHP 6.2 billion between 1981 and 1983, "an amount roughly equivalent to 25% of the country's money supply and 30% of tax collections by the Bureau of Internal Revenue in 1981."[57] At any rate, former minister of industry Roberto Ongpin (who later took over the CDCP) said that the bailout was the "most obscene, brazen and disgraceful misallocation of taxpayers' money in the history of the Philippines." *Time Magazine*, at the time, called it a "Chrysler-size package put through without any debate or publicity."[58]

Note that the CDCP was only one of the many crony companies bailed out by the Marcos regime in the early 1980s, even as the economy was already tumbling toward a full-blown crisis. Like a person who drives more recklessly knowing that her car is insured,[59] the availability of government bailout money during martial law meant that crony companies had little to no incentive to be efficient with their ways. In the end, the public paid for their misdeeds.

But alongside the inefficiency came the corruption. According to reports, Marcos "received millions of dollars in kickbacks on government construction contracts from Cuenca's company and others."[60] In 1987, the Corazon

Aquino administration filed a case against the Marcoses and Cuenca for alleged corrupt acts. Specifically, the government alleged that Cuenca,

> by himself, and/or in unlawful concert with defendants Ferdinand E. Marcos and Imelda R. Marcos, [took] undue advantage of his influence and association and with the active collaboration and willing participation of above defendant spouses, engaged in schemes, devices and strategems designed to unjustly enrich themselves and to prevent disclosure and discovery of ill-gotten assets.[61]

The government sought PHP 50 billion in moral damages and PHP 1 billion in exemplary damages[62] since Cuenca and cohorts obtained "favored public works contracts" for projects like the LRT, "secured loans and financial assistance" from government banks without enough capital, and "secured a favored rescue arrangement at the behest of defendants Ferdinand E. Marcos and Imelda R. Marcos in the form, among others, of conversion of multimillion peso debt in favor of NDC into equity."

But in 2018, the Supreme Court finally dismissed the case against the Marcoses, Cuenca, and other defendants since the government "failed to prove by preponderance of evidence." The high court even pointed out that the case lost because the government had resorted to mere *photocopies* of their pieces of evidence, which are inadmissible in court.[63] This decision frustrated a lot of people. Some progressive leaders said that the Supreme Court "disregarded" the history of Marcosian crony capitalism and decried the decision as a "sharp insult" to martial law victims.[64]

FAST-FORWARD TO THE 21ST CENTURY, MYTHS AND exaggerations about Marcosian infrastructure, sadly, still abound. For instance, one viral post said that there were no mass transit projects built by the government after Marcos Sr.'s term. This is nonsense, of course. Although Marcos Sr. had built LRT Line 1, there were other railways built and are still in existence, including the Metro Rail Transit (MRT) Line 3 along EDSA and the LRT Line 2 from Recto to Antipolo.[65] Aside from these, there are also other railways under construction, including the MRT Line 7 along Commonwealth Avenue and the Metro Manila Subway of the Duterte administration. We have not even mentioned the other types of mass transit, including the roll-on/roll-off (RORO) ships and point-to-point buses popularized under the Arroyo and Noynoy Aquino administrations, respectively.

Sometimes, too, the misconceptions come in the form of credit-grabbing. For instance, a viral post said that Marcos Sr. planned the Skyway Stage 3, a project that was allegedly stymied by Corazon Aquino and only pushed through under Rodrigo Duterte's term.[66] The truth, though, is that the project was first crafted during the Ramos administration in the 1990s and was finally approved during Noynoy Aquino's term in 2013 as a public-private partnership (PPP) with San Miguel Corporation. Marcos Sr. never had any hand in it.

THIS BRINGS US TO ONE LAST—AND ESPECIALLY symbolic—infrastructure myth: that former president Benigno Aquino III had ordered the destruction of the infamous 30-meter-high concrete bust of Ferdinand Marcos's face at Tuba, Benguet.

FIGURE 8.5 Baguio-based activists holding a protest at the defaced Ferdinand Marcos bust in 2021 to commemorate the fifth year of the dictator's burial at the Libingan ng mga Bayani (Photo by Sherwin De Vera of *Northern Dispatch*)

Finished between 1978 and 1980, costing around PHP 3 million at the time, and said to be modeled after Mt. Rushmore, the Marcos bust is perhaps the best manifestation of the narcissistic and egotistical edifice complex of Ferdinand and Imelda. It was meant to be part of an abortive 355-hectare Marcos Park, situated on Ibaloi ancestral land (several Ibaloi families were displaced during the bust's construction). But contrary to social media posts, the bust was blasted by unidentified people way back in December 2002—nearly eight years before Noynoy Aquino took office.[67]

Right after the People Power Revolution, there were plans to have the bust blown up. It is quite understandable why many locals have long wanted to do so. First, the bust was built even as the road infrastructure in the town where it was located (Tuba, Benguet) still had poor roads—yet another indication of the double standards in Marcos's infrastructure spree. Rose Laboten, one of the Ibaloi locals, said in 1986: "We have a joke we tell to explain why our roads are not paved in Tuba. It's because the president was sick and they kept using more and more concrete to fill in his cheeks."[68] More seriously, the bust came to be a painful reminder of the dictatorship and the displacement it entailed. Laboten added: "Imagine living with this huge Marcos head staring down at you for the next many years—long after he's gone . . . . All it reminds us of is the damage and the pain he caused to all of us."

Despite this, former president Corazon Aquino thumbed down that proposal to demolish the bust (she did however allow the displaced Ibaloi to conduct rituals to "exorcise" the bust).[69]

Fast-forward to 2021, the blasted Marcos bust found a new purpose as the site of a protest by groups such as the Cordillera People's Alliance to protest the 2022 presidential bid of the dictator's son, Bongbong Marcos.[70] One of the protesters said: "The North remembers, the North resists. Marcos was and will never be a hero."[71]

IN SUMMARY, MARCOS DID BRING ABOUT WHAT could objectively be called a "golden age" of infrastructure and architecture. But the various edifices and other infrastructure projects he and Imelda had built came into being because of ballooning debt, were often inefficient and needless, and served as vehicles for various acts of corruption. The projects were also often used to wrap around the Philippines an image of prosperity and stability under Marcos's rule. But hidden behind these grand projects is the true state of society: widespread and increasing poverty coupled with mounting unrest. Big and sprawling as these were, the edifices could only do so much to hide the larger truth that we were by no means a developed country under martial law. Will the newer generations of Filipinos learn to see beyond the spectacle of it all?

09 Marcos signed the 13th-month pay law? Contractualization did not exist?

CLAIM 1 Marcos signed the 13th-month pay law.	**VERDICT** MISSING CONTEXT
CLAIM 2 Contractualization did not exist during martial law.	**VERDICT** FALSE

MARCOS LOYALISTS ON SOCIAL MEDIA CLAIM THAT labor, too, benefited during martial law. They say, for instance, that it was Marcos who should be credited for the 13th-month pay that Filipino workers enjoy today—even going as far as saying that those opposing Marcos should refuse to receive their 13th-month pay come Christmastime. Loyalists also claim that labor contractualization was nonexistent during the Marcos years and that Corazon Aquino passed a law establishing such practice.

As with the other golden age myths, these notions are a mix of half-truths or flat lies.

While it is true that Marcos signed in 1975 a presidential decree requiring all employers to give their workers a 13th-month pay, it only covered workers "receiving a basic salary of not more than P1,000 a month."[1] In other words, the pay was by no means universal. President Corazon Aquino corrected this policy through a memorandum order signed in August 1986 that made the 13th-month pay a benefit for all workers.[2]

Also, Marcos himself was not at all the proponent of the concept of the 13th-month pay. In various instances, it is credited to labor leaders in Congress such as Zoilo de la Cruz (regarded as the "father of the 13th-month pay" and who supposedly drafted the bill and lobbied it to Marcos, with whom he was deemed to be "close") and Eulogio Lerum (who was said to have led the "labor delegation to the 1975 National Tripartite Conference").[3]

At any rate, the 13th-month pay was not the brainchild of Marcos. More importantly, we need to contrast his "achievement" against the devastation that his regime wrought on the labor sector. For instance, the fast rise of prices—also called inflation—led to an erosion of the real value of workers' wages as early as 1970, even before martial law was imposed. Prices rose rapidly: from a low inflation rate of 1.4 percent in 1969, inflation skyrocketed to 15 percent in 1970.

Such acceleration of prices, caused by the forced devaluation of the peso (see chapter 2) and the unabated rise of global oil prices, meant that workers could buy fewer goods with the same salaries or wages they earned. Figure 9.1 shows how much the real value of workers' wages plummeted throughout the Marcos years (from 1969 to 1985): by 71 percent for skilled labor and 76 percent for unskilled labor. Agricultural wages also fell by a third from 1962 to 1986.[4]

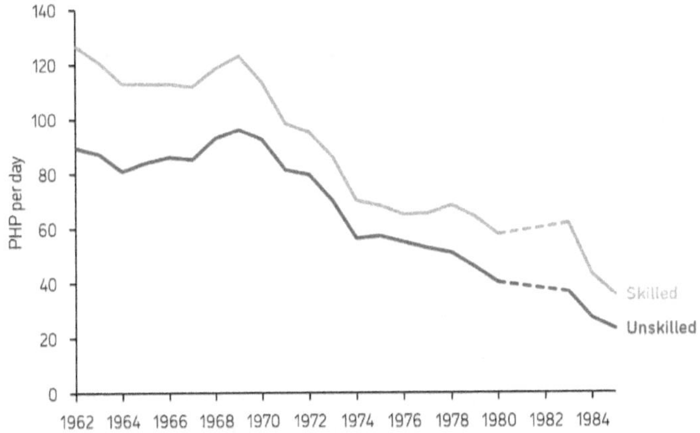

FIGURE 9.1 Real wages for skilled and unskilled labor, 1962–1985 (Note: In constant 1986 prices, converted using CPI; data for 1981 and 1982 not available; source of data: James K. Boyce, *The Philippines: The Political Economy of Growth and Impoverishment in the Marcos Era* [Hampshire: The Macmillan Press Ltd., 1993], 28.)

The decline of real wages in the 1970s and 1980s was "on a magnitude with few precedents in modern economic history," according to Boyce.[5] He also called it "immiserizing growth"—that is, whatever growth that happened at the time had failed to trickle down to the masses. Of all the indicators coming from that time, the decline of real wages is arguably the clearest manifestation of the rise of inequality during martial law.

This is somehow corroborated by income data from that time, based on the Family Income and Expenditure Survey (FIES)—but only if one makes the necessary adjustments to fix certain biases present in the data. Economist Jona Estudillo, using FIES data, showed that there was in fact a reported *fall* in inequality in 1985 (using the Gini coefficient), "due to the rise in the income shares of the two lowest and middle quantiles at the expense of the two highest quintiles."[6] But there are caveats to this. First, the FIES has long been criticized for failing to capture the incomes of the highest income groups.[7] Second, to make sense of this seemingly anomalous result, one needs to account for the differing levels of income underreporting across income classes. That is, one needs to keep in mind that income underreporting may have been more severe among the rich rather than the poor (e.g., due to capital flight among the rich or better reporting of non-cash income among the poor). Bearing this in mind, and making some data adjustments, Boyce found that "rather than a 45 percent rise in the real incomes of the poorest 30 per cent between 1961 and 1985, Series C shows a 23 percent decline."[8] Also, the ratio of the population share of the richest ten percent to the poorest 30 percent would rise, rather than fall, over the same period. The same finding applies to both rural and urban areas. Murky income data mean that conclusions about income distribution from the FIES are "necessarily conjectural."[9] But one can see from the analysis of Boyce that from 1961 to 1971, the rich became richer and the poor became poorer. Then from 1971 to 1985, everyone got poorer somehow, but those who were already poor suffered more than the rich—again, immiserizing growth.

AT ANY RATE, IT SHOULD COME AS NO SURPRISE that these trends toward increasing inequality sparked widespread social unrest and discontent. This was exemplified by the First Quarter Storm of 1970, which kicked off with massive protests outside the Legislative Building in Manila (now the National Museum of Fine Arts) on 26 January 1970, when Marcos delivered his State of the Nation Address (having just won his historic second term in office).[10] Although primarily led by student groups, labor organizations were also represented well in that protest.[11] After the speech, Ferdinand and Imelda emerged from the building and were pelted with several objects like bottles and stones and even "a cardboard coffin and a papier-mâché crocodile."[12] The violent dispersal led to several injuries and at least two deaths; more protesters would get injured and die during the First Quarter Storm.[13]

Apart from being more common in the 1970s, labor strikes also became a lot more violent because of the involvement of state forces. And Marcos slyly used the chaotic events to partly justify his declaration of martial law in 1972. Once martial law was imposed, Marcos banned labor strikes and cracked down on labor activists. Labor leaders who voiced out labor concerns were hunted down or killed like animals.

The labor sector continued to endure "systemic harassment by government forces" well into the late years of martial law, until the early 1980s. As the economy descended to even greater depths, strikes became more frequent again. From August to September 1982 alone, some 50 trade unionists were apprehended in Metro Manila by the military in coordination with "private company guards."[14] Activists were regularly beaten and shot at when they resisted during these confrontations and those apprehended were routinely charged with conspiracy to commit rebellion or sedition. Later, in 1984 and 1985, there would be a massive rise of unemployment and underemployment and even more OFWs would flee the country—encouraged by Marcos's long-standing "labor export policy."[15]

As for contractualization, the fact is that it existed during Marcos's time.[16] The Labor Code of 1974, issued by Marcos via a presidential decree, provided for "probationary employment" for a period not exceeding six months. An employee hired this way "may be terminated for a just cause or when he fails to qualify as a regular employee in accordance with reasonable standards made known by the employer to the employee at the time of his engagement."[17] This provided an opportunity for firms to lay off workers before they became permanent and entitled to benefits for regular employees. At any rate, it was Marcos, not Corazon Aquino, who laid the foundations for contractualization—a policy that succeeding governments would find difficult, if not impossible, to undo because of strong pushback from the business sector.[18]

Long story short: the Marcos years were far from the workers' paradise that some people are painting it to be.

10 Crime went down? Only one person was executed by the regime?

CLAIM 1	VERDICT
Crime plummeted during martial law.	FALSE

CLAIM 2	VERDICT
Only one person was executed during the regime.	FALSE

CLAIM 3	VERDICT
No one was arrested for criticizing the government.	FALSE

AS FAR AS MARCOS LOYALISTS ARE CONCERNED, aside from being a "golden age" for the economy, martial law was also a time when criminality went down. To them, it ushered in an unparalleled era of peace and order, which supposedly contributed to the flourishing of the economy under Marcos's Bagong Lipunan (New Society).

Although such claims have been going around for quite some time, these were echoed on 20 September 2018 in a YouTube interview—or more of a tête-à-tête—by Bongbong Marcos himself with Juan Ponce Enrile, his father's former defense minister, one of the architects of martial law, and whose fake ambush in 1972 supposedly triggered its declaration (as discussed in chapter 16, Enrile was also a major crony, enjoying several timber concessions and other business privileges throughout martial law).

As one would expect, the interview was soaking wet with lies. For instance, Enrile claimed that no one was killed apart from the Chinese drug lord Lim Seng[1] and that there were no massacres committed by the regime.[2] Enrile also denied the claim that 70,000 persons were arrested—except, he said, if one were to count curfew violators and jaywalkers. "People could go out at night. They can go out to fish, they could go out to farm, they were free in fact," he added.[3] Lastly, Enrile claimed that not one person was arrested because of "political or religious belief." He even dared critics: "Name me one person who was arrested simply because he criticized Marcos. None."

FIRST, ON THE ALLEGED DECLINE OF CRIME: WHILE there is truth to this, the decline of crime was short-lived. As early as 1984, in a groundbreaking white paper, UP economists noted that from 247 per 100,000 people in 1971, the crime rate dropped to 236 in 1972 upon the declaration of martial law and by 1976, it fell further to 183.[4] At face value, there was indeed some improvement in the crime situation. This was supported by official reports by former president Fidel Ramos, who served as chief of the Philippine Constabulary during martial law (there was no Philippine National Police yet at that time).[5]

But over time, said the economists, "the peace and order situation deteriorated."[6] By 1980, the crime rate was back up to 279 per 100,000 people and further rose to 313 per

100,000 people by 1982. These numbers were even higher than in 1971, before martial law was declared. Moreover, the economists noted there was a significant rise in the number of dissident encounters with the military in the media: from 245 in 1977, there were 852 by 1982. Although it was hard to document accurately, there was also an "increasing number of reports regarding summary executions of persons, popularly known as 'salvaging.'"[7] Finally, they noted as well that the disposal rate of pending cases slowed down from the 1970s to the 1980s, and naturally there was a commensurate rise in the number of backlog cases—suggesting that the wheels of justice at the time seem to be "grinding ever more slowly." All in all, the economists said, "the country in fact appears to be worse off now than before the advent of authoritarian rule as far as peace and order is concerned."[8]

Note as well that violence permeated Philippine society in the years in the run-up to the declaration of martial law in 1972. In August 1971, there was the Plaza Miranda bombing, where two grenades were thrown at a proclamation rally of the Liberal Party, killing nine and injuring almost a hundred people including some senatorial candidates for the 1971 midterm elections. One of the injured was Jovito Salonga, who was then running for reelection as senator (he sustained injuries in his eye and ears, but lived on and even topped the senatorial race).[9] After this incident, Marcos quickly suspended the privilege of the writ of habeas corpus, so anyone could be imprisoned by the government even without court permission. (Habeas corpus was reinstated later, after its suspension incited massive protests.) Meanwhile, between March and September 1972, about twenty other explosions rocked Metro Manila, including the one at Joe's Department Store at Carriedo, Manila. These incidents would in fact be enumerated in Marcos's martial law proclamation itself, Proclamation No. 1081.[10] Aside from these horrifying incidents, operations of the Communist Party of the Philippines (CPP) and its armed group, the New People's Army (NPA), also increased during this time,[11] and they became Marcos's scapegoat for the fake ambush of Juan Ponce Enrile in the same month, which also led to the eventual declaration of martial law.

FAR FROM KILLING JUST ONE PERSON, THE REGIME killed thousands. According to American historian Alfred McCoy, there were at least 3,257 people killed during martial law, based on various sources he culled. This comprised 2,427 "salvagings," 737 disappearances, and 93 "extrajudicial killings" based on data and testimonies. Furthermore, McCoy noted that there were about 35,000 people tortured and 70,000 arrested during the period.[12] Although skeptics have doubted McCoy's figures—primarily because they included *recorded* killings at a time when the media was controlled by the government—these have rather stood the test of time. Other estimates have been put forward. For instance, Amnesty International's figures vary only slightly: they estimated 3,240 people killed from 1972 to 1981, 34,000 tortured, and 70,000 imprisoned.[13] Meanwhile, legal scholar John van Dyke counted the number of abuses from 1972 to 1986 and tallied at least 5,531 instances of torture, 2,537 summary executions, 783 disappearances, and 92,607 "public order violation arrests."[14]

Fast-forward to May 2018, the Human Rights Victims' Claims Board gave reparations to 11,103 people who were confirmed (using solid evidence) to have suffered human rights abuses during the Marcos regime.[15] Here is the breakdown of the approved cases:

- 2,326 killed/disappeared
- 238 raped/forcefully abducted
- 217 tortured to point of mutilation, insanity, or sexual abuse
- 1,467 tortured to point of psychological harm
- 182 tortured with seduction/acts of lasciviousness
- 669 detained for more than six months
- 1,417 detained for 15 days to six months
- 1,239 detained for 36 hours to fifteen days
- 579 involuntarily exiled from the Philippines (with physical injuries)
- 2,739 involuntarily exiled from the Philippines (with no physical injuries)

Some of the most egregious abuses happened against Muslims in Mindanao. By 1977, as many as 40,000 Moro militants were said to have been killed, on top of the 10,000 non-combatants who died and the 1.7 million displaced.[16] What more in the succeeding years during martial law?

Even though the estimates are at times inaccurate and discrepant, it cannot be denied that the human rights abuses numbered thousands.

LOOKING AT NUMBERS IS ONE THING. BUT IT IS another thing to listen to the stories of actual human rights victims—activists, journalists, and in many instances, mere students—who either died in the hands of the regime or survived to tell their tales today.

As there are many victims of the regime's atrocities, we do not have enough space here to recount all of their tales.[17] But among the most prominent deaths include Macli-ing Dulag (a Kalinga leader assassinated by the military in

1980 for opposing the Marcos government's infrastructure projects, notably the Chico River Dam Project), Archimedes Trajano (a 21-year-old who criticized Imee Marcos in an open forum, then later summarily carted off the event, tortured, and killed), Boyet Mijares (tortured and salvaged son of Primitivo Mijares, former top propagandist of Marcos and author of the damning book *The Conjugal Dictatorship of Ferdinand and Imelda Marcos*), and, of course, Senator Ninoy Aquino (killed at the tarmac of the Manila International Airport on 21 August 1983, and whose death was said to have catalyzed the downfall of the regime[18]). The names of many heroes of the martial law period are memorialized on the Wall of Remembrance at the Bantayog ng mga Bayani along Quezon Avenue.

Horrible stories also emerged from the Marcosian massacres that undeniably happened during the Marcos dictatorship, contrary to Enrile's claims.

One is the Palimbang Massacre (or the Malisbong Massacre), which happened at Barangay Malisbong, Palimbang, Sultan Kudarat on 24 September 1974—almost exactly two years since Marcos declared martial law. The entire barangay was "razed to the ground" by soldiers and "allies," destroying some 300 houses. Worse, over the course of a month, some 1,500 males—from teens to senior citizens—were massacred inside the Tacbil Mosque.[19] It caused unimaginable trauma to the community. According to one survivor,

> Every day in the mosque, the Army would get 1 to 10 persons. Those who were inside the mosque would hear shots of fire hours after these people were taken outside. And those who were taken outside never came back.[20]

The atrocities were the stuff of nightmares:

> My grandfather (father of my mother) was buried alive and another relative was nailed to a cross like Christ. . . . I had relatives taken—seven to nine relatives were taken outside, but only the brother of my father survived. All of them were stripped of their clothes; they were brought to the beach; they were made to dig for their own graves; and when they were done, they were shot and killed.[21]

At the same time, women and children were gathered and put in boats, with several women (aged 9 to 60) raped by the perpetrators. When they were released, "most of them lost their sanity."[22]

Another infamous massacre happened on 18 March 1968—well within Marcos's first term as president, and similarly against Muslims. The context of this killing is the Philippine government's covert plan to destabilize Sabah and wrest it from Malaysia through what was called "Project Merdeka." In 1967, army generals—with the complicity of Marcos himself—formed a secret commando unit called "Jabidah" (named after a beautiful woman of Moro lore) to implement the plan. At one point, this operation involved bringing about 180 Tausugs from Basilan, Sulu, and Tawi-Tawi all the way to Corregidor Island to receive training in guerrilla operations and jungle warfare, among others.

However, at Corregidor, the Tausugs were ill-treated. They endured discrimination, lack of compensation, and poor living conditions. Many were also hoodwinked, thinking that their training was in view of being eventual soldiers of the armed forces. The recruits started to become restless and aired their grievances. At one point, they were heard, giving the impression everything was fine. But soon after, the recruits were carted off Corregidor in batches. Some batches were told to start packing for home and were brought to the island's airport, but death awaited there. One survivor, Jibin Arula, recounted:

> When we reached the airport, our escorts alighted ahead of us. Then Lt. Eduardo Nepomuceno ordered us to get down from the truck and line up . . . . As we put down our bags, I heard a series of shots. Like dominoes, my colleagues fell. I got scared. I ran and was shot at, in my left thigh. I didn't know that I was running towards a mountain . . . . By 8 AM, I was rescued by two fishermen on Caballo Island, near Cavite.[23]

All in all, about 60 Tausug recruits were killed. What was to be called the Jabidah Massacre was far from a small, hushed-up massacre. It would cause ripples in the Philippines' political landscape and would reverberate up to the present. In fact, the Jabidah Massacre is said to have sparked the Moro insurgency in Mindanao and the formation of the Moro National Liberation Front (MNLF).

Besides the Palimbang and Jabidah massacres, there were many others: the Manili Massacre (1971) in North Cotabato, the Daet Massacre (1981) in Camarines Norte, the Sag-od Massacre (1981) in Northern Samar, and the Escalante Massacre (1985) in Negros Occidental.[24]

FAR FROM BEING A PEACEFUL UTOPIA, THE Marcos years were drenched in blood. However, despite the abundance of historical and legal evidence of the regime's human rights abuses, many Filipinos today still deny that such atrocities happened. Are the survivors' tales of suffering mere figments of some people's imagination? Other Marcos loyalists have knowledge and actually admit that there were abuses, but they nonetheless brush them off as historical footnotes of little to no consequence—even justifying such atrocities as necessary for the greater good. Worse, these brutal incidents are also rarely discussed, if not entirely absent, in the history books of our students.

If we forget about the past—unwittingly or deliberately—we are bound to repeat it. Indeed, huge waves of human rights abuses would again plague the Philippines under the Duterte administration (2016–2022) nearly half a century after martial law, which would result in even more killings. We can put an end to the wanton bloodshed. How? By remembering and never forgetting the past.

PART 2

CRISIS MISMANAGEMENT

11 Filipinos' purchasing power fell after EDSA?

CLAIM 1	**VERDICT**
Prices were low throughout the Marcos dictatorship; electricity was even free.	FALSE
CLAIM 2	**VERDICT**
While the average "spending power" of Filipinos was PHP 100/day before the Marcoses, that dropped to PHP 27/day after the Marcoses left.	FALSE
CLAIM 3	**VERDICT**
High inflation during the dictatorship was good.	FALSE

ONE OF THE ECONOMIC ARGUMENTS THAT MARCOS loyalists seem to be most confused about revolves around prices and inflation—or the rate of increase of prices. On the one hand, some of them parrot the notion that prices were low throughout the Marcos dictatorship. In fact, some even say that electricity back then was free.[1] Alternatively, they

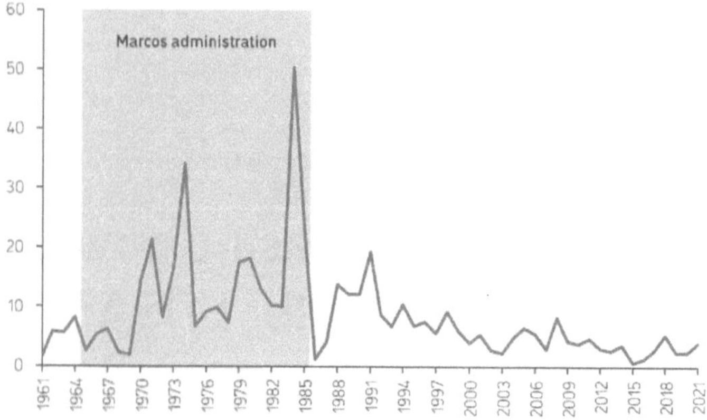

FIGURE 11.1 Inflation rates (in percent), 1961–2021 (Note: Base year 2010; source of data: World Bank)

say that the purchasing power of the peso was significantly lower after Marcos "left" Malacañang than when Marcos first came to power. Some seem to at least accept the notion that prices were astronomically high during the dictatorship but justify them nonetheless as "good" or beneficial for Filipinos.

First, it is not at all true that prices were low and stable during the dictatorship. In fact, prices during that time were exceedingly volatile and inflation even reached historical highs that would simply be unimaginable today. Figure 11.1 shows that the highest annual postwar inflation rate of the Philippines was recorded in 1984, when it reached 50 percent. (In October that year, inflation even peaked at 63.8 percent.[2]) Yearly inflation also exceeded 20 percent in three other years: in 1974 (31.8 percent), 1985 (22.6 percent), and 1971 (20.7 percent). In total, from 1965 to 1985, or in the span of the two decades of Marcosian rule, inflation reached double-digit annual figures in 12 years (thus 60 percent of the regime). And those 12 years accounted for 71 percent of the years that the Philippines recorded double-digit inflation rates since recording of prices began in 1957.[3]

The fact that inflation rose dramatically during the martial law years meant that prices actually accelerated, or rose faster and faster—like your car would when you put the pedal to the metal. One of the starkest increases in inflation then was in 1970, when inflation reached 15 percent, from a very low 1.4 percent the year before. As mentioned in chapter 2, this particular spike of inflation contributed to the widespread social unrest that led to the First Quarter Storm and many other protests in the run-up to the declaration of martial law on 23 September 1972.

High and rising inflation is a problem because it leads to a rapid decline of the purchasing power of the peso. This simply means that your peso income can buy fewer goods and services: with a fixed budget, your shopping bag becomes lighter, and you can fill up fewer liters of fuel in your car or motorcycle.

In figure 11.2, it is evident that the purchasing power of the peso deteriorated rapidly during martial law, especially from 1970 to 1974. It only dropped even more since then. By 1985, or right before EDSA, the purchasing power of the peso was so low that what PHP 100 could buy in 1965, you can only buy PHP 8.10 worth of goods and services by 1985, or twenty years later. That was a whopping 92 percent decline in the peso's purchasing power.

While it is true that the purchasing power of the peso after the Marcos years was much lower than before it, loyalists fail to mention (or understand) two things: first, that the purchasing power of the peso *necessarily* goes down over time (because overall demand rises over time, and so do

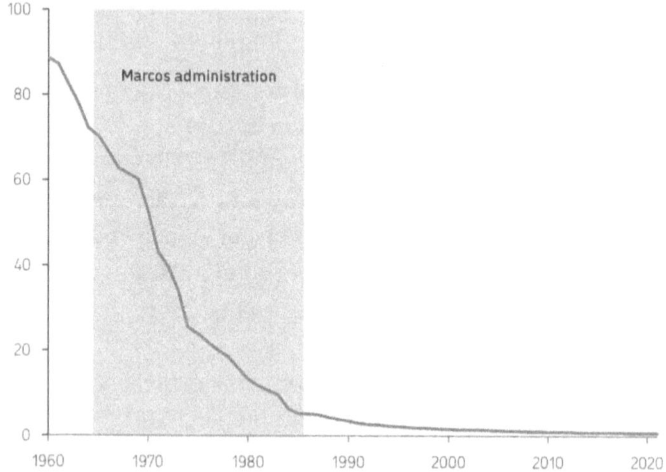

FIGURE 11.2 Purchasing power of the peso, 1960–2021 (Note: Base year 2012; source of data: Philippine Statistics Authority)

the prices of goods and services), and second, that Marcos's mishandling of the economy during the dictatorship was to a large extent responsible for the steep decline of purchasing power.

To be fair, bad luck was partly responsible for the rapid rise of prices during the Marcos years. For example, there was a steep rise of world oil prices in 1974, 1979, and 1980. In 1973, against the backdrop of the Arab-Israeli War, the Organization of the Petroleum Exporting Countries (OPEC) imposed oil embargos against the US and other countries sympathetic to Israel, essentially cutting off their oil supplies and, at the same time, restricting oil production.[4] Another oil price hike occurred in 1979 and 1980 because of the drop in oil production in conflict-ridden countries in the Middle East. In 1979, there was the Iranian Revolution, while in 1980, there was the Iran-Iraq War.

As a result of these spikes in world oil prices, annual inflation in the Philippines rose from 15.7 percent in 1973 to 31.8 percent in 1974—the second highest postwar inflation rate, next to the record 50 percent in 1984. Meanwhile, in 1979 and 1980, inflation spiked again at 17.4 and 17.5 percent, respectively.

But by far, the biggest jumps of inflation were due to Marcos himself, particularly due to the abrupt devaluations of the peso vis-à-vis the US dollar in 1970 as well as in 1983 and 1984.[5] In those instances, the International Monetary Fund (IMF) instructed the Marcos regime to devalue the peso to stabilize the economy, which was hemorrhaging too many dollars because of massive importation as well as profligate government spending (leading to massive budget deficits and debt). The country was coming from a long period of fixing the peso-dollar exchange rate, a policy that Marcos refused to change because of tremendous pressure from the domestic industrialists—specifically importers—whose profits might be ruined by devaluation. Marcos himself earned money from appointing cronies to these industries, so he had a personal stake in not devaluing the peso—for as long as he can do so. Were it not for the economy's perennial shortage of dollars, as well as pressure from the IMF, maybe Marcos would not have devalued the peso voluntarily. But the price of his dilly-dallying was abrupt devaluations, which made the peso weak, made imports expensive, and made the prices of domestic goods rise very steeply—hence, swelling inflation.

One of the major ways the dictatorship tried to abate inflation was the setting up of the Oil Price Stabilization Fund (OPSF).[6] But it came in quite late, having been established in October 1984, the year inflation spiked to a record 50 percent. Basically the OPSF was tasked to give petroleum companies huge subsidies whenever world oil prices increased, so that petroleum can be sold cheaper here at home. But the flip side of this was that the OPSF needed to increase petroleum taxes whenever oil prices went down. In principle, this arrangement sounded good. But in practice, it represented a huge drain on public coffers and the government never found the courage to increase oil taxes. Economist Nimfa Mendoza found that from 1990 to 1997, the government shelled out PHP 17.6 billion in subsidies, all coursed through the OPSF.[7] Worse, the OPSF itself had to be saved by the Philippine National Oil Company for the amount of PHP 10 billion. In 1998, alongside the oil deregulation law, the OPSF was abolished. But it left a debt of PHP 2.6 billion to the "big three" oil companies.

All in all, Marcos's OPSF translated to a huger public sector deficit that ate away funds that could have been spent on social services like education and health.

NEITHER WAS ELECTRICITY FREE DURING MARTIAL law. One of the first things Marcos did after declaring martial law was to seize the businesses and assets of the powerful Lopez family. This included the takeover of electricity distributor Meralco by Imelda's brother Kokoy, who ran the company to the ground and whose leadership of the firm resulted in exorbitant rises in the price of electricity. As recounted by Manapat:

> As soon as Kokoy acquired Meralco, the electricity rates, controlled by the government when the Lopezes were in charge, were increased by 100%,

> with the rates continually increasing throughout the whole time Kokoy assumed control . . . . Thus, merely a year after Kokoy's takeover, Meralco grossed the biggest sales in the country, and outdid San Miguel, the country's biggest corporation.[8]

In particular, they made a killing from a new pricing scheme that allowed electricity rates to jump if oil prices rose or the peso depreciated. This presented yet another source of economic suffering for consumers, considering that Meralco had (and continues to have) a monopoly of electricity distribution in Metro Manila and nearby areas.

SOME LOYALISTS SEEM TO BE AWARE OF THE HIGH inflation rates during the Marcos years, but content themselves with saying that the acceleration of prices was good or beneficial for Filipinos.

True, inflation is not always bad. For one thing, it is natural for prices to rise over the span of decades, as economies grow, and along with it, demand for goods and services. When the population grows, more people demand goods and services, and this tends to raise prices in the long run. Inflation, therefore, is part of the normal march toward progress.

However, inflation becomes hurtful when it rises too fast. The extreme example of this would be episodes of *hyper*inflation as seen in other countries at different points in history. Recent examples would be Zimbabwe in 2008 (when annual inflation peaked at 87.9 *sextillion* percent in November that year) and Venezuela in 2018 and 2019 (with annual inflation peaking at 2.69 million percent in January

2019). In both instances, money was just as valuable as toilet paper (if not less), and even beggars refused to accept paper bills that already nominally amounted to billions worth of the local currency.

In the Philippines, the closest thing to hyperinflation happened during the Japanese occupation in World War II. The Japanese government issued significant volumes of fiat money, later pejoratively called "Mickey Mouse money." There was so much of it that each paper bill had so little value, and people reportedly brought with them *bayongs* (native handwoven bags) to buy the simplest commodities. The Japanese government had to issue peso bills with denominations of PHP 100, PHP 500, and PHP 1,000, whereas before this the largest peso bill in circulation was PHP 10. The Philippines saw hyperinflation from January to December 1944, peaking at a monthly inflation rate of 60 percent. Back then, prices doubled in less than 45 days.[9]

Compared to the Japanese-occupation hyperinflation, Marcos's 50-percent inflation rate in 1984 is of course smaller, but it was still quite bad. And by today's standards, a 50-percent inflation rate is simply unimaginable. At present, the Bangko Sentral ng Pilipinas (the new agency that replaced the old Central Bank) targets an annual inflation rate of just three percent (plus or minus one percentage point), and we already consider a four- to six-percent inflation rate quite high and painful. Imagine double-digit inflation—let alone 50 percent!

In his popular book, *The Conjugal Dictatorship*, Primitivo Mijares, Marcos's former top propagandist, noted how crucial inflation was as a social issue. He wrote, "the runaway inflation that afflicts us, which was brought about more by the inflationary policies of the martial law regime than by world economic conditions, has battered the poor much more than it has hurt the rich." It also "impoverished the masses and eroded the income of laborers and employees." Mijares wrote this in 1976. He added, "all economic forecasts indicate that there will be greater economic difficulties in the late '70s." True enough, inflation rose to new heights in 1979 and 1980. Rather presciently too, Mijares said that inflation—apart from other forms of economic hardship—"will contribute to [Marcos's] downfall." Just as inflation had fanned the flames of protest in the early 1970s, it is not far-fetched to think that historic inflation seen in 1984 and 1985 fanned the flames of social unrest that culminated in the EDSA People Power Revolution in 1986. And in the decade prior, inflation was already spiking to record high after record high.

ALL IN ALL, THE DOUBLE-DIGIT INFLATION RATES during martial law certainly did more harm than good for most Filipinos, especially the poor. Runaway inflation also went against the objectives of good macroeconomic policy, and this is precisely why these days most central banks adhere to inflation targets.

But the temptation to dismiss high inflation persists to this day. For instance, during the spell of relatively high inflation in 2018, the Duterte government's economic managers were quick to dismiss such episode as "transitory" or one that would go away quickly enough. Some pundits and academics took the view that it was a sign that the economy was healthy.[10] But that spell of inflation meant more economic misery especially not just for the poor but also for the middle class.[11] As it turns out, inflation did subside after about a year, with policies like the Rice Tariffication Law letting in substantially more rice imports to quell the shortages. But the suffering of people *during* spells of high inflation should not be dismissed—more so if inflation reaches a double-digit rate (even 50 percent!), as it undeniably did during martial law.

Echoes of Marcosian inflation reverberated in 2022, during Marcos Jr.'s first year as president. In December 2022, inflation reached 8.1 percent, the highest in 14 years and more than double the upper inflation target of the Bangko Sentral.[12] Meanwhile, during his campaign, Marcos Jr. talked of bringing back the OPSF in light of a huge spike of world oil prices (chiefly owing to the Russian invasion of Ukraine) and rising inflation.[13] But that seemed ill-advised, especially with the public coffers already strained and the total government debt already exceeding a record PHP 13 trillion in nominal terms. Will we ever learn from the lessons of the past?

12 Unemployment rate was 66 percent because of EDSA? EDSA led to more OFWs?

CLAIM 1	VERDICT
Unemployment reached 66 percent in 1986.	FALSE

CLAIM 2	VERDICT
EDSA removed regularization, and this led to an increase in overseas Filipino workers (OFWs).	FALSE

APART FROM GLORIFYING THE MARCOS dictatorship, loyalists are also keen to put the succeeding administrations—especially the administration of former president Corazon Aquino—in the worst possible light. In the process, they often arrive at absurd claims. Here, let's address myths pertaining to the labor sector during martial law, especially in the years leading up to the economic crisis.

For example, one particularly vile piece of disinformation spread in 2021 involves a table or matrix filled with made-up economic statistics.[1] It claimed, for one, that the unemployment rate was 7.2 percent in 1965

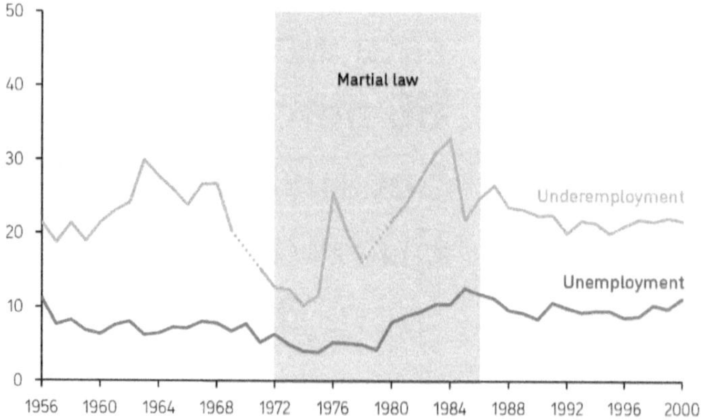

FIGURE 12.1 Unemployment and underemployment rates (in percent), 1956–2000 (Note: Underemployment rate for 1970 and 1979 missing; source of data: Philippine Statistics Authority)

(when Marcos first took power), then rose to a whopping 66 percent in 1986 (implying that 2 in 3 people in the labor force at the time had no job).

This is plainly false. One need only look at the economic records. While it is true that unemployment in 1965 was 7.2 percent, in 1986, it was just 6.7 percent, or smaller by nearly a factor of 10 compared to what loyalists say.

But there is a lot more to be said. Data clearly show the massive deterioration of the labor sector during martial law. Figure 12.1 shows that throughout martial law, there was a tremendous rise in the unemployment rate. In 1972, the unemployment rate stood at 6.3 percent. But by 1985, at the height of the economic crisis, the rate *doubled* to 12.6 percent.

During martial law, you were lucky to keep your job. But those who did keep their jobs had a hard time, too.

Apart from the rise of unemployment, there was an even more serious rise in the *under*employment rate, which comprises people with jobs but working too few hours or receiving too little pay compared to what they want. De Dios and Dinglasan have argued that underemployment matters more for the Philippines than unemployment if one were to look at the plight of the poor—simply because the poor cannot afford to be unemployed.[2] From 12.7 percent in 1972, the underemployment rate rose to as much as 32.9 percent in 1984, or by a factor of 2.6. This means that at the height of the crisis, nearly a third of employed Filipinos were dissatisfied with their jobs, and wanted to work more or needed more pay just to get by. Both the unemployment and underemployment rates reached record highs during the Marcos years, alongside the record decline of our economy in the 1980s.

Both the steady rise of joblessness and the fall of real wages during martial law[3] prompted many Filipino workers—from blue-collar workers to professionals—to leave the country and seek greener pastures abroad, hence the so-called overseas Filipino worker (OFW) phenomenon.

Of course, the exodus of workers started many decades ago: in the early 1900s, several Filipinos, mainly from the Ilocos region, fled to Hawai'i to become agricultural workers. The trials and tribulations of early migrant Filipinos were captured in Carlos Bulosan's classic novel, *America Is in the Heart*. But there was a resurgence of this wave of emigration during martial law.

Figure 12.2 shows a steady and significant rise of OFWs as a portion of the population, especially from 1975 to 1983. Over that duration, the share of OFWs in the population grew by 9.33 times or nearly tenfold. (The next time such a significant rise was seen was in the late 2000s.) Put another

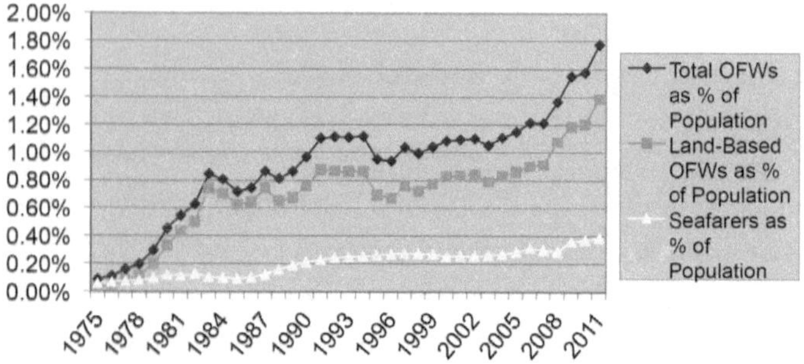

FIGURE 12.2 OFWs as percent of population, 1975–2011 (Source of data: *Philippine Statistical Yearbook*, various years; reprinted from Neil G. Ruiz, "Made for Export: Labor Migration, State Power, and Higher Education in a Developing Philippine Economy" [PhD diss., Massachusetts Institute of Technology, 2014], 15.)

way, the average annual growth of OFW deployment from 1974 to 1985 was 23.7 percent, the highest ever and one that is unmatched in the years since. The data shows that the OFW phenomenon grew in earnest during martial law, and not after it. "There is no evidence to suggest an upsurge during the time of Cory's administration or a result of the EDSA Revolution," said statistician Jose Ramon Albert.[4]

MIGRATION IS OFTEN SAID TO BE CAUSED BY PUSH and pull factors. One can easily see the deteriorating economy in the 1970s and 1980s as important push factors that drove many Filipinos to foreign lands to look for decent jobs and pay.

But in fact, the Marcos dictatorship saw fit to *encourage* this exodus itself, through what is now called the

Philippines' "labor export policy." This was jumpstarted by the Labor Code of 1974, which sought, among its policies, "to insure careful selection of Filipino workers for overseas employment in order to protect the good name of the Philippines abroad."[5] That Labor Code also set up new government agencies specifically tasked to help OFWs (then known as overseas contract workers or OCWs) to find jobs abroad. These include the Overseas Employment Development Board, the Bureau of Employment Services, and the National Seamen Board.[6] By 1982, these agencies would be merged into the Philippine Overseas Employment Administration (POEA), which in 2023 was subsumed under a new agency called the Department of Migrant Workers.

The reason for Marcos's labor export policy is twofold.[7] First, it was a convenient way for the government to find jobs for a growing rank of educated Filipinos who cannot find work at home and faced dire labor market conditions. In that sense, promoting migration was also a way to quell rising unrest among Filipinos. Second—and more crucially—the remittances sent back by OFWs to their families was a convenient way for the Marcos dictatorship to rack up dollar supplies needed to pay off its massive debt and import bill. Remember that the Marcos regime was perennially running out of dollars since the 1960s,[8] primarily because of the heavy importation by domestic industries. But such need was amplified by the regime's profligate spending and prolific borrowing. The dollar earnings of OFWs provided a steady inflow of much-needed dollars, which shored up our economy during the crisis years.[9]

The Marcos dictatorship's desperation for OFW dollars was underscored by an executive order in December 1982 that forced OFWs to send back 50 to 70 percent of their remittances home through "official channels."[10] OFWs who did not comply with the directive risked non-renewal of their passports and even of their employment contracts. Worse, they may be deported back to the Philippines, with their employers held liable. By May 1985, this was reversed by another executive order, which instead gave incentives to OFWs sending their money through the official channels.[11]

The OFW phenomenon affected a generation of young children—including myself—whose parents went abroad to work and, hence, had to be left to the care of close relatives.

In 1990, at the tender age of one, my parents (before leaving for the US) left me to the care of my grandaunt and granduncle, who lovingly raised me to adulthood and treated me as though I were their own child (they had no biological children).[12] My two closest first cousins, meanwhile, were left to the care of my maternal grandmother and grandfather. This peculiar family arrangement was experienced by thousands of other children around our age. Luckily for me and many others from my generation, we turned out okay: my adoptive parents raised me in the best way they could. But the OFW phenomenon came at the price of severe disruptions in normal arrangements in many other families. There is empirical evidence to show, for example, that the absence of parents due to work migration tends to hurt the academic performance of the children who were left behind. Such parental absence may also increase the risk of early sexual initiation among the children they left behind.[13] Such drastic changes in family life would not have happened for millions of families if, to begin with, good jobs were available in the country during the Marcos dictatorship and the economic crisis had not happened.

FINALLY, LET'S ADDRESS THE LINK BETWEEN THE OFW phenomenon and regularization. At the outset, we have to be clear what regularization means: typically it means regularizing probationary employees after six months of work. This was codified in Articles 280 and 281 of the 1974 Labor Code and was not removed even after EDSA. Maybe what some people are referring to are the unfair and unlawful labor practices such as "end-of-contract" (or "endo") scheme, where firms circumvent the regularization requirement by hiring workers with contracts that end in five months.[14] This was said to have been enabled by later amendments to the Labor Code. But at any rate, there was still regularization after EDSA, and EDSA should not be blamed for the rise of OFW deployment that was seen during the martial law years.

In sum, the Marcos years saw neither a cornucopia of jobs nor steadily rising wages. Instead, decent jobs were increasingly scarce, wages plummeted in value, and millions were forced to flee the country for employment opportunities elsewhere—wreaking havoc among millions of Filipino families in the process. Labor conditions deteriorated during martial law, and the data bear this out.

13 The economy tanked after the Marcoses were ousted?

CLAIM 1 The Philippine economy got worse after Marcos was ousted.	**VERDICT** FALSE
CLAIM 2 The economy crashed in 1983 due to US sanctions imposed by "deep state" agents.	**VERDICT** FALSE

THE OVERARCHING NARRATIVE DEVELOPED BY loyalists is that the Philippines enjoyed being a great "tiger economy" until Marcos left office, and that everything went downhill when former president Corazon Aquino, head of the *dilawans* (yellows), took office after the EDSA Revolution. Some people even allege that the economic crash was due to the punitive sanctions (in the form of tariffs) imposed by US "deep state" operatives.[1]

But all available evidence point to the fact that the economy tanked and reached a record low *during* the Marcos regime, not after it, and that no US sanctions or deep state agents were involved.

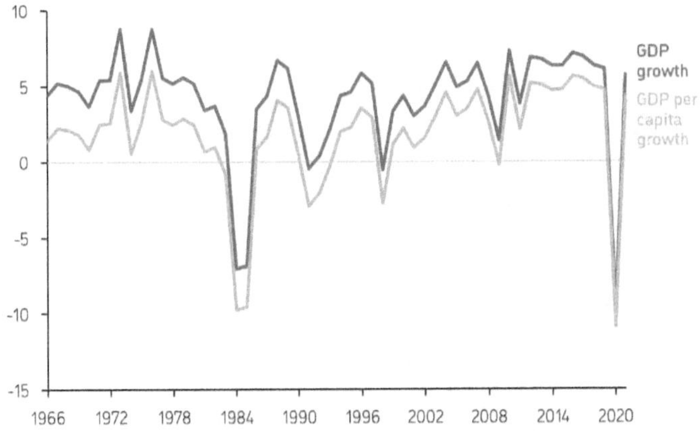

FIGURE 13.1 Annual GDP and GDP per capita growth (in percent), 1966–2021 (Source of data: Philippine Statistics Authority)

First, it is clear from the data (figure 13.1) that we experienced our worst economic crisis or recession in 1984 and 1985—years that fall squarely within the Marcos regime. In those two consecutive years, total production as measured by the GDP fell by seven percent per year, for a total of 14 percent. Sure, there were two other recessions in the 1990s: one in 1991 (when the GDP dropped by 0.44 percent, caused by a combination of a power crisis and a plethora of coup d'états) and another in 1998 (when the GDP fell by 0.51 percent due to the Asian financial crisis). But both these episodes paled in comparison with the Marcosian economic crisis. In fact, we never experienced a recession as bad as the Marcosian one until 2020, 35 years after Marcos's ouster, during the COVID-19 pandemic, when GDP sank by almost 10 percent. But even with the pandemic, the Marcosian crisis can still be legitimately called the worst economic crisis that befell the Philippines since World War II. At the height of the COVID-19 lockdowns, we experienced negative growth but only for five consecutive quarters.[2] In contrast, during the Marcos regime, we experienced decline for *nine* consecutive quarters. In addition, the total damage to the economy during the Marcosian crisis was 14 percent, overshadowing the ten-percent drop in 2020 due to the pandemic.

Turns out that even a pandemic cannot beat the economic damage wrought by the particularly bad dictator.

Even greater damage can be seen if we focus on GDP per person or capita: as early as 1982, it started dropping so that by 1983, it recorded a 0.83-percent decline, the first since 1960. This is nothing, though, compared to what came next: in 1984 and 1985, GDP per person collapsed by 9.76 and 9.56 percent, respectively. The total damage, then, from 1983 to 1985, was 19.3 percent. It took us more than two decades—until 2003—to recover the per-person income we already enjoyed back in 1982. As mentioned in chapter 1, this sorry episode in our economic history, laden with missed opportunities, has been called by economists the "lost decades of Philippine development."

THESE FACTS RAISE THE ALL-IMPORTANT questions: What happened? Why did our economy have to tank so badly? How did Marcos mismanage the economy? What were the things he did wrong?

The reason, as one can imagine, is quite complex. In fact, at the UP School of Economics, it can take an entire semester to discuss what had happened to our economy in the 1970s and 1980s. But here, let us focus on the six most important factors:

1) Perennial lack of international reserves;
2) Explosion of inefficient government spending, leading to massive budget deficits;
3) Massive and irresponsible accumulation of debt;
4) Rise in global interest rates in 1980, induced by the "Volcker disinflation;"
5) Crony capitalism; and
6) Capital flight.

First, the government perennially lacked international reserves because, more often than not, more dollars were leaving the country than those that were coming in. For one thing, as discussed in chapter 2, the prevailing industrial strategy at the time (called import substitution industrialization or ISI) was heavily import-dependent. Even before Marcos took office, we were importing way too many goods and inputs, and this required a significant dollar supply. Basic economics tells us that strong demand for dollars ought to be accompanied by a weakening of the peso. Yet, at the same time, the peso was deliberately fixed by the government at a certain level (we had a "fixed exchange rate regime"). This policy spelled a huge dollar shortage. Marcos continued ISI as well as the fixed exchange rate, both of which he had inherited from previous administrations. It is no wonder, then, that the government was also running out of dollars during his time in office. Moreover, many of the industries protected by the Marcos regime from international competition never grew to become export powerhouses, and the anemic increase of exports prevented the country from earning much-needed dollars that the government could have used to pay for its mounting debts. Exports thus could have been a strong source of dollars. In 1969 and 1971, the Marcos government passed laws to promote investments and exports, apart from the establishment of export processing zones. But although we started to see more "non-traditional" exports like semiconductors and garments, these were still low value-added and imported parts with little to no tariffs.[3] The rest of Philippine industries would fail to grow more efficient and would still be sheltered by protectionist policies that they have grown used to.[4] Meanwhile, we relied too much on primary commodities, such as sugar and coconuts, for exports. When the world prices of these commodities rose, so did our dollar earnings. But in reverse, price crashes hurt our reserves considerably.

Second, Marcos significantly expanded government spending and investments. As we discussed in chapter 8, this is all well and good in normal times, were it not for the fact that many such investments went into projects that were highly inefficient, grandiose, and even outright needless (for instance, Imelda's designer hospitals and other projects meant to satisfy her "edifice complex"). While its spending spree exploded, the Marcos government failed to raise revenues to finance such spending. Hence, the government naturally incurred a growing budget deficit or revenue shortfall, which the regime financed with loans left and right—especially foreign loans.

Third, there was a plethora of loans in the 1970s that developing countries could borrow, owing to the explosion of revenues in oil-exporting countries that ultimately found their way in the global commercial banking system. Marcos took advantage of this surplus of loanable funds, otherwise known as "petrodollars." From 1965, the year Marcos took his oath as president for the first time, to 1985, or Marcos's last full year in office, the country's external debt grew by a staggering USD 25.45 billion. If we count starting from 1972, the year of the declaration of martial law, it would still be large at USD 23.52 billion. Many of Marcos's projects were financed using such debt and it led to some growth, hence the terms "debt-driven growth" and "debt for development." From 1972 to 1982, or about a decade since martial law was declared, the economy grew on average by a rather decent 5.5 percent each year. Note that in previous years and administrations, aggressive spending would have resulted in a shortage of dollars, which turned into a balance-of-payments crisis. In fact, that happened as well during the first term of Marcos as president. But the petrodollars allowed the Marcosian economy to continue to grow for some time.

But here is the catch: the country's debt accumulated at an exceedingly fast rate and soon, it became obvious that it was simply unsustainable. At the same time, most of the debt-financed projects were also inefficient, so the borrowings did not yield as much new production and new national income as one might expect. Debt, in short, was growing at a much faster rate than our national income. All the debt indicators were flashing red, yet the Marcos regime ignored them.

Fourth, interest payments exploded as well. This is not just because of the sheer size of the Marcosian debts, but also because of a concurrent steep rise in world interest rates in the 1980s due to US monetary policy, which was directed by US Federal Reserve chair Paul Volcker. The US, at the time, faced sky-high inflation and its government decided to treat it as "public enemy number one." The Fed fought inflation in 1980 by implementing tight monetary policy, which meant higher interest rates in the US. Soon after, rates across the world rose, too.[5] The US sneezed and the rest of the world caught this cold, including the Philippines which, apart from seeing massive debts, fell victim to the rising world interest rates. The unfortunate timing of the so-called Volcker disinflation—at a time when the Marcos regime was borrowing tremendous amounts of money—bled our country of scarce dollars and exacerbated our already dire shortage of international reserves. In fact, Marcos's economic managers had to declare a "debt moratorium" in 1983, essentially admitting to the world that our country can no longer pay for its debts. (We will discuss the loans in detail in chapter 14.)

Fifth, the system of crony capitalism was a channel by which the Marcos regime extended its influence in the private sector and looted it—just as it effectively looted the public sector. Ostensibly, many businesses were set up by the Marcos cronies to boost domestic industry, rev up the economy, and promote national development. But blanketed by layer upon layer of protection from international competition and heavily subsidized by public monies, these industries and businesses had no real incentive to be efficient. Marcos also instructed government financial institutions—like the Philippine National Bank, Development Bank of the Philippines, and even the Central Bank—to lend huge sums directly to these crony businesses even if the prospects for return were minimal. These loans later came to be known as "behest loans"—that is, ordered at the behest of Marcos himself. This led to a massive wastage of public funds and the bankruptcy of public financial institutions, most notably (and paradoxically) the Central Bank itself.

Sixth, so much capital left the country in the 1970s and 1980s. Aside from looting the private sector, Marcos's crony capitalism also led to a substantial reduction of competition and confidence in the Philippine business landscape. People close to the Marcoses had a leg up in business. It was a "golden age" as far as they were concerned. But there was no level playing field to speak of. This eroded non-crony investors and businesses' confidence in the Philippine economy, leading to massive capital flight in the 1970s and 1980s. This also contributed to the hemorrhaging of dollars due to Marcos's trade policies and his colossal debt.

The above points are just the tip of the iceberg of factors that led to the Marcosian debt and economic crisis in the 1980s. In the next chapter, we will discuss at length the Marcosian debt; in chapter 15, we will talk about large-scale corruption; and in chapter 16, we will cover crony capitalism and capital flight.

14 Marcos added just USD 1 billion to the national debt?

CLAIM 1	**VERDICT**
Marcos contributed only USD 1 billion to the Philippine debt during his years in office. Moreover, former president Corazon Aquino amassed even greater debt totaling PHP 1 trillion.	FALSE
CLAIM 2	**VERDICT**
The Philippines' foreign loans were collateralized by Marcos's gold deposits worldwide, and we paid zero interest on World Bank loans.	FALSE
CLAIM 3	**VERDICT**
We never defaulted on our loans.	FALSE
CLAIM 4	**VERDICT**
Marcos built a lot of good projects with the loans, justifying his huge debts.	FALSE

EFFORTS TO MINIMIZE OR JUSTIFY THE MASSIVE accumulation of debt during the Marcos regime are rife on social media. For instance, some people claim that Marcos, in his more than two decades in power, merely added USD 1 billion to the national debt—not the "inflated" figure of USD 24 billion as stated by "detractors."[1] Loyalists also say that several things ought to be deducted from the USD 24-billion figure, including the USD 13.5 billion that Marcos had "inherited" from the nine presidents before him, the USD 7 billion borrowed by the private sector throughout his reign, and the USD 2.5 billion of international reserves that he left with the Central Bank right before he was ousted in 1986. Hence, we were just left with USD 1 billion. In contrast, they say, Corazon Aquino amassed even greater debt, totaling PHP 1 trillion.[2]

Meanwhile, one post claimed that the Philippines paid zero percent interest for its loans from the World Bank and that the Marcos regime easily got foreign loans because of strategic gold reserves that Marcos supposedly deposited or "positioned" in banks worldwide.[3] In addition, the same post said that the idea of generations of Filipinos paying for the Marcos regime's loans is but a "brainwashing statement" of "dilawans" and "communists" to tarnish the Philippines' image.

In addition, some people stubbornly insist that the Philippines never defaulted on its loans during martial law.[4] Finally, others admit that Marcos had indeed borrowed tons of money during his time, but nonetheless proceed to justify such borrowings by saying that Marcos did a lot of good with that money—mainly building highways, bridges, hospitals, and schools, among others. Hence, on the whole, such borrowings ought to be viewed as a net positive for the country and not a net negative.

FIRST, A CURSORY LOOK AT THE DATA WILL instantly debunk the spurious and frankly silly claim that Marcos just borrowed USD 1 billion. In 1965, the total outstanding external debt of the Philippines amounted to just USD 0.8 billion (this also instantly debunks the claim that Marcos had "inherited" debt of USD 13.5 billion). By 1985, or Marcos's last full year in office, the external debt ballooned to a whopping USD 26.25 billion (figure 14.1). Hence, the total outstanding external debt added by Marcos in the 20 years of his rule amounted to a staggering USD 25.45 billion. Even if we start counting in 1972, the year martial law was declared, the additional debt would still be sizable at USD 23.52 billion.[5]

As early as this point, we can also debunk the idea that Corazon Aquino amassed even greater debt than Marcos, which they say amount to PHP 1 trillion. Data from the Bureau of the Treasury show that from 1986 to 1991, the total outstanding debt (both domestic and external) went up by only PHP 240.12 billion, or just under a quarter of the supposed PHP 1 trillion that she amassed.[6] This is way lower compared to the debt in tens of billions of *dollars* that Marcos had accumulated.

Some people might say that the gargantuan sum of the Marcosian debt was unfairly inflated by the private sector's debt and that we should only focus on the debt incurred by the government itself. But even if we focus only on the public sector's debt, we're still left with a net increase of debt totaling USD 18.66 billion (from 1965 to 1985) or USD 18.01 billion (from 1972 to 1985). This is still a far cry from the USD 1 billion stated by the loyalists. And from figure 14.1, it should be evident that the rise of public debt, especially during martial law, was driven primarily by public (and not private) debt.

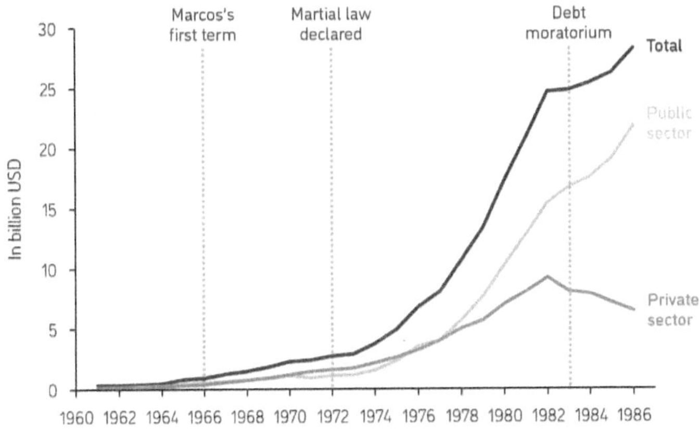

FIGURE 14.1 Outstanding external debt, 1961–1986 (Source of data: James K. Boyce and Lyuba Zarsky, "Capital Flight from the Philippines, 1962–1986," *Philippine Journal of Development* 15, no. 2 [1988]: 191–222.)

Nonetheless, there is a legitimate reason to include both the public and private sector's debt when assessing Marcosian debt: remember that the regime had established a system of crony capitalism, and a lot of crony businesses were able to secure loans from international creditors with the backing of the Marcos government. In fact, all private companies wishing to borrow from abroad had to secure permission from the Central Bank's Monetary Board.[7]

Loyalists also argue that, on an annual basis, the debts incurred by Marcos would still turn out to be less than the debts incurred by succeeding presidents. This is misleading. If we extend figure 14.1 to the present, we see that the country's total outstanding debt has continued to increase to new heights. But that is only natural as a country grows: we have more needs now than ever before, and

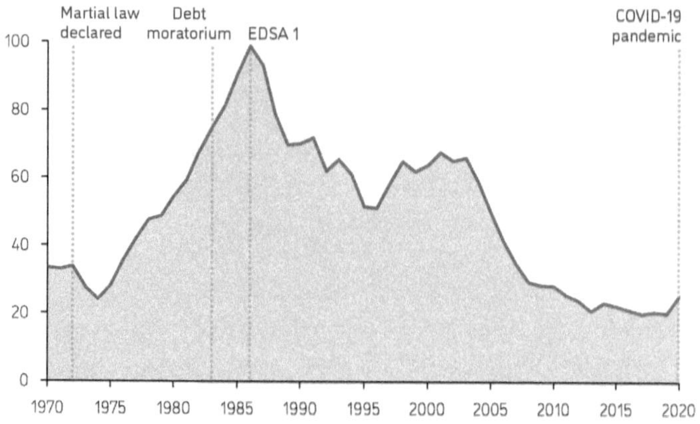

FIGURE 14.2 Debt as percent of gross national income (GNI), 1970–2020 (Source of data: World Bank)

prices around the world naturally go up due to growth and inflation.

This is precisely why increases in debt must be contrasted with increases in our national income, and why economists much prefer to look not at absolute levels of debt but the so-called debt-to-GDP ratio (or a ratio with some other income measure like GNI). Figure 14.2 shows that the country's debt as a percentage of our GNI rose steeply from a little over 24 percent in 1974 to as large as 90.55 percent by 1985. This means that right before the Marcos regime was toppled, our total external debt was more or less equal in size to our economy's total income—even taking into account the substantial incomes coming from overseas Filipino workers.

This, more than anything else, tells us just how rapid and unsustainable debt accumulation was during martial law. It took us many *decades* to bring down the debt-to-GDP ratio to around 20 percent. Although there was a spike in 2020 due to the intense borrowings of the government amid COVID-19, it is still nowhere near the steep ascent of debt during the Marcos years.

Significantly, the Marcos regime continued to borrow heavily even in the late 1970s, when there was a second global oil price shock and when the country was already hemorrhaging dollars and incurring a widening current account deficit ("roughly, a situation where the country is dissaving"). One might expect that such red flags should have given Marcos and his economic team pause in borrowing. However, de Dios, Gochoco-Bautista, and Punongbayan noted that Marcos and his technocrats were overcome by overconfidence—emboldened by the country's respectable growth during the first oil price hike as well as by the "positive advice from multilateral creditors, such as the World Bank and the IMF."[8]

What about the claim that Marcos had left USD 2.5 billion in our international reserves before his exile to Hawai'i? Data from the Bangko Sentral ng Pilipinas show that by December 1985, our international reserves amounted to just USD 1.087 billion. In contrast, the total external debt then was USD 26.6 billion. Clearly, the little reserves we had then was by no means adequate to pay for Marcos's colossal loans.

In fact, this inadequacy of reserves was another key feature of our public finances throughout martial law: the ratio of our reserves to our external debts steadily fell from the mid-1970s to the mid-1980s. Figure 14.3 shows that by 1984, our reserves were a puny 3.5 percent of our external debt; in 1984, it was still puny at just 4.1 percent. Sure, there was a spike in our reserves in 1974, but this was on account of a sudden rise of world sugar and coconut prices, which boosted our exports of (and dollar earnings

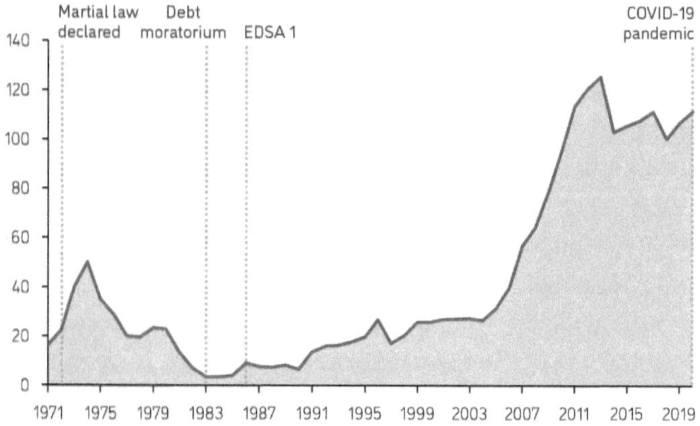

FIGURE 14.3 Philippine international reserves as percent of external debt, 1971–2020 (Source of data: World Bank)

from) these commodities. From 1970 to 1972, sugar and copra prices tripled, while copper and lumber prices doubled.[9] This led to a rare current account surplus in 1973. But that spike was quite small: the extra dollars we earned from such exports were offset by the concurrent rise of world oil prices due to the OPEC embargo (specifically, the oil import bill jumped and the current account surplus quickly turned into a deficit). In fact, the price of our commodity exports shot up, largely thanks to the concurrent rise of oil and petroleum prices. In the end, the 1973 current account surplus proved temporary, as sugar and copra prices crashed soon after. The current account deficit ballooned from 1974 all the way to 1983 (it suddenly dropped in 1984 once the IMF intervened and finally lent us money after protracted negotiations).

Apart from reducing the number of months in which we could pay for our imports (another measure of the adequacy of our reserves), the sheer hugeness of the Marcosian loans naturally meant larger interest payments as well. After all, the price of any loan is the interest, which is a percentage of the total principal. But rising interest payments were exacerbated by the fact that world interest rates in the early 1980s shot up dramatically.

For context, the US was reeling from another round of oil price hikes (a sequel of sorts to the oil price hikes in the mid-1970s). And the US Federal Reserve, then headed by Paul Volcker, viewed inflation as public enemy number one. In response, Volcker hawkishly combatted high inflation by setting record high interest rates. This raised the costs of borrowing, dissuaded people from taking out loans for houses or cars, and dampened demand—and hence, prices. Such policy, however, pushed global interest rates through the roof—such was the global influence of the Fed's monetary policy (even today).[10]

Since much of the Marcosian debts were denominated in dollars and had flexible interest rates, the rise of global interest rates meant that we expended more of our precious dollars on interest payments: figure 14.4 shows that from under two percent, the share of interest payments to our GNI more than tripled to over six percent from 1981 to 1984. Such interest payments represented funds that could have been spent instead on much more useful projects and programs, such as education and health, but were rapidly depleted because of Marcos's insatiable hunger for debt. Obviously, contrary to the myths, it is not at all true that we paid zero interest on World Bank loans, or any loan for that matter. According to former Central Bank governor Jose Cuisia Jr., the Marcos debts were not fully paid until 2018, or 32 years after the dictatorship's downfall.[11]

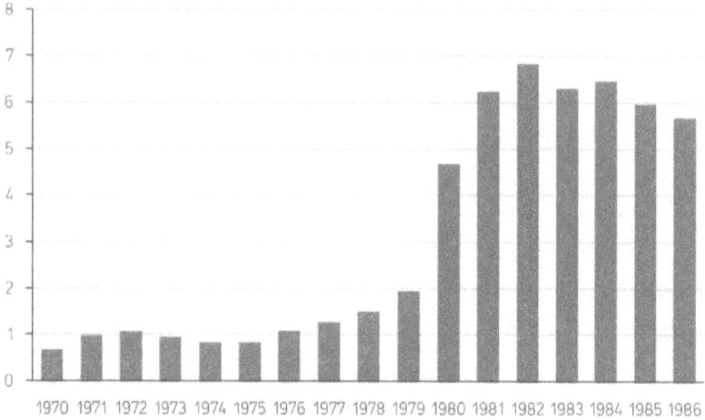

FIGURE 14.4 Interest payments on foreign debt as percent of GNI, 1970–1986 (Source of data: World Development Indicators)

WHY AND HOW DID MARCOS ACCUMULATE SO MUCH debt in the first place? As with many things, it is a combination of demand and supply.

The first factor is demand. A key feature of the Marcos regime is that it significantly expanded government activities and investments (e.g., ambitious big-ticket infrastructure projects). By 1973, a year after martial law was declared, government spending immediately doubled (from PHP 1.2 billion to PHP 2.28 billion), notably on infrastructure spending. The investments of government—including both the national and local governments as well as public corporations—went up dramatically from two percent of the GNP in 1972 to 6.6 percent in 1976. Put another way, from 1974 to 1976, or in just two years, domestic investments rose by 35 percent.[12] This accounted for the record 8.8-percent GDP growth in 1976, which, along with a similar growth rate in 1974, would turn out to be the highest growth of the country's GDP in a single year after World War II. But at the same time, Marcos's spending spree was not accompanied by a commensurate increase in government revenues. Hence, his government incurred significant budget deficits. Simply put, he was already spending beyond his means.

But note that this is not new for Marcos. He already spent beyond his means—and went on to mismanage the economy—even in his first term as president, from 1965 to 1969. From 1964 to 1968, government spending had already risen by a significant 43 percent and the budget deficit began to rise as early as then.[13] Aside from spending on infrastructure and other large-scale programs, Marcos also expended huge sums for his reelection campaign in the 1969 elections, which, by the way, were said to be one of the costliest, dirtiest, and most violent elections in our history. The results were said to have been determined by the three G's: "guns, goons, and gold."[14] The Commission on Elections itself had to flag Marcos's overspending. Later, it was found that from 1968 to 1969 alone—in just one year—government spending jumped further by 25 percent and the budget deficit tripled. According to the late former senator Jovito Salonga,

> Marcos used up the foreign exchange reserves [for the elections] and so depleted the National Treasury that not enough resources were left to service the mounting external debt and cover a huge trade deficit.[15]

Salonga also claimed that Marcos's reelection bid was supported and "marred by shameless raids on the public treasury, amounting to almost a billion pesos."[16]

In the face of large budget deficits, Marcos had three options. First, he could simply instruct the Central Bank to print more money. And in fact, in the last four months of 1969, at the height of the Marcos's reelection bid, money supply jumped by about 20 percent.[17] But economics tells us that such a policy is unsustainable in the long run because it is a surefire recipe for stoking inflation. Although Marcos's spending spree, which relied on the growth of money supply, did not cause hyperinflation, the mass printing of money would boomerang by contributing to sky-high inflation in 1970—right after Marcos had won his second term.

Second, Marcos could choose to slow down spending and roll back his pet projects. But this was politically unfeasible, since Marcos was really bent on securing a second term as president. He thought that he could buy his way for a second shot at the presidency—and he did exactly that.

Third, Marcos could continue with such projects and just finance the growing deficits by borrowing money, especially from abroad. He heavily banked on this third option.

But where could Marcos borrow money from? Marcos had another choice to make: to borrow domestically (by issuing government securities in the domestic markets) or to borrow from abroad.

This brings us to supply. It is not at all true that the Marcos regime was able to obtain so many loans because of the president's gold reserve deposits worldwide, which, according to myths, had allegedly served as the nation's collateral.[18] Instead, when the regime was grappling for loans to finance his big-ticket projects, there was a huge surplus of loanable funds from abroad, coming chiefly from

the surplus of dollars earned by oil-producing countries in the Middle East because of OPEC's oil price hikes in the 1970s.[19] These excess foreign exchange reserves, later known as "petrodollars," were "recycled"[20] and found their way into global commercial banks, which in turn lent them at low (at times even negative[21]) interest rates. Governments of developing countries—including the Marcos regime—that were eager to finance their own development projects grabbed this opportunity to borrow massive loans on the cheap. Banks simply needed guarantees from government that they would be repaid. And they also set adjustable interest rates for the loans they gave out as a hedge against inflation (that is, such interest rates would be recalculated regularly, say, every six months over the duration of the loans).[22]

Aside from these commercial loans, multilateral agencies like the World Bank and Asian Development Bank were also eager to lend out monies to poor countries. This continues to be part of their mission and business model to this day. The World Bank, in particular, shifted its goals decidedly after World War II, away from supporting the reconstruction of Europe toward funding infrastructure and development projects worldwide. This was especially the case under the leadership of Robert Strange McNamara, who served as the World Bank's fifth president from 1968 to 1981. Indeed, Marcos cultivated a special relationship with McNamara, impressing and winning him over by "skillfully deploying a cadre of technocrats."[23] McNamara ended up supporting the regime and was elated when Marcos had lifted through a presidential decree the existing limits on public indebtedness. This opened the floodgates for loans from the World Bank and other multinational organizations. From 1973 to 1981, the Philippines got about USD 2.6

billion in loans from the World Bank, an eightfold increase from the total loans we got from 1950 to 1972. By 1980, we were also eighth among 113 countries in terms of total loans received from the World Bank. So taken was McNamara with martial law that he agreed to hold the 1976 annual meeting of the World Bank and IMF at the Philippine Plaza Hotel (now Sofitel Philippine Plaza Manila).[24]

Indeed, one key reason Marcos was able to rack up huge loans was that such borrowings were legitimized by Marcos's cadre of technocrats, which included Cesar Virata (finance minister, who would later become the country's first and only prime minister in the middle of—and, in fact, largely because of—the debt crisis), Gerardo Sicat (the first economic planning minister[25]), Jaime Laya (governor of the Central Bank), Roberto Ongpin (commerce and industry minister), Manuel Alba (budget minister), Vicente Paterno (minister of industry), and Placido Mapa (chair of the Development Bank of the Philippines and second economic planning minister). Decked with doctorates and other advanced degrees from elite universities here and abroad,[26] the Marcos technocrats had a veneer of legitimacy about them and leveraged such legitimacy as they presented the case for the Marcos regime's loans before the international community—particularly before private creditors and multilateral agencies, such as the World Bank and IMF.[27] Invariably, these technocrats would end up deodorizing the regime and propping it up to the extent that it lasted. Interestingly, the technocrats had a testy relationship with Marcos's cronies. As put by one businessman at the time, if Marcos were a wheel's hub, the technocrats and cronies were different "spokes" that "never touch except through the President."[28] "If the Benedicto and Virata spokes did touch, Virata would resign," he added.

TO SUM, THE MARCOS DICTATORSHIP OBTAINED A windfall of dollars because of the glut of petrodollars at the time, as well as support from multilateral organizations. So even if commodity prices dropped like a rock in 1975 and exports remained weak, the regime had plenty of dollars to go around with by way of the new loans. This averted a lack of funds for the regime's pet projects and further emboldened the regime to spend aggressively. Indeed, government spending rose by 40 percent by 1975, and private investments—by, say, businesses supported by the regime—also jumped by 35 percent between 1974 and 1976. Exports of manufactured goods like clothes, commodities, and semiconductors also rose by 13 percent annually from 1974 to 1980.[29] Even so, the current account deficit widened because of continued heavy importation of capital goods. This further fed the need for more loans, in a sort of vicious cycle.

Marcos's profligate spending and irresponsible borrowing would lead to not just one, but two economic crises during his two decades in power.

The first occurred as early as the end of his first term in 1970. Intense spending and borrowing that was not backed by enough dollars led to "twin deficits": a budget deficit (revenue shortfall) and a current account deficit (crudely, a dollar shortfall because imports way exceeded exports). We had difficulty repaying our creditors, which, in January 1970, the first month of Marcos's second term as president, formed a consultative group[30] that approved a restructuring of our loans. They agreed to the loan restructuring only if the Marcos government agreed to undergo a "stabilization program" under the International Monetary Fund or IMF.[31] In other words, we would get a hefty loan from the IMF only if we implemented policies to correct the mini economic crisis caused by Marcos's economic mismanagement. The stakes rose further when our private creditors said that they would only lend more money to the Philippines if the Marcos government complied with the IMF's conditions.

The looming crisis was so bad that Marcos had no choice but to concede to the IMF's "conditionalities." First and most crucially, his government had to deliberately devalue the artificially strong peso from PHP 3.9 to PHP 6.4 per US dollar, in order to mitigate the dollar shortage.[32] Second, the country also had to shift from a fixed exchange rate regime to a "managed float." This basically means that the dollar-peso exchange rate was to be determined more by supply and demand and less by the government. Third, Marcos had to put a brake on spending: indeed, government investments dropped in 1970 and 1971.

As expected, the Philippine economy was stabilized by these policy changes: exports recovered as the peso weakened and the current account deficit vanished (it even turned into a *surplus* in 1973). However, the peso's devaluation came at the price of a huge spike of inflation, which, together with the fast growth in money supply in 1969, led to economic hardship and social unrest in 1970, contributing to the declaration of martial law in 1972 (see chapter 2).

But this episode in our economic history, however painful, did not deter Marcos from pursuing aggressive spending during his second term as president and, later, during martial law. In fact, he even ramped up government spending during martial law. And as the deficit swelled further, he also ramped up his borrowings well into the 1980s. But this would only escalate to a full-fledged debt and economic crisis—one that was presaged by the crisis at the end of his first term and one that would end up being even larger and deeper.

THIS BRINGS US TO THE NEXT MYTH: THAT THE Philippines never defaulted on its loans. We did. Marcos's borrowing binge during martial law led to the country's declaration of a "debt moratorium" in 1983. This, in essence, meant that we declared to the world that we could no longer pay for our debts.[33] Around the same time, a number of Latin American countries like Argentina and Mexico also fell victim of the global rise of interest rates and similarly declared their own debt moratoria. The ensuing years of economic crisis were even called *la década perdida* ("the lost decade"). So we were not alone, but that does not mean that Marcos was any less bad in managing the economy. Neighboring countries in the ASEAN also did not experience a debt crisis to the extent we did.

In October 1983, two of Marcos's economic managers (namely prime minister Virata and Central Bank governor Laya) flew to New York City to talk to some of our private creditors, seeking a way to postpone the repayment of the country's massive debts.[34] They specifically requested for a 90-day debt moratorium on the country's principal payments due that year. In itself, the declaration of a debt moratorium tarnished our reputation in the international community. No one wanted to lend us any money anymore, thereby cutting us off from much needed external money. Today, some argue that requesting or declaring a rescheduled repayment of debt was not equivalent to default. But as once opined by former Supreme Court Senior Associate Justice Antonio Carpio, "mere suspension of repayment, like declaring a debt moratorium, is already an 'event of default.' "[35]

The October 1983 debt moratorium heralded a tipping point for our country. Before that, the country had been accumulating massive debt and the regime got away with it by borrowing even more to pay for past loans. But upon the declaration of the moratorium, we could no longer borrow new debt to pay for past debt. In economic parlance, from "positive net transfers" we began to incur "negative net transfers" (Boyce 1993).

Just like what happened in 1970, it was only the IMF that was willing to lend us via another stabilization program—but only if Marcos once more implemented policies to correct the economy. Again, Marcos had no other choice but to submit to the IMF's conditions. These were the major steps that he had to take:[36]

1) Stem the country's hemorrhaging of dollars;
2) Cut back on spending to reduce the deficit; and
3) Restrict money growth.

First, Marcos had to accumulate as much dollars as possible to abate the dire shortage of dollars. Marcos did everything to get its hands on dollars. He was desperate for it. As described by Jesus Estanislao, an economist who served as the National Economic and Development Authority (NEDA) director-general and finance secretary during the Corazon Aquino years:

> If you wanted to get dollars in order to travel abroad, you cannot easily get dollars because the dollars were reserved for the privileged . . . . You could not easily buy apples, grapes, oranges outside of Christmas because that was not allowed in. That was part of the rule. And why? Because dollars were rationed. And in the rationing of

> dollars, who do you think would get first crack at getting dollars?[37]

Marcos also reimposed the old policy of rationing foreign exchange that our country resorted to in past balance-of-payments crises. He required all banks to surrender their dollars to the Central Bank, forming a central pool of money from which the latter allocated scarce dollars to pay for our foreign obligations. Among the prioritized payments were raw materials imported by domestic industries, imports of grain and oil, and payments for our loans from multilateral organizations like the World Bank.[38] In December 1982, Marcos even issued an executive order mandating OFWs to send 50 to 70 percent of their remittances through official channels, or banks under the supervision of the Central Bank.[39] To further stem the outflow of dollars, the Marcos government also imposed even more restrictions on imported goods in 1983 and 1984. Import taxes served an added purpose of raising much-needed revenues for government (later, export taxes were raised as well). In June 1984, Marcos issued a presidential decree criminalizing "dollar-salting" or "dollar blackmarketing," defined as the illegal transfer of dollars abroad without the consent of the Central Bank.[40] (Funnily enough, his wife, Imelda, would later be charged with several counts of dollar-salting in relation to their ill-gotten wealth, but would eventually be acquitted.[41])

But even as the Central Bank required everyone to pitch in with their dollars in a so-called "exchange surrender system," there was a massive loophole: some exporters could import raw materials as long as these were not financed by foreign loans and were not on the government's priority list. At the time, there was a thriving black market for foreign currency, and transactions were done mainly by Chinese-Filipinos in Manila's Binondo district. This was otherwise known as the "Binondo Central Bank."[42] Some importers bought dollars at the government's official exchange rate (PHP 14 per US dollar at the time), but others bought it at much higher rates (say, PHP 30 per dollar). This "dual exchange rate" led to a premium on the black marketeers' exchange rate, spelling massive profits for them. But more importantly, it meant that the government was not getting as much dollars from imports as it should; it was a massive leakage from their point of view.

If the Marcos government's exchange surrender system were to have any chance of success, they had to step in to control this black market. And they did: at one point, the black marketeers were "rounded up" by the National Intelligence and Security Agency and told of the government's plan to stabilize the currency.[43] The black marketeers were also ordered to buy and sell dollars at the government's own rates, allowing traders to keep some minimal profit. People who disobeyed would be arrested. The heavily regulated operations of the Binondo Central Bank went on from early 1984 up until Marcos's ouster in 1986 and somehow worked to reduce the black-market premium on the exchange rate.

Moreover, and still as part of the IMF's conditions before lending us money again, the time came for another round of peso devaluations, akin to the one in 1970. From May to July 1983, the peso went from PHP 10.30 to PHP 11 per US dollar, and from September to October 1983, it went down even more to PHP 13.7 per dollar. As discussed in chapter 2, these movements in the exchange rate (there were more of these later in Marcos's reign) led to a skyrocketing of prices and inflation, which led to much suffering. It was a bitter pill that the Marcos government force-fed to the Filipino people in order to cure the illness that was caused by Marcos in the first place.

Second, apart from preventing the deadly hemorrhaging of dollars, Marcos also had to curtail his aggressive spending in order to stem, in turn, the ballooning deficit, which peaked at about 5.5 percent of the GNP in 1981 and 1982.[44] For one, the government needed to raise more revenues, and this was accomplished through new import and export taxes as well as higher excise taxes on products like petroleum. On the other side of the equation, spending, too, needed to be cut, including investment spending (for instance, the halting of Marcos's famed eleven industrial projects launched in 1979[45]), operations and maintenance spending, as well as lending and equity transfers to government corporations—which, for the longest time, have been swimming in government funds. But it was quite difficult to rein in the spending of public corporations: those in water, power, oil, and transportation continued to invest heavily and borrow abroad (to the greatest extent possible). It was only in late 1983 that the Marcos government was able to tame the spending of public corporations to help the national cause.

Third, the Central Bank also had to restrict the growth of money supply. In so doing, it would make the peso relatively scarcer, thereby driving up its value and returns vis-à-vis the US dollar, inducing people to hold on to peso assets rather than dollar assets, and dissuading people from hoarding dollars (especially when they expect the peso to weaken vis-à-vis the dollar). Ideally, all this would serve to stem the depletion of dollars. Indeed, the Central Bank curbed money growth by raising its key interest rate, raising the proportion of cash that private banks had to keep in their reserves (that is, raising the "reserve requirement ratio"), and limiting the banks' ability to borrow from the Central Bank through the so-called rediscount window.[46]

But despite such policies, money supply—particularly cash and equivalents—still grew by 40 percent in 1983, largely due to the peso's devaluation (which led to losses in the Central Bank's swap and forward contracts) and the Central Bank's continued massive lending to government and non-bank financial institutions (mostly thrift banks).[47] In basic macroeconomics, fast money growth spells high inflation. So, the unintended rise of money growth in late 1983 only worsened the already high inflation brought about by the peso's devaluation earlier that year.

Dohner and Intal claim that the Central Bank's failure to stem money growth proved to be "the most damaging" part of the Philippines' adjustment to the lack of credit and the IMF's conditions.[48] By late 1983 and early 1984, inflation rose to historic levels of about 50 to 60 percent.

In 1984, in a bid to stem sky-high inflation—as well as capital outflow and the steep drop in reserves—the Central Bank issued its own certificates of indebtedness called "Jobo bills" (named after the Central Bank governor at the time, Jose "Jobo" Fernandez Jr.). Such bills had interest rates that were artificially higher than most other financial instruments—about 40 percent per year[49] or even as high as 43 percent[50]—precisely because the Central Bank wanted investors to invest in them, therefore giving money (or providing liquidity) to the cash-strapped Marcos government. But as the issuance of these high-interest Jobo bills encouraged people to take their money out of their bank deposits and invest in these bills, this dried up the supply of loans and discouraged spending by the private sector in the real economy.[51] This exacted a heavy toll on the economy and turned out to be the last piece of the puzzle that finally pushed the economy toward a recession.

FROM OCTOBER 1983, THERE WERE SEVERAL extensions to the 90-day moratorium asked by Marcos's economic managers. This proved to be the IMF's longest negotiations with any debtor country at the time. And it was not as if the IMF's "standby loan" was gargantuan: in fact, at "just" USD 650 million, it was modest compared to previous standby programs by the IMF to the Philippines.[52]

Why did the negotiations take so long? There were various reasons. For one, the Marcos regime had a difficult time complying with the conditionalities set by the IMF. Aside from the usual prescriptions (e.g., building up dollar reserves, reducing deficit, stemming money growth), the IMF also required the Marcos regime to implement structural corrections to the economy. The most controversial of these was the loosening of the regime's firm grip on the sugar and coconut industries, which for several years have been monopolized by Marcos's top cronies—Roberto Benedicto and Danding Cojuangco, respectively. There were some half-hearted efforts to comply with this here and there: for instance, through the greater representation of sugar planters in PHILSUCOM and NASUTRA and the transfer of the coconut export monopoly to UNICOM. But on the whole, Marcos resisted such reforms and only pushed for marginal changes at best.

Also, a huge scandal erupted from the Central Bank. In December 1983, Central Bank governor Laya was found to have manipulated statistics concerning the country's foreign reserves. In a bid to conceal the truth about our ability to repay our loans and to make the economy's situation appear less dire than it really was, Laya basically overstated our reserves by 50 percent (translating to amounts ranging from USD 600 million to USD 1.1 billion, based on various estimates).[53] As former Central Bank governor Jose Cuisia Jr. recalls, at one point, our reserves even went down to as much as *minus* USD 400 million.[54] This blatant attempt at window dressing and deception "angered" our private creditors and induced them to leave the negotiating table: they were waiting for us to secure the IMF loan before finally approving the debt rescheduling that we originally requested. We had a "junk rating" and, as a result, said Cuisia Jr.,

> We could not borrow from the international market. For ten years we were absent from the international financial markets. The multilaterals stopped lending to the Philippines—the IMF, the World Bank, the ADB. This is why we were [in] such a deep, deep hole at the time. It was really very excruciating for the officials like governor Fernandez to be able to convince the banks that we were still a credit-worthy country. They did not believe us, so our credibility was really shot . . . . It was only in 1993 that we were able to get back and borrow from the international capital markets.[55]

But apart from stalling our negotiations with our creditors, Laya's lies also derailed our negotiations with the IMF: in no time, the latter sent a team to Manila to investigate the Central Bank's books, and ordered an independent audit later carried out by prominent accounting firm SyCip Gorres Velayo & Co. (SGV). In a fact-finding report dated 19 October 1984, it was found that transactions by the

Central Bank "have been found to be fictitious without any funding, in effect generating non-existent reserves for the CB." These transactions ultimately "misrepresented the CB's gross and net international reserves."[56] Overall, Laya's deception further diminished what little reputation and credibility we still had on the international stage.[57] Unfortunately, Gerardo Sicat, in his 2014 biography of Cesar Virata, downplayed the window-dressing episode and said that it was "sensationalized" by media and was "blown out of proportion."[58] He chalked it up to the Central Bank's "aggressive" foreign exchange operations that led to an "error in the statistics." But how could anyone have simply conjured USD 600 million from thin air?

It was not until December 1984—more than a year since the debt moratorium—that the IMF finally signed an agreement giving us the USD 650-million standby loan (remitted in tranches and conditional on frequent assessments by the IMF on whether we were reaching stated targets for stabilization). Later, in May 1985, our private creditors—a group of about 330, but the economic managers were negotiating with a committee of about a dozen representatives—followed suit and finally agreed to have our debt restructured and rescheduled. But this came a full 19 months since Virata and Laya first announced the debt moratorium in October 1983. Among other things, the restructuring entailed a rescheduling of the USD 5.88-billion debt we owed them in the period October 1983–December 1986, a new loan of USD 925 million payable in nine years (with a grace period of five years), and a "revolving trade facility" amounting to USD 2.97 billion (which basically means a credit line from which we can always borrow money, limited by a maximum value, and which we can pay at our own convenient schedule).[59] In 1990, the negotiations continued and our debts were restructured to be repaid in two tranches—USD 11 billion and USD 6.8 billion, respectively—with some debts restructured to be paid for as long as 25 years. Hence, "all the [Marcosian] debts were fully paid by 2018," according to former Central Bank governor Cuisia Jr.[60]

DESPITE ITS EXCRUCIATING PROCESS, THE IMF'S stabilization program fixed the Marcosian economy quite well as intended and, surprisingly, rapidly.

For one, we accumulated much-needed dollar reserves to pay for our external obligations—even in excess of what the IMF required. The current account deficit was also eliminated (and even became a surplus), mainly because of the decline of the import bill as the peso became weaker. Meanwhile, owing to tight monetary policy, the sky-high inflation rates in 1984 were quickly dampened by 1985 to low levels not seen since the 1960s. The Philippines—particularly the private sector—also substantially reduced its reliance on foreign loans.

But just like the stabilization in 1970, the 1984–1985 stabilization came with a huge economic cost—a much huger one at that. As the Marcos dictatorship took steps to satisfy the IMF's conditions—especially to tame inflation—it issued the high-interest Jobo bills. But the rise of real interest rates—even as we were sitting on the negotiating table with our creditors—put a hard brake on the economy. Indeed, the very tight monetary policy of this time was the most important factor for the recession, linking the debt crisis to a broader economic crisis.

Why is the real interest rate so crucial? While the *nominal* interest rate is what is usually quoted by banks,

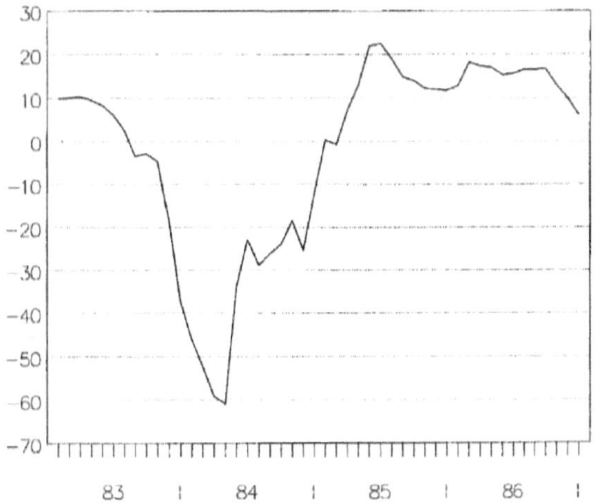

FIGURE 14.5 Real interest rates (in percent), 1983–1986 (Note: Treasury bill rate less CPI inflation rate; reprinted from Robert S. Dohner and Ponciano Intal Jr., "The Marcos Legacy: Economic Policy and Foreign Debt in the Philippines," in *Developing Country Debt and Economic Performance*, vol. 3, *Country Studies—Indonesia, Korea, Philippines, Turkey*, eds. Jeffrey D. Sachs and Susan M. Collins [Chicago: University of Chicago Press, 1989], 552.)

the *real* interest rate is nominal interest less inflation. It is the latter, more than the former, that determines the pace and level of investments. Because of tremendous inflation in 1984, the real interest rate was often negative that year (see figure 14.5). But with the issuance of high-interest Jobo bills, nominal interest rates increased. At the same time, the peso devaluation required by the IMF reduced import prices and inflation. The combination of higher nominal interest and lower inflation meant that the real interest rate became less and less negative. In fact, it reached more than 20 percent by mid-1985, and that high level was sustained until

1986. But a very high real interest rate does not bode well for an economy. This had the effect of "drying up" private credit, which "drove many firms to the wall . . . and left the financial system unwilling to take on anything but the most minimal lending risk."[61] In essence, businesses could not borrow loans from banks and, on the other hand, banks imposed strict requirements to the few businesses to which they lent.

Unsurprisingly, many businesses went in the red and many of them failed to repay their outstanding loans. Banks, too, were in trouble: about 23 went under in 1984 and 58 more added in 1985, while about 100 rural banks became insolvent. In hindsight, the Marcos government ought to have relaxed its overly tight monetary policy in 1984 and 1985. But at any rate, this is how the country's worst postwar recession came about.

GDP shrank by a record seven percent in *both* 1984 and 1985, for a total of 14 percent. Investments in particular were hard-hit, dropping by as much as 50 percent. Exports were supposed to increase at this time to contribute to growth, but this did not materialize: even though the peso was a lot weaker than the dollar, such decline was offset by the high inflation rate during this time. In fact, in real terms, the peso *appreciated* or strengthened in late 1984 and early 1985. Hence, exports did not take off as expected.

Note that industry output was already flagging in 1983, even before the IMF-led stabilization, because of the tight conditions that prevented many firms from importing the raw materials that they needed for their production. The resulting scale-down of their operations—and in many instances, downright closure—resulted in the record recession, unemployment, and poverty during this period.

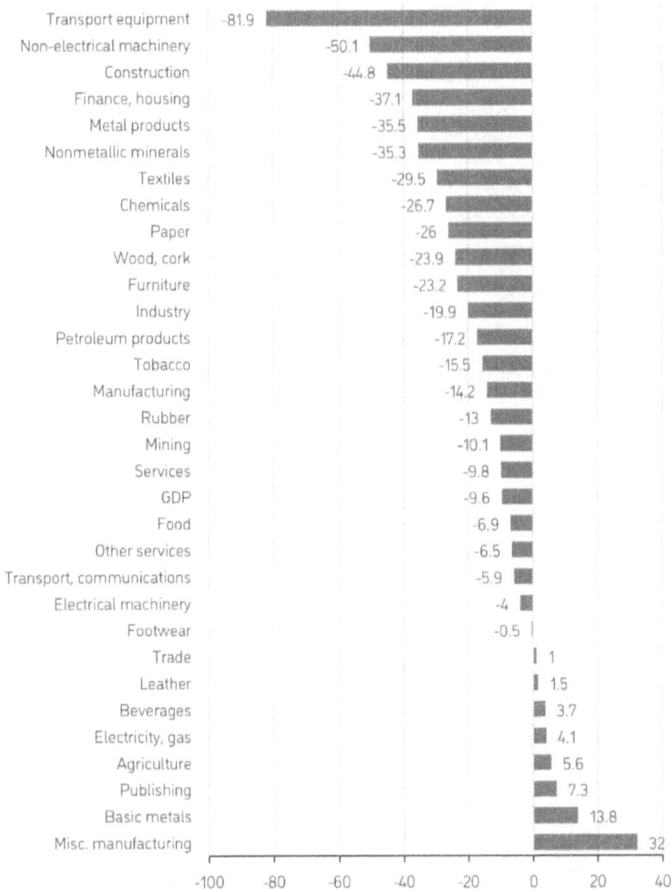

FIGURE 14.6 Decline of Philippine economic sectors as measured by percent change of real gross value-added, 1983–1985 (Source of data: Robert S. Dohner and Ponciano Intal Jr., "Debt Crisis and Adjustment in the Philippines," in *Developing Country Debt and the World Economy*, ed. Jeffrey Sachs [Chicago: University of Chicago Press, 1989], 169–92.)

People from all walks of life were not spared. Many consumers, for instance, would often panic and hoard items from groceries in fear of imminent and actual shortages. This was captured on the cover of the 9 December 1983 issue of *Mr. & Ms.* magazine, featuring actress Bibeth Orteza clutching several packs of tissue paper in a grocery trolley, with a text cloud above her: "What me, panic?"

Zooming in on specific sectors, industry contracted the most from 1983 to 1985 (by almost 20 percent), particularly the manufacture of transport equipment, non-electrical machinery, and construction (see figure 14.6). When the peso was devalued, import-dependent manufacturers were also hit. Agriculture continued to grow, except for the sugar sector, which collapsed tremendously—chiefly owing to the decline of world sugar prices and the government's (particularly NASUTRA's) failure to pay sugar millers and producers, culminating in a full-blown famine (see chapter 4). Expectedly, the labor sector also crashed during this time: unemployment went up to 12.6 percent by 1985, while underemployment skyrocketed to 33 percent by 1984 (see chapter 12).

The steep cost of the IMF stabilization and the resulting economic crisis led economist Manuel Montes to offer a grim prognosis in 1987:

> The prospects for the Philippine economy for the rest of the decade of the 1980s are not bright. The recent adjustment programme left many of the old industries at 40 per cent capacity utilization and very high incremental capital/output ratios (ICOR) . . . . An ICOR of 4, the historical ICOR from 1960 to 1980, would permit 5 per cent annual growth. Even if such a growth rate were to be

> sustained until 1990, per capita income in 1990 would still be 13.7 per cent lower than it was in 1980.[62]

Indeed, the country's "lost decades of development" lasted not just in the late 1980s but throughout the 1990s and well into the early 2000s. It was not until 2003 that per-person income exceeded the level back in 1982, or 21 years prior.

IN SUM, THE PHILIPPINES' DEFAULT ON ITS LOANS was the inevitable fallout of Marcos's wanton and irresponsible borrowing spree, which eventually snowballed into the country's worst economic crisis in history. Put another way, we would not have experienced such a drastic shrinking of our economy if we had not defaulted on our loans—which, in turn, would not have happened if Marcos and his cronies and technocrats responsibly managed the public coffers.

Despite the drastic and unforgettable debt and economic crisis in the mid-1980s, some loyalists still try to justify in vain Marcos's debts by saying that at least he had lots of projects done. But as we discussed in chapter 8, the Marcosian investments grew more and more inefficient over time and these projects were grandiose yet often useless. At the same time, even if some debt-driven projects contributed to growth of national output and income, such growth paled in comparison to the growth of the country's external debt, which rapidly became unsustainable—hence, the debt crisis.

Of course, there is also the issue of whether the subsequent Corazon Aquino administration should have pushed for the repudiation of the Marcosian debts. In a "yellow paper" by economists (many of whom co-authored the more famous 1984 UPSE white paper), they said, "The approach to managing external debt should proceed from what is required for reasonable growth, not what the creditors impose . . . it is time the government refuse to subordinate growth to an overly burdensome debt service."[63] They further "urge[d] the monetary authorities to be cognizant of the country's need for economic recovery and less compliant with the requirements of the IMF and foreign creditors for debt servicing." The NEDA director-general at the time, Solita Monsod, argued for "selective repudiation" and linking debt payments with the country's economic performance.[64] But Aquino ultimately rejected calls for debt repudiation and settled for debt restructuring instead; thus, generations of Filipinos had to live with the debt payments. But as the automatic debt payments ate up huge chunks of the national budget, Filipinos had to endure and live with budget cutbacks on key government programs and services. Was this the best move? Could we have gotten away with debt repudiation? This is still being debated.

Interestingly, the country's collective trauma with Marcosian debt in the late 1970s until the mid-1980s seems to carry over to this day. In the middle of the COVID-19 pandemic, for instance, the national debt would exceed PHP 13 trillion and the debt-to-GDP ratio would exceed 60 percent—both record highs. Economists have explained that these figures are not as dire as they seem if viewed together with the debts racked up by almost every other country in the world, and if seen in proportion to the massive spending needs of government due to the pandemic (including spending for the pandemic response itself, economic relief, and aid for businesses). Also, the debts are justifiable so long as government spent the borrowed funds. Yet monthly news about ever higher debts and debt ratios send people (especially netizens) in a panic, proceeding to automatically rail against government officials.

I wonder: how much of this deep-seated and collective aversion to debt would go away if only Marcos Sr. had not profligately borrowed during the 1970s and 1980s and had he not sent the country into a downward spiral because of his regime's debts? What would the nation be like if we were not collectively traumatized by Marcosian debt?

PART 3

CRAZY RICH FILIPINOS

15 Marcos riches came from hard work, not from large-scale plunder?

CLAIM 1 Marcos was rich before becoming president, so he had no interest in getting richer and could not have stolen from Filipinos.	**VERDICT** MISLEADING
CLAIM 2 Marcos's riches came from hard work, not from large-scale corruption.	**VERDICT** FALSE
CLAIM 3 There is no proof that the Marcoses stole billions from the Filipino people.	**VERDICT** FALSE
CLAIM 4 Kris Aquino stole Imelda's jewelry.	**VERDICT** FALSE

SOME PEOPLE WILL STOP AT NOTHING TO JUSTIFY the large-scale corruption of the Marcoses. For instance, many claim that even before becoming president, Marcos was wealthy and had no reason to steal from the public coffers. According to one version of the story, spread by Imelda herself, her husband Ferdinand traded in gold early in his career and that she herself saw Ferdinand's stash of gold at a bank near Jones Bridge in Manila.[1] Later, the couple allegedly made a fortune from the rise of gold prices in the 1970s.

Another version of this was that the Marcos riches and jewelry collections came from hard work. In an interview in 2019, Imee was quoted saying that her father was a great lawyer who defended "multinationals" and "big-time corporations," and was a top taxpayer as a result of the substantial lawyer fees he had earned. Imee added, "We've always been a hardworking family" and they never became poor—except after EDSA (which she described as "pagdurusa talaga," or real suffering on their part).[2]

And why would they be guilty if not one of them has ever been convicted nor jailed? Some say there is absolutely "no proof" of plunder, that they are "not guilty" of anything. Said one viral post, "If Ferdinand Marcos stole billions from Filipinos, why do the succeeding presidents after him cannot show any proof at all? How come Imelda won every corruption case that was thrown to her?"[3]

FIRST, MARCOS WAS BY NO MEANS POOR BEFORE becoming president. But that is because he had already engaged in traditional, run-of-the-mill corruption as a legislator. (Here is a quick recap of his political career before his first election as president in 1965: in 1949, at age 32, he became representative of Ilocos Norte's Second District and served in that role for a decade, until 1959; then in 1959, at age 42, he became senator, and later served as senate president from 1964 to 1965.[4])

Marcos had plenty of opportunity to play dirty in his early political career and engage in corrupt acts that were considered ordinary even then. For instance, Marcos, as district representative, filed a bill about import controls. Back then, the government was desperate for dollars and wanted to control which items could and could not be imported. After the said import control bill was passed, Marcos was appointed to head the special congressional committee on import and price controls that determined what essential items could be imported or not.[5] But this power to grant import permits offered Marcos a chance to get kickbacks from people who wanted such permits:

> Apparently, the norm was to part with ten percent of the amount applied for, handed over in cash to a bagman in Ermita, Manila. Marcos was believed to own the bagman, body and soul . . . [6]

Then in 1960 and 1961, there was the infamous "Stonehill 'blue book' scandal," involving prominent US businessman Harry Stonehill. At the time, Stonehill owned 18 big companies, but was charged of tax evasion. Upon the orders of then justice secretary Jose "Pepe" Diokno,[7] Stonehill's offices were raided. The raid unearthed a "blue book" wherein Stonehill wrote down the bribes he made to ranking Filipino politicians, bureaucrats, media personalities, and police and military officials. Most of the politicians implicated in the damning document were from the Nacionalista Party, but some were affiliated with the Liberal Party—including Marcos himself in his capacity as Senate president.[8]

Marcos was also corrupt in his first term as president. For example, he profited from his administration's support to the US in the Vietnam War, which involved sending thousands of troops under the so-called Philippine Civic Action Group or PHILCAG. There is evidence that the US Embassy in Manila was remitting "quarterly checks, each in the amount of several thousand dollars" to the Marcos regime, under an agreement "between officials of the Department of State and President Marcos that the Philippine government could conceal the receipts of these payments from the Philippine public in its national defense budget."[9] Officials denied there was anything illicit or underhand about this and claimed that such checks—usually deposited at the Philippine Veterans Bank at Camp Aguinaldo—were part of "intelligence funds for national security."

Marcos also allegedly skimmed money from Japanese loans and war reparations. Japanese corporations contracted for such loans and reparations would give kickbacks totaling USD 53 million from 1965 to 1986. A bagman would receive commissions from Japanese corporations and that bagman would then pass on the money to the head of the Reparations Commission, which finally deposited such proceeds into the Marcoses' offshore accounts.[10]

Marcos also made a lot of money from stock and other market manipulations. For instance, in the publicized "XYZ scandal," Marcos used his powers as president to manipulate Benguet Mining Corporation's stocks in exchange for shares in the company and in casinos in the Bahamas. Complicit in this were the men X, Y, and Z, who made "sizeable killings" from what is now called insider trading.[11] Later, these men were found out to be Marcos cronies Roberto Benedicto, Honorio Poblador, and Potenciano Ilusorio.[12]

Marcos also intervened in a big transaction of the US company General Telephone and Electronics Corporation (GTE)—specifically, GTE's sale of its 28-percent equity shares in telecom monopoly PLDT. GTE was originally in talks to sell such shares to a group of Filipinos. However,

> in or about 1966, officials at the highest levels of the government of the Philippines urged GTE for political and purported security reasons not to sell its interest in PLDT [to one group] and told GTE to deal with another group of Philippine nationals . . .[13]

This second group turned out to be the Philippine Telecommunications Investment Corporation (PTIC), 46 percent of which was owned by Marcos himself through a shell corporation set up by one of his cronies.[14]

On 20 and 21 March 1968, Ferdinand and Imelda signed contracts pertaining to accounts with Credit Suisse, where they notoriously used pseudonyms to hide their identities: "William Saunders" for Ferdinand and "Jane Ryan" for Imelda. We know about these because the signed documents bearing such pseudonyms were found in Malacañang in 1986 right after they had fled to Hawai'i.[15]

The corrupt acts of Marcos only scaled up to unbelievable extents once Ferdinand declared martial law on 23 September 1972 and formed his cabal of cronies (more on this later).

AND THEN THERE WAS IMELDA'S EXCESSES. IT IS one thing to be wealthy. But it is another to ransack the public coffers to buy extravagant stuff that no ordinary person needs—especially when Filipinos at large were suffering precisely as a result of those excesses and greed. This is what Imelda did with the money their family stole from Filipinos. In fact, her prodigal ways led to the coining of a new word in some dictionaries: "Imeldific," meaning "ostentatiously extravagant."[16] As quipped by a US lawmaker involved in hunting down the Marcos riches, "Compared to [Imelda], Marie Antoinette was a bag lady."[17]

Take for instance what had happened after the Marcoses were booted out of Malacañang. The family managed to carry with them 67 racks full of Imelda's clothes and left behind 55 more. Among the clothes and articles Imelda left were 1,060 pairs of shoes (apart from 1,800 more in Tacloban City, making the total 2,860—not quite 3,000 as the public commonly believes), 508 floor-length gowns, 427 dresses, 888 handbags, 464 scarves, 664 handkerchiefs, 71 pairs of glasses, 65 parasols, 15 mink coats, and 1 swan feather gown. Imelda also bought expensive perfumes "not by the ounce but by the gallon," explaining the huge jars of French perfume found in Malacañang after their family's exile, as well as a gallon of Mitsouko made by Guerlain in her New York Olympic Towers condo in New York.[18]

Imelda also had huge hoards of jewelry. There was so much of it that some of the most prized pieces were hurriedly carted off in suitcases—even in diaper boxes—when they fled Malacañang and flew to Hawai'i, leaving behind the less prized pieces in Malacañang. In 2014, the so-called Malacañang Collection was forfeited by the Sandiganbayan in favor of the Philippine government—yet another indelible, unassailable proof of the Marcoses'

corruption and extravagance.[19] During her heyday, Imelda or her aides would buy pieces of jewelry studded with huge gems as though they were buying candy from the *sari-sari* store. For instance, authorities discovered a brooch with a 150.01 carat Burmese ruby surrounded by diamonds and mounted in yellow gold. It was accompanied by a note indicating that the piece was worth USD 290,000. The note was written by Imelda's personal secretary, Fe Gimenez, who wrote to Ferdinand: "Sir— Ma'am liked this when she saw this in New York but she couldn't afford this!"[20] Apparently, Gimenez later bought the piece in Imelda's behalf and notified Ferdinand of the purchase.

Besides the Hawai'i and Malacañang jewelry sets, another set was in the care of the Greek national Demetriou Roumeliotes, an associate of Imelda. After the ouster in 1986, Roumeliotes was caught by airport authorities trying to smuggle jewelry out of the country.[21] All in all, there are three jewelry collections—namely the Hawai'i, Malacañang, and Roumeliotes collections—estimated to have a total value of USD 8 million (possibly a conservative estimate). All were eventually forfeited in favor of the government and are supposedly in the vaults of the Bangko Sentral ng Pilipinas for safekeeping. The keys to the vaults are held by four different government agencies—namely the PCGG, the Bureau of Customs, the Commission on Audit, and the Office of the President—and the vaults cannot be opened by any single one of them. This belies another myth circulating online that Kris Aquino, the youngest daughter of President Corazon Aquino, somehow managed to steal Imelda's jewelry.[22]

Even more incredibly, Imelda and her family had wantonly spent public funds on many other excesses even in the late 1970s to early 1980s, when the economy was already diving straight toward chaos.

In 1976, following a trip of the first couple to Kenya, around 254 Tagbanua families were displaced from Calauit Island, Palawan. This was to clear the island for more than a hundred animals—giraffes, impala, gazelles, and zebras, among others—shipped straight from Africa in order to populate a Philippine safari envisioned by Imelda and enabled by Ferdinand.[23] Although ostensibly a conservation effort of the regime, it served as a hunting ground for the dictator's son, Bongbong Marcos, who flew in to hunt wild boar.[24] For this, Calauit was even called "Bongbong's Safari Park." It cost about USD 200,000 per year to maintain—and that was in 1986 US dollars. Fast-forward to the twenty-first century, Calauit survives but funds are all extinguished and the surviving giraffes are covered in wounds infested by screwworm flies.[25] At any rate, Calauit "became a symbol of Marcos's profligate dictatorship."[26]

Other examples of the Marcoses' extravagant lifestyles abound. In 1979, when a new beach resort was inaugurated at Caylabne Bay in Cavite, Imelda invited several distinguished guests, including members of European royalty. But she realized that the sand was not white enough. This led her to order a military plane to go to Australia and fetch some white sand.[27]

In June 1983—mere months before the economic managers declared the debt moratorium—Imelda basically renovated the entire town of Sarrat, Ilocos Norte (the hometown of Ferdinand's mother) in preparation for the "wedding of the century" between Irene Marcos and Gregorio Araneta. In just 45 days, five new buildings of seventeenth-century Spanish design were erected in the otherwise sleepy and nondescript town, alongside a new international airport, and a five-star hotel. On the day of the wedding itself, Irene rode an ornate carriage brought in from Austria and drawn by seven white horses imported straight from Morocco.[28] The whole affair was said to be a vain attempt to display the Marcos wealth and outshine the recent wedding of Princess Diana and Prince Charles in 1981. (There were rumors that Imelda wanted Imee to marry Prince Charles himself. But when this did not come to pass, Imelda reportedly went berserk.[29])

Later in 1983, Imelda went on a trip and shopping spree at New York, Copenhagen, and Rome. In New York alone, Imelda spent a dizzying USD 4.5 million, USD 3 million of which was supposedly spent in a day.[30] The total bill for the entire trip was said to be USD 70 million. Most infamously, numerous accounts say that Imelda ordered a plane to make a U-turn mid-flight and return to Rome immediately when she realized they had forgotten to buy any cheese (this was later dubbed the "Great Cheese Scandal").[31]

Evidently, Imee picked up on this habit of her mother. When sister Irene visited London in 1984, she was asked by a British travel writer (the former wife of National Artist BenCab) how Imee was able to breastfeed her child back in Manila while traveling in Europe. Irene responded as if it was the most natural and obvious thing to say: "She just expressed her milk everyday and then Daddy sent a Philippine Airlines plane to wherever she was and it would bring the milk back!"[32]

In the regime's last two years in power, the Marcos family had spent about USD 68 million for personal consumption,[33] USD 11 million of which went to "clothes, paintings, antiques, handicrafts, and other items," USD 3 million on clothes alone, and USD 2.4 million on "food, hotel accommodations, and transportation expenses."[34]

In the same period, the Marcoses' chartered flights aboard Philippine Airlines totaled a whopping USD 2.7 million.[35] Talk about conspicuous consumption!

WAS MARCOS SIMPLY HARDWORKING, THUS explaining his wealth? Not true.

In 2003, the Supreme Court in the landmark case *Republic of the Philippines v. Sandiganbayan* already ruled that the Marcoses' legitimate or lawful wealth from 1966 until February 1986—the span of Marcos's entire reign in power—totaled only PHP 2.32 million or USD 304,372.43. This constituted the salaries of Ferdinand as president and Imelda as governor of Metro Manila. Their lawful wealth beyond these amounts could not be established by any court because the Marcos couple failed to submit supporting income tax returns as well as their Statements of Assets, Liabilities, and Net Worth (SALNs). In addition, the two constitutions in effect during Marcos's terms as president also prohibited Marcos from earning more than that. As quoted in the case:

> Besides, under the 1935 Constitution, Ferdinand E. Marcos as President could not receive any other emolument from the Government or any of its subdivisions and instrumentalities. Likewise, under the 1973 Constitution, Ferdinand E. Marcos as President could not receive during his tenure any other emolument from the Government or any other source.[36]

So any amount beyond PHP 2.32 million was—as far as the law is concerned—ill-gotten.

And the government did recover massive ill-gotten wealth. For instance, the 2003 ruling affirmed an earlier decision by the Sandiganbayan finding that amounts in excess of USD 658 million—previously deposited by the Marcoses in five Swiss bank accounts—were ill-gotten. The amounts, 25,809 percent larger than their lawful income, were recovered by the Philippine Commission on Good Government (PCGG)—tasked by Corazon Aquino in her Executive Order No. 1 to recover the Marcoses' ill-gotten wealth—and deposited in escrow in the Philippine National Bank (PNB). In 2014, an additional USD 29 million would be recovered from other Swiss deposits.

Years before, in 1990, the Swiss Federal Supreme Court had already found that the Marcoses did stash USD 356 million worth of ill-gotten wealth in Swiss banks via foundations.[37]

The PCGG's recovery of the Marcoses' Swiss deposits is said to be one of the most important and successful asset recovery cases in history. It was so successful that it sparked a global movement to go after the ill-gotten wealth of other despots worldwide. A *New York Times* report in 1998 says,

> The [Marcos] case prompted Swiss bank regulators to make significant changes in banking's inner sanctums, which had routinely welcomed enormous sums with few, if any, questions asked. For the first time, banks were obliged to scrutinize funds from foreign political figures. Banks also had to take greater steps to ascertain the true owner of funds before accepting them for deposit.[38]

Besides these funds, other Marcos assets were forfeited by the Philippine government, and the Marcoses were found guilty in other court cases. For instance, the three jewelry collections of Imelda have all been forfeited in favor of the government.[39] Also, Imelda was convicted for graft in 1993 and 2018. The 1993 conviction was for two counts of graft over lease contracts between the Light Rail Transit and the Philippine General Hospital Foundation (although she was later acquitted by the Supreme Court in 1998). In 2018, she was convicted for seven counts of graft for the setup of private "foundations"—really *entities*, for those were not really charitable at all[40]— in Switzerland during the time she was a government official.[41] The reason Imelda is not in jail is that she has since paid PHP 300,000 in bail and was allowed by the court temporary freedom while appealing her case to the Supreme Court.[42] To this day, as of writing, the Supreme Court has not decided on this case.

Other notable successes by the PCGG include a USD 10-million award by a Hawai'i court to 7,526 martial law victims (arising from a settlement with the owners of Marcos properties in Texas and Colorado)[43] and a 2012 Supreme Court ruling that a 24-percent block share (equivalent to more than PHP 70.2 billion, including dividends) in San Miguel Corporation belongs to the Philippine government.[44] This 2012 Supreme Court grant would be the biggest one-time recovery of the PCGG to date.

All in all, as of December 2020, the government has recovered over PHP 174.23 billion from the Marcoses' ill-gotten wealth,[45] coming from the Swiss bank accounts, shares in various companies like PLDT and San Miguel Corporation, as well as properties like jewelry, paintings, and real estate here and abroad, including several buildings in New York—like a seven-storey skyscraper in New York

City also called the "Trump Building," and a waterfront mansion in Long Island.[46] Included as well are properties in New Jersey[47] (later sold off once the PCGG was able to secure the titles from the New Jersey Supreme Court), as well as in Beverly Hills in California and Honolulu in Hawai'i. The PCGG's sequestration of these properties was enabled by many court decisions—proving even more the mass corruption of the Marcoses.

The gigantic loot of the Marcoses led to a huge estate tax liability that the family still has not paid until today. In 1991, the Bureau of Internal Revenue (BIR) determined the estate tax to be PHP 23.293 billion. But despite several notices, the Marcoses did not pay the amount. They reacted only in 1993 when the BIR auctioned off some of Marcos's properties in Tacloban City, Leyte in order to pay for the unpaid estate tax. But despite Bongbong Marcos's remonstrances—as he was the appointed administrator of his father's estate—the Court of Appeals said the estate tax was "final and unappealable." Fast-forward to 2021, the unpaid estate tax liability has ballooned—due to a mountain of interest and penalties—to a mind-boggling PHP 203.819 billion. Still, they have not paid, and seem to have no intention of doing so—nor do they seem willing to return the remaining ill-gotten wealth that the PCGG says is still under litigation.[48]

Now that Marcos Jr. has won the presidency at last, the chances of them paying their obligations have disappeared completely. This, at a time when the Philippine government incurred massive debt from the COVID-19 pandemic and is in dire need of "fiscal consolidation." Former finance secretary Carlos Dominguez III suggested to the incoming Marcos Jr. administration the imposition of new taxes, and proposed several ways of doing so. It turns out that the Marcoses' unpaid estate tax liability of PHP 203.819 billion is already about three-fourths of the total revenues that can be earned if Marcos Jr. would implement Dominguez's tax proposals. But where is Marcos Jr.'s credibility here? How can he expect people to pay new taxes if he himself had evaded doing so for more than three decades?

THE RECOVERED ILL-GOTTEN WEALTH OF THE Marcoses has gone to much social good. Most of it has been given to three big groups of beneficiaries: the Comprehensive Agrarian Reform Program (for, say, irrigation facilities, farm-to-market roads, credit assistance to farmers, scholarships, etc.), the Coco Levy Trust Fund, and human rights victims during martial law. The last is especially notable since it arose from Republic Act No. 10368, otherwise known as the "Human Rights Victims Reparation and Recognition Act of 2013." This law is remarkable and groundbreaking in many respects. For one, it officially acknowledges that human rights abuses were perpetrated by the regime of Ferdinand Marcos Sr. It states:

> it is hereby declared the policy of the State to recognize the heroism and sacrifices of all Filipinos who were victims of summary execution, torture, enforced or involuntary disappearance and other gross human rights violations committed during the regime of former President Ferdinand E. Marcos covering the period from September 21, 1972 to February 25, 1986 and restore the victims' honor and dignity. The State hereby acknowledges its moral and legal obligation to recognize and/or provide reparation to said victims and/or their families for the deaths, injuries, sufferings,

> deprivations and damages they suffered under the Marcos regime.[49]

For this alone, one might say that the administration of former president Benigno Aquino III did well in pushing Congress to pass this law. Even more significantly, this law set aside PHP 10 billion from the recovered Swiss deposits for the benefit of human rights victims identified by the Human Rights Victims' Claims Board.[50] In 2018, at the end of the Claims Board's operations as mandated by law, it was able to give out reparations for a total of 11,103 victims.[51]

But the job is far from done. The PCGG has yet to recover PHP 125.98 billion in ill-gotten wealth.[52] Even the government, however, is clueless how much of the wealth is yet to be found. There is likely more out there, says former PCGG commissioner Ruben Carranza. In 1998, Imelda blurted out that "there is more Marcos wealth that this government is not yet aware of, but for the time being I can admit that there is only USD 800 million kept in various international banks, but I cannot reveal them." She added, "If you know how rich you are, you are not rich. But me, I am not aware of the extent of my wealth. That is how rich we are."[53] This is a lot similar to a previous statement she made, as quoted in *Some Are Smarter than Others*: "If you know how much you've got, you probably don't have much."[54]

FINALLY, SOME PEOPLE CLAIM THAT THE MARCOSES are innocent because they have never been convicted nor jailed. Another version of this is that the Marcoses won every case hurled against them.

This is utterly false. To recap, table 15.1 shows a list of the convictions involving the Marcoses as defendants (this list

TABLE 15.1 Selected court cases won against the Marcoses and associates

Year	Court	Nature of case/amounts involved
1989	Sandiganbayan	Unexplained wealth of Fernando Timbol, presidential photographer close to the Marcoses
2003	Supreme Court	Forfeiture of USD 658-million Swiss deposits (plus interest and other accrued amounts); follows a 1990 case in the Swiss Federal Supreme Court regarding USD 356 million hidden in Swiss entities
2005	Supreme Court	Shares of Cojuangco, Campos, and Zalamea declared as ill-gotten wealth of the Marcoses
2006	Supreme Court	Reconveyance to Philippine government of 111,415 PTIC registered in the name of Prime Holdings Inc. (PHI)
2010	Sandiganbayan	Pilfering of PHP 10 million from NFA funds to the Marcoses' private account
2012	Sandiganbayan	Decision stated that coco levy funds are public funds and anything bought with it should be treated as public funds/property as well
2012	Supreme Court	Preferred shares in San Miguel Corporation ordered reconveyed to Philippine government to benefit coconut farmers and the coconut industry

Year	Court	Nature of case/amounts involved
2014	Sandiganbayan	Danding Cojuangco's shares of stock in FUB/UCPB declared owned by the Philippine government and to be used only for the development of the coconut industry and the welfare of coconut farmers
2018	Sandiganbayan	Imelda's conviction for seven counts of graft for illegal creation of Swiss entities; Imee, Irene, and Bongbong explicitly named as beneficiaries
2019	Sandiganbayan	Marcos Sr.'s use of dummies to obtain shares in Eastern Telecommunications Philippines, Inc. (EPTI)
2021	Sandiganbayan	Royal Traders Holding Co. Inc. ordered to return to the Philippine government more than PHP 1 billion worth of bank certificates absconded by the Marcoses when they were exiled to Hawai'i
2022	Sandiganbayan	Reversal of 2019 decision, clarifying that the Marcoses recovered only 4 properties out of PHP 200 billion worth of real properties, bank deposits, stocks, and paintings forfeited in favor of the government

excludes other cases with the Marcoses not impleaded as defendants).[55]

Note that most of the convictions are civil cases. Why has there been no conviction regarding any bigger criminal case, for instance, plunder and "dollar-salting" (or the illegal transfer of dollars abroad without prior consent by the Central Bank, an act criminalized by Marcos himself in 1984 precisely because of the dire shortage of dollars then)?

The answer is that plunder was not a crime until the passage of Republic Act No. 7080 in July 1991. And although Imelda was charged with 32 counts of dollar-salting, she was acquitted by a lower court in 2008, and this decision was affirmed later by the Supreme Court in 2018, citing not so much the merits of the case but the weak case of the prosecution. Said Associate Justice Marvic Leonen, who penned the decision, "Apathetic prosecution allows impunity . . . . Prosecutors must not only be courageous but must also show their dedication to public interest through their competence."[56]

This brings us to the sad realities of the Philippine judicial system and the legal profession. Clearly, there have been lapses in the way the authorities have tried to hold the Marcoses accountable. Former PCGG commissioner Carranza admitted in an interview with Rappler that "in many ways [it's] not as strategic as it should have been, not as comprehensive as it should have been."[57] Some recent cases were dismissed simply because evidence provided by prosecutors were mere photocopies and hence inadmissible before courts. Apart from this, Carranza said that much more could have been done to prosecute the Marcoses and find them guilty in more cases—maybe even force them to spend time in jail—were it not for the corruption in the judiciary and the "tentacles" of the Marcoses spread all

over it. Cases remain unresolved for decades, and in many instances, deliberately delayed by the Marcoses by hiring cadres of lawyers deploying every delaying tactic possible. (Alas, in the dollar-salting cases, flimsy delaying tactics were deployed by the prosecution itself.)

At any rate, the landmark 2003 decision *Republic of the Philippines v. Sandiganbayan* ruled with finality that the Marcoses acquired ill-gotten wealth, and prosecutors as well as the PCGG can use the ruling to go after any other properties or assets or accounts that they may want to run after in the future. Also, several cases are still being pursued in various courts. Let us see what the future will bring.

16 Marcos fought the oligarchy?

CLAIM 1	**VERDICT**
Marcos fought the oligarchy.	FALSE
CLAIM 2	**VERDICT**
No one among the Marcos cronies has been found guilty of corruption.	FALSE

FANS AND LOYALISTS PRAISE MARCOS TO THIS DAY for supposedly standing up against the Philippine oligarchy. An oligarchy is defined as "a government in which a small group exercises control especially for corrupt and selfish purposes."[1] In fact, when Marcos declared martial law in 1972, he anchored his Bagong Lipunan (New Society) on a "revolution from the center" led by government—ostensibly pushing back against both the communist left and the elite, oligarchic, conservative right.[2]

But although Marcos did outshine, outrank, and overturn the old Philippine elite, he was nowhere close to defeating them. Instead, he put his own family and friends (collectively, his "cronies") on top of the food chain that was Philippine society, supplanting the old elite (which they arguably envied and aspired to become) with a new elite of their own making. This was the basis of so-called *crony capitalism* from which the Marcoses and their cronies profited immensely, plundering the public sector while at the same time lording over the private sector. Note that this is very much the crucial point when talking about the Marcoses' economic and political power: they spread their reach not just in the public sector, but also very much in the private sector. The Marcoses are proud of this feat. In 1998, Imelda was quoted as saying in an interview for the *Philippine Daily Inquirer*:

> We practically own everything in the Philippines, from electricity, telecommunications, airlines, banking, beer and tobacco, newspaper publishing, television stations, shipping, oil and mining, hotels and beach resorts, down to coconut milling, small farms, real estate and insurance.[3]

The scale of crony capitalism was also aptly described by Corazon Aquino's erstwhile NEDA director-general and finance secretary, Jesus Estanislao:

> It was not Filipino first. It was family first, friends first, and cronies first. So it was a government where everything was stacked up against everybody who did not belong to friends, family, and cronies. So competition was not allowed.[4]

Not coincidentally, the original cover of *Some Are Smarter than Others*—the landmark 1991 book on Marcos's crony capitalism by Ricardo Manapat—features a menacing octopus with huge, writhing tentacles.[5] Meanwhile, the original cover of Primitivo Mijares's *The Conjugal Dictatorship* featured Ferdinand and Imelda's heads sprouting from a giant claw hand clutching the Philippine archipelago.

Corruption, of course, was nothing new when the Marcoses came to power. As we mentioned in chapter 15, even before becoming president, Ferdinand was already an established figure of the old political elite and was quite adept at run-of-the-mill corruption—in the form of kickbacks from projects, privileges and exemptions, concessions, and the like. Everybody else was doing the same thing; Ferdinand was doing what most people were expected to do at the time.

But all of that scaled up during the dictatorship and the regime even found new—if innovative and ingeniously complex—methods to improve upon the corruption of old, to make it a lot more blatant but also more efficient. In the words of journalist George M. Taber, who claimed to have coined the term "crony capitalism" in 1980:

> I was struck by the Philippine distortion of the capitalist system. This was not capitalism. It was a weird distortion of the free market that benefited a few and kept the masses in poverty. The cronies got rich, and the poor stayed poor. So early that morning I wrote the headline: "A Case of Crony Capitalism."[6]

Corruption, in short, reached unprecedented heights during martial law. The sky was the limit as far as the Marcoses and their cronies were concerned. This would earn Ferdinand the unsavory distinction of holding (to this day!) the Guinness World Record for the world's "greatest robbery of a government"—for an estimated loot totaling USD 5 billion to USD 10 billion.[7]

(Let me add two quick sidenotes regarding Guinness. First, there is also an absurd myth alleging that Marcos was awarded the Guinness World Record for being "the best president of all time."[8] Second, in the months leading to the 2022 elections, the webpage for Marcos Sr.'s "greatest robbery" Guinness World Record suddenly disappeared. Guinness said they took it down to "ensure its accuracy."[9] Why only then?)

Unsurprisingly, Marcosian crony capitalism led to a concentration of wealth and power in the country's political and business elite. According to de Dios et al., this was "the main characteristic distinguishing the Marcos years from other periods in our economic history."[10] And without a doubt, this contributed in no small measure to the continual rise of income inequality from the 1960s to the 1980s.[11]

IN THE FIRST PLACE, HOW DID THE MARCOSES create the system of crony capitalism? It will do well to look at the various means and schemes by which they ransacked the public coffers and extracted money well in excess of what they were due as government officials. Here we defer to the wisdom of former Senate president and former PCGG chair Jovito Salonga,[12] who made an extensive documentation in his 2000 book, *Presidential Plunder: The Quest for the Marcos Ill-Gotten Wealth.* Salonga outlined nine principal "techniques" by which the Marcoses obtained their ill-gotten wealth,[13] which we paraphrase as such:

1) Creation of *monopolies* in vital industries (e.g., sugar, coconut, and bananas) under the control of Marcos cronies;
2) *Behest loans* awarded by government financial institutions to cronies even with little to no collateral;
3) Forcible *takeover* of large public or private firms/agencies/assets (e.g., Lopez assets in media and power, such as ABS-CBN, *Manila Chronicle*, and Meralco);[14]
4) *Raiding of the public coffers*, specifically the Treasury and other government financial institutions (e.g., PNB, DBP, SSS, and the Central Bank itself);
5) *Presidential decrees and orders* favoring cronies and their businesses with privileges, tax exemptions, and concessions in land and natural resources (e.g., timber and mining concessions for Juan Ponce Enrile);
6) *Kickbacks and commissions* from firms doing business in the Philippines (also known as "front-loaded corruption");
7) *Shell corporations/dummy companies* used to launder money and make investments abroad (e.g., in Hawai'i and New York);
8) *Skimming off foreign aid* and other forms of assistance; and
9) *Deposits* in banks here and abroad using code names and pseudonyms ("William Saunders" and "Jane Ryan").

There are of course several other excellent texts that dive deep into the world of Marcosian crony capitalism, the lives of the cronies themselves, how they came into the Marcoses' orbit and thrived there, and what happened to them after EDSA. The best reference, bar none, would still be Ricardo Manapat's *Some Are Smarter than Others.*[15] It is an astonishing and authoritative work of investigative journalism, completed over a decade, although it was originally published in 1979 as a much thinner 48-page pamphlet, which Ninoy Aquino called "the most explosive document to have rocked the city of Manila."

We shall not dream of replicating here what was done masterfully by previous authors. But we will try to highlight some of the egregious acts done by the cronies—acts that best illustrate how corruption flourished during martial law. Moreover, in this chapter, we will focus on the first five techniques outlined by Salonga. (We already discussed kickbacks and commissions when we described the cronies Herminio Disini and Rodolfo Cuenca in chapter 8 on infrastructure; we already talked about the money laundering, skimming of foreign aid, and use of pseudonyms in chapter 15.)

Monopolies

Martial law saw an extraordinary rise of monopolies in nearly all major sectors of the economy. The ensuing lack of competition made the everyday lives of Filipinos difficult—and this alone is a strong argument against the idea of the martial law years as a "golden age." As wonderfully put by Dr. Jesus Estanislao, one of Corazon Aquino's former economic managers:

> Those golden years never existed. They existed in the mind of people, in the propaganda machine of the dictatorship, but they were never real. Take a look at the life of ordinary people. If you wanted to fly Philippine Airlines to various destinations, for example Singapore, you could not easily get a ticket because the seats were rationed, because Philippine Airlines was a monopoly, there was no competition. Take a look at [the situation] now. Take a look at PLDT at that time: in order to get a phone, you had to wait several years, and if you get a phone you probably had it party line. Take a look at the situation now. Those were the golden years? When you had to wait three . . . four . . . five years in order to get a telephone line with a party-line? And you had to shout "Tubig!" in the morning because there was [no] water flowing through your faucet. And [now], we have after privatization, the liberalization program that we initiated, you now have water all throughout Metro Manila. So these are some of the benefits that the change has made. Going back to the past would be a terrible situation for us, because we were really a dark Third World country out in the dumps.[16]

It was not until the administration of former president Fidel V. Ramos (1992–1998) that the Philippine government decidedly broke down the martial law-era monopolies. For instance, PLDT's monopoly in telecommunications ended with Republic Act No. 7925 or the Public Telecommunications Policy Act of the Philippines. After that, a flurry of other competitors like Digitel and Bayantel arose, albeit with fleeting success. Now, Globe is the main competitor of PLDT-Smart; the industry is still largely a duopoly, but at the very least, gone are the days when PLDT was the only option for Filipinos.[17] Meanwhile, Philippine Airlines's monopoly in air travel ended when President Ramos signed in 1995 Executive Order No. 219, which allowed other domestic and international players to compete in the industry. This eventually democratized air travel and allowed for more budget-friendly flights and even "piso fare" promotions for people. One of these newer airlines now uses the catchphrase, "It's time every Juan flies!"[18] But this scenario would have been impossible during martial law because of PAL's long-standing monopoly.

Two of the biggest monopolies created during martial law were related to the Philippines' primary exports. Apart from sugar,[19] coconuts proved to be a juicy source of rents and profits for the dictatorship.[20] Both commodities made up about a third of our export earnings during martial law.[21]

For a long time, the coconut industry was neglected. At the start of the 1970s, the government discriminated against the export of our primary goods in general, favoring and promoting instead the import-dependent manufacturing sector in keeping with the strategy of import substitution industrialization (ISI). Around the time Marcos took office, the government barely paid any attention to the plight of coconut farmers (especially against greedy middlemen), as well as the development of their sector in terms of, say, exports or research. But in 1971, the country's largest group of coconut farmers (Coconut Producers Federation, or COCOFED) managed to successfully lobby for a new law creating a Coconut Industry Investment Fund (CIIF) that, among other things, aimed to set up regional banks to help along investments in coconut processing and marketing. This fund was to be created from a new levy or tax on coconut sales (at PHP 5.50 per metric ton).

Then in 1973, there was a shortage of copra worldwide, jacking up its price to sky-high levels and leading to a domestic shortage of coconut-based products like cooking oil and margarine. To tame prices here at home, the government set price caps. But this injured domestic producers, so they were compensated by the government from a supposedly temporary Coconut Consumer Stabilization Fund (CCSF). This stabilization fund was financed from yet another coconut levy of PHP 150 per metric ton. Later, it was ordered to set aside a portion of its proceeds for the development of the coconut industry, and much later, a new Coconut Industry Development Fund was created out of the joint levies from the sale of copra and stabilization, which was already at PHP 200 per metric ton then.

Enter Marcos's cronies. In 1973, Marcos created the Philippine Coconut Authority (PCA), which allowed coconut levy funds to be used to buy a bank meant to serve as the coconut industry's bank. The PCA ended up buying First United Bank, which was later renamed into United Coconut Planters Bank (UCPB). The UCPB grew tremendously since much of the coconut investment fund and the entire stabilization fund were deposited in this bank. Note that it was headed by Danding Cojuangco, while its board was chaired by defense minister Juan Ponce Enrile. By 1979, the UCPB created a new entity, United Coconut Oil Mills (UNICOM), that channeled levy funds to make investments in coconut milling and buy existing mills. By 1980, UNICOM controlled 90 percent of the country's coconut milling capacity. By the way, in

1978, the CIIF (which was controlled by UCPB) used money from the stabilization fund to buy 47 percent of San Miguel Corporation.

By taxing or levying the coconut industry and placing cronies in strategic positions, Marcos had created a perfect environment in which to siphon money from this sector. Crony Danding Cojuangco was not only president of UCPB and UNICOM, he was also a director of COCOFED, head of PCA, and owner of a hybrid coconut[22] seed nut farm that was believed to be financed by diverted coconut levy funds. In 1985, the NEDA estimated that the coconut levies collected by government amounted to a whopping PHP 10 billion.[23] Yet only a tenth of the fund was used to reimburse local producers and an even smaller proportion was spent for the benefit of coconut farmers and their families (usually in the form of life insurance and scholarships).

Just like in sugar, the government (through UNICOM) "monopsonized" (not monopolized) coconuts for export by being the sole *buyer* of it (in contrast, if you are the sole *seller* of something, you monopolize it). Economists have shown that because of this tremendous exercise of market power, copra farmers received significantly lower prices than they ought to have received.[24] Rather than benefit from the government, the farmers suffered huge losses for the trouble of producing coconuts. Despite colossal sums collected ostensibly for the benefit of coconut farmers, they benefited too little from it. In contrast, cronies were alleged in past cases to have been the primary beneficiaries of the coconut levy funds.

Fast-forward to 2012, the Supreme Court ruled that certain shares of San Miguel Corporation, which were purchased with coconut levy funds, belonged to the Philippine government.[25] This yielded PHP 71 billion in recovered ill-gotten wealth—the single largest recovery made by the PCGG to date. That amount has since been used for the benefit of the coconut industry, as originally intended.

Behest loans

A lot of Marcos's cronies profited as well from the so-called *behest loans*—loans awarded by government banks at the behest of the dictator himself. You can think of this as one of the "innovations" by which Marcos raided the public coffers. In November 1992, former president Fidel Ramos, while creating an ad hoc committee to investigate the Marcosian behest loans, laid down the definition of a behest loan:

1) It is undercollateralized.
2) The borrower corporation is undercapitalized.
3) Direct or indirect endorsement by high government officials like presence of marginal notes.
4) Stockholders, officers or agents of the borrower corporation are identified as cronies.
5) Deviation of use of loan proceeds from the purpose intended.
6) Use of corporate layering.
7) Non-feasibility of the project for which financing is being sought.
8) Extraordinary speed in which the loan release was made.[26]

Whereas the typical firm borrows money directly from the bank—presenting collateral to give the bank something to hold on to in case of default—the cronies' businesses borrowed money differently. Marcos himself, abusing his power as president, would instruct government financial institutions (like the Philippine National Bank or Development Bank of the Philippines—at times even the Central Bank) to lend to the cronies' businesses in which the Marcoses may have some shares or other form of interest. This, even though the amounts of the loans were well in excess of the expected output of the business, even if the businesses were not expected to be profitable in the long run, and even if the government banks themselves ran the risk of declaring bankruptcy. The amounts in the behest loans that were well in excess of the crony businesses' needs would go straight to the cronies' bank accounts. The cronies did not care if the business or the banks go under. It was free money as far as they were concerned and that was what they were after.

In some rare instances, the borrowed funds were invested. But more often than not, they were absconded by the beneficiaries in part or in full. Jose Mari Velez, a former head of the Development Bank of the Philippines (DBP), had this to say:

> Persons seeking the loan would just come around here and say that we need 100–200 million dollars for this project which looks viable. It's not viable but Marcos says it is viable. When he says that then it better be viable. For instance, we were recently sent an account for 65 million dollars that we are supposed to pay. Now, apparently this money was supposed to have put up a steel mill, a

> factory . . . . So we asked to see where the factory is, and to this day, after several months, nobody has found it. In short, this factory does not exist.[27]

Several behest loans went on unnoticed by most Filipinos and were freely allowed by the authorities, including Marcos's economic managers—not until this system ultimately spelled financial ruin for government banks and it was too late to do anything. Former prime minister Cesar Virata in 1984 belatedly admitted that:

> We were quite liberal in guaranteeing loans, so that investors could go on with their projects on the basis of commercial loans. We found out later that their motives were not as pure as we would have liked. In other words, some of the companies really wanted to make money out of purchases of equipment rather than by operating it. This has been one of the major faults in our system.[28]

The behest loans played a particularly large role during the economic crisis in the 1980s: many of the crony businesses that underperformed were saved by government banks such as the PNB and DBP. But the banks themselves had to be rescued by new capital coming from private and public pension funds, namely from the Social Security System and the Government Service Insurance System. According to the following account from China Bank:

> By 1986, the PNB and the DBP had given out behest loans amounting to P119 billion. When the banks were rehabilitated in 1986, DBP assets had been reduced by 86% and PNB assets by

> 67%. Many leading businessmen felt that the government was throwing away public money to prop up the president's cronies—at a time when sounder, more productive firms badly needed and better deserved the capital. The Philippine banking industry, already undergoing many challenges, was weakened even further.[29]

Even the Central Bank came to the rescue of the embattled banks. Over time, the Central Bank's credit became concentrated on PNB and DBP and, ultimately, the Central Bank became embarrassingly and ironically bankrupt. By the end of the regime had incurred losses amounting to around PHP 300 billion[30] (in 1982–1985 alone, it lost PHP 57.6 billion[31]).

The Nobel Prize-winning economist and *New York Times* columnist Paul Krugman came to the Philippines in the 1990s to study what had happened with the Central Bank of old. Krugman and his team said,

> In essence the problem is that the Central Bank is itself insolvent. Abuse of its domestic credit creation during the Marcos era has left the Central Bank with a portfolio consisting largely of uncollectable loans—effectively fictitious assets—while past borrowing leaves the Central Bank with real liabilities. The result is that the monetary authority runs a substantial deficit, and must be supported by the Treasury.[32]

Ordinarily, in times of crisis, it is the Central Bank that is supposed to help the Treasury (just like what happened during the COVID-19 pandemic). But during martial law, it abnormally went the other way around. The Treasury supported the Central Bank. Eventually, the behest loans later morphed and contributed directly to the gargantuan Marcosian debt. According to former finance secretary Estanislao, "the national treasury had to assume them because in effect they were guaranteed by the national treasury, and therefore guaranteed by the Philippine Republic, and therefore they became public debts."[33]

Ultimately, the Central Bank was ruined by its complete lack of independence from Marcos himself. Marcos "strongly influenced" the Monetary Board, the Central Bank's highest policymaking body, by packing it with his cabinet ministers.[34] The Central Bank's colossal losses and tarnished reputation (exemplified by Laya's window dressing of the reserves), led to the establishment of an entirely new monetary authority, the Bangko Sentral ng Pilipinas, in 1993. To allow the Bangko Sentral to start with a clean slate, the old debts of the Central Bank were shouldered by a body called the Board of Liquidators (CB-BOL).[35] And in order to pay for these debts, the BSP Charter provided that the BSP shall "remit seventy-five percent (75%) of its net profits to a special deposit account (sinking fund) until such time as the net liabilities of the Central Bank shall have been liquidated." Believe it or not, it was only in July 2018 that the CB-BOL was abolished. And as of 2016 it still owed the national government a debt of PHP 413.45 billion.[36] In effect, the country felt the aftershocks of the Marcos dictatorship's mismanagement of the Central Bank at least a quarter of a century after the regime's end.

Takeovers

Right after Marcos declared martial law on 23 September 1972, he ordered the forcible takeover of the Lopez clan's assets in power (the Manila Electric Company or MERALCO) and media (ABS-CBN and *The Manila Chronicle*). Whereas Enrile's fake ambush happened at 8:00 p.m. of 22 September 1972, the daily broadsheet *The Manila Chronicle*—which was quite critical of Marcos—was shut down minutes before midnight of 23 September. Soldiers took over MERALCO just thirty minutes past midnight, and by 1:00 a.m., an army captain and his soldiers went to ABS-CBN to shut it down as well.[37]

Why did Marcos target the Lopezes' businesses as one of his first deeds under martial law?

The Lopezes were very much part of the old elite that Marcos claimed and appeared to rail against. Originally from Iloilo, the Lopezes grew wealthy because they were among the families that dominated the sugar industry in Negros Island and acquired immense economic power there. So wealthy were they that, for example, Eugenio Lopez Sr. celebrated his and his wife's ruby or fortieth wedding anniversary with a literal fountain of champagne.[38] The Lopezes' economic power translated to political power as they began to enter politics. In fact, Marcos and the Lopezes used to be allies: Marcos rode on the Lopezes' influence by picking Fernando Lopez, sole brother of Eugenio Sr., to be his vice president in both the 1965 and 1969 elections.[39]

The Lopezes, however, grew increasingly critical of Marcos and come martial law, Marcos retaliated against the family big-time. Through Letter of Instruction No. 1, s. 1972, Marcos had instructed the military to take over the biggest media outlets, primarily ABS-CBN and

Associated Broadcasting Corporation (ABC).[40] Allegedly, the owners were "engaged in subversive activities against the government" and were "participants in a conspiracy to overthrow the government." This takeover rang the death knell for press freedom under martial law.[41] ABS-CBN later fell into the control of Marcos's crony and "Sugar King" Roberto Benedicto.

Apart from this, ABS-CBN's president, Eugenio "Geny" Lopez Jr., was arrested on 27 November 1972, about ten weeks after the declaration of martial law, due to eight trumped-up charges regarding supposed assassination attempts against Marcos. Geny Lopez was imprisoned in Fort Bonifacio along with Sergio "Serge" Osmeña III, son of Marcos's political rival, Sergio Osmeña Jr. In 1972, both of them famously embarked on a hunger strike. Geny's father, Eugenio Lopez Sr., was then living in exile in the US and did not speak openly about his son's arrest until in January 1975, when he said, "Our property was given to the Marcos family through its front men in exchange for the release of my son and for the safety of our family."[42] But even though they succumbed and surrendered their assets to the Marcoses, Marcos never let Geny Lopez free. Don Eugenio Lopez died while his son was still under prison in Fort Bonifacio.

In fact, Geny and Serge had to *escape* from prison. The manner of their prison break in the late hours of 30 September 1977 seemed to have come from a movie (in fact, the incredible tale would later be turned into a 1995 film called *Eskapo*, starring Christopher de Leon and Richard Gomez, and produced by Star Cinema). Here is how the prison break began:

> That night at 9, Serge and I donned our camouflage suits, went into my bathroom and took off the

> iron grills welded to a steel frame. After the iron bars were removed, the six glass louvers were next. Then we cut out the wire screen behind the louvers. I went out first, Serge followed. Serge then pulled the steel frame back in place, using a rope he had looped over the shower head, using the shower head as a pulley. We started replacing the louvers, but stopped at five out of six because wedging the last one back into place was making a lot of noise. We also reattached the screen with masking tape.[43]

After that, Geny and Serge were able to crawl past guards; reach a low point of the prison walls; meet up with Geny's sons, Gabby and Raffy (aged 25 and 20 then), who were waiting with a vehicle; climb into the trunk of the said vehicle; get past another checkpoint; head to an apartment at Ayala Avenue; and travel early in the morning all the way to Lingayen, Pangasinan, where a Cessna plane carted them off to Hong Kong, where they would finally fly to Los Angeles and seek asylum.

Geny Lopez's kidnapping and imprisonment is also crucial in understanding how the Marcos regime took over MERALCO. Marcos's henchmen prepared documents to the effect that Eugenio Lopez Sr. would sell their shares in Meralco Securities Corporation in exchange for Geny's freedom. Specifically, the shares were to be sold to the Meralco Foundation, a private foundation controlled by Imelda's brother, Kokoy Romualdez. The Lopezes would receive a down payment of USD 1,500 for the shares (that was about PHP 10,000 with prevailing exchange rates then) and the balance of USD 6 million was to be paid over in the span of ten years. But Meralco Foundation defaulted on its payments by 1985, and the shares—which were at that point still not paid for—were reverted to the Lopezes' First Philippine Holdings Corporation.

Kokoy Romualdez's takeover spelled disaster for MERALCO. He and his family merely used it as a milking cow:

> Kokoy and other members of the Romualdez family bled Meralco, thereby reducing its cash flow, with the result that no further payments were ever made beyond the initial $1,500. Expenses for Imelda's 2 July 1974 birthday party, for example, were shouldered by Meralco; the catering personnel of the Meralco restaurant and cafeteria, including the expensive silverware, china, and glassware of the company, were marshalled and flown from Manila to Leyte using company planes to serve Imelda's guests. The following year, a new private nine-seater jet costing more than a million dollars was ordered using company funds.[44]

Moreover, it is said that Imee Marcos's fake graduation photo from the UP College of Law (where its former dean, Froilan Bacungan, allowed her to attend classes despite the lack of an undergraduate degree) was staged at Meralco Theater. The photo was shared by Imee herself on social media. Dean Bacungan would later admit, "There was indeed some kind of a ceremony held which looked as if she graduated. I was there. It was a little bit PR that, strictly speaking, we should not have participated in."[45]

By the end of martial law, the Lopezes were able to regain a small but still sizable share of MERALCO's shares (about 16 percent, the second largest next to the shares of government itself). But the mere fact that Marcos forcibly took over MERALCO—with no intention of running it efficiently and profitably—is a stark example of the lengths that the dictatorship went just to satisfy its craving for power.

Raiding of public coffers

The Marcoses dipped their hands directly into the huge sums of money lodged with the country's biggest financial institutions. We already discussed above the behest loans that enriched the cronies, as well as the infamous bankruptcy of the Central Bank by the mid-1980s.

But other ways of corruption were just as blatant—maybe even worse.

For instance, coming from just his first term as president, Marcos's reelection campaign in 1969 was supposedly financed (at least in part) by money printed directly by the Central Bank[46]—leading to substantial money growth and inflation by 1970. This practice went on until the very last months of martial law, in the run-up to the snap elections in February 1986. According to Corazon Aquino's budget minister Alberto Romulo, "Marcos, in his last two months in power, 'raided' the government treasury of hundreds of millions of dollars to pay off local officials and voters for their part in the February 7 presidential election campaign," and that this had "left the new government with a budget deficit of USD 250 million for the first quarter of 1986."[47]

Meanwhile, later in the dictatorship, the Philippine National Bank (PNB) had a branch in New York City that Imelda would frequent to get money for her luxurious shopping sprees (e.g., jewelry, clothes, art, antiques), her grand parties at Waldorf Towers, and even her daughter

Imee's expenses during her stay at Princeton. The total amounts withdrawn from PNB New York—and deposited in Imelda's private bank accounts—was about USD 20 million. And there is evidence to suggest that the funds withdrawn from PNB New York can be traced directly to President Marcos's intelligence funds. Essentially, "the New York branch was nothing but a great big personal piggy bank for Marcos and the First Lady," said one of former president Corazon Aquino's investigators.[48] In *Presidential Plunder*, Salonga further noted that "our information was that both PNB Manila and PNB New York had been deeply involved in the remittances of huge public funds to pay for the New York buildings bought by the Marcoses, through their dummies and agents, particularly the Bernsteins and the Tantocos."[49]

One of Imelda's most trusted agents abroad was Vilma Bautista. At the time, she was "first secretary" at the Philippine Consulate at New York but in effect, she was Imelda's secretary. In 2013, Bautista was convicted of stealing Impressionist paintings that she attempted to sell in an auction. This set off alerts in the Art Loss Register—"the world's largest private database of lost and stolen art"—as well as the PCGG.[50] Previously, in 2010, Bautista sold an expensive Monet painting (titled *Le Bassin Aux Nymphéas* or *Water-Lily Pond*) that used to be owned by her boss and was allegedly gifted to her. She sold it for USD 32 million to a Panamanian company, which sold it to a London gallery, and later went into the hands of a Swiss billionaire and hedge fund manager.[51] For this transaction, Bautista failed to pay USD 28 million in New York taxes and was convicted of tax fraud. She was sentenced in 2014 but only started to serve prison time in December 2017. As of 2020, she was New York City's "no. 2 most delinquent taxpayer."[52]

Presidential decrees and orders

Several cronies made tons of money from the privileges they received straight from Malacañang, inked by Marcos's pen.

For instance, two of the biggest cronies were retail magnates Bienvenido "Benny" Tantoco Sr. and Gliceria "Glecy" Rustia-Tantoco, the founders of Rustan's (which is in fact a combination of Rustia and Tantoco; the company almost came to be known as "Tanrus").[53] At present, the Tantoco family is known for—among others—Stores Specialists Inc., which brought into the Philippines international consumer brands like Zara, Burberry, MAC (in 1997, they also brought Starbucks into the Philippines through Rustan Coffee Corporation).

But back during martial law, the Tantoco couple memorably owned Tourist Duty-Free Shops Inc. (TDFS), whose retail outlets were located in airports and hotels. Marcos Sr., through Presidential Decree No. 1193, granted the TDFS a special permit to operate duty-free shops and the exclusive franchise to operate for 25 years (the decree was drafted by the Tantocos themselves and was sent to Malacañang, "ready for the signature of Marcos"[54]). Crucially, the TDFS was exempted by Marcos from paying the usual customs duties and regulations. Rather than pay regular taxes, it was merely instructed to pay seven percent of its net sales: two percent went to the national government, while five percent went straight to the Nutrition Center of the Philippines, one of Imelda's "foundations." From this single deal, Imelda's foundation obtained USD 6 million from the Tantoco couple.

What's more, to "facilitate Rustan's access to Italian luxury goods," Marcos appointed Benny Tantoco as ambassador to the Vatican. Glecy also happened to be one of Imelda's "Blue Ladies," in charge of managing Imelda's overseas bank accounts as well as multimillion dollar transactions involving art and real estate. In 1980, as the Philippine economy was about to spiral out of control, Glecy wrote to renowned shoemaker Ferruccio Ferragamo about Imelda's request for customized shoes. Ferragamo replied, "As a policy we do not make special orders but, as an exception, we will be glad to produce the styles Mrs. Marcos will select."[55] Imelda rewarded the Tantocos' unwavering loyalty by patronizing Rustan's and turning the couple into the country's retail magnates. In return, the Tantocos allegedly showed their heartfelt appreciation to Imelda by sending over "crates of cash" come Christmastime.[56] The Tantocos' closeness to the first couple would be instrumental to the success of their retail empire which continues to thrive today. Said Rodolfo Cuenca in his 2010 biography, "The House of Rustan's would not be what it is today if not for the owners' friendship with and closeness to Imelda."[57]

Cronies also swam in money from the profits they made in the logging industry. Marcos issued timber license agreements (TLAs) to his small cadre of cronies "as a tool of political patronage."[58] From about 58 in 1969, the number of TLAs exploded to 461 by 1976,[59] aided primarily by Presidential Decree No. 705, which in 1975 set the tone for illegal logging during martial law. The extent of favoritism and cronyism in the industry was stark: some five million hectares were estimated to have been leased to only 114 individuals, with defense minister Juan Ponce Enrile alone obtaining at least four concessions in 1977—each about 80,000 to 90,000 hectares, while the average at the time was just 30,000 hectares.[60] Aside from Enrile, Herminio Disini (most notorious for his brokerage of the

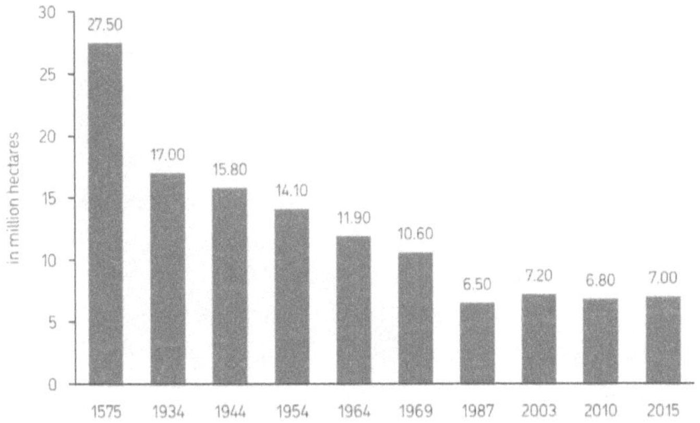

FIGURE 16.1 Philippine forest cover, 1575–2015 (Reprinted from Karol Ilagan, "7M Hectares of Philippine Land are Forested—And That's Bad News," Philippine Center for Investigative Journalism, 12 May 2021, https://pcij.org/article/6504/the-philippines-has-7m-hectares-of-forests-why-thats-bad-news.)

Bataan Nuclear Power Plant) also made a fortune from 200,000 hectares of logging and paper-pulp concessions that overlap with the ancestral lands of the Tinggian indigenous people in the Cordilleras.[61] TLAs also covered about two-thirds of all public forest lands, up from about 40 percent in previous governments after World War II.[62] (Apart from his interests in logging, Disini also effectively monopolized the importation of cigarette filters after Marcos issued a presidential decree in 1975 that raised the import tariff rate paid by his competitors from 10 to 100 percent.[63])

The exploitation of forest resources was worsened by a policy that restricted log exports to a fourth of total log production. By setting such a maximum, timber concessionaires were incentivized to extract even more timber from their concessions, conduct illegal logging activities (including logging well beyond their concessions and smuggling the excess timber abroad), and conceal their misdeeds in their books (as detected by discrepancies in the value of logging shipments from the Philippines and upon their entry into foreign borders). This policy environment created an illegal economy at the local level, with actors like military agents receiving bribes from concessionaires in exchange for keeping silent about (or even facilitating) illegal logging and smuggling.[64] At one point, Marcos even used TLAs to entice Muslim rebels to come into the light by giving them their own logging concessions.[65]

All of these led to the country's worst and most rapid case of deforestation in modern history: from 1968 to 1984, some 312,000 hectares of forest land were lost each year.[66] The forest cover of the Philippines dwindled from 10.9 million hectares in 1970 to just 7.4 in 1980—and dwindled further to 6.7 million in 1990, and 5.4 million in 2001 (figure 16.1). Although there were some reforestation efforts during martial law—embedded, in fact, in PD 705, for "no person shall be given a permit to export if he has not complied with the requirements on replanting and reforestation"[67]—they were puny, poorly enforced, and mainly just paying lip service. From 1975 to 1985, the reforestation rate was only about 57,000 hectares per year—not even a fifth of the annual rate of deforestation.

WE CAN GO ON AND ON ABOUT THE MARCOS cronies, and in fact, entire books have been written about them and the various ways by which they have immensely, disgustingly profited from martial law. But it will suffice to say that the rampant monopolization of industries and the largesse they extracted from their closeness to the Marcos regime had irreversibly warped the Philippine economy and made it a lot less efficient and innovative, and a lot more costly. In short, the cronies' laziness and inefficiency hurt the Philippine economy at large, making it vulnerable and infirm. This is a textbook example of what one might expect from the typical monopoly. In the words of Dohner and Intal,

> The intervention, monopolization, and acquisition of the martial law government and Marcos cronies changed the nature of the economy in the Philippines, weakened the efficiency and profit motivation of its actors, and postponed or made more difficult economic adjustments to an increasing adverse international environment.[68]

Even worse, as many crony businesses went under, they were bailed out by the Marcos regime at great cost to the already tenuous and cash-strapped public coffers. Take, for instance, the whopping bailout of Rodolfo Cuenca's Construction Development Corporation of the Philippines, which cost around PHP 5 to 6.2 billion. In addition, government banks like the PNB and DBP had to be bailed out as well (with money from the national budget or the Central Bank) when the crony businesses in which they had made several investments began to fold. By 1986, these government financial institutions were exposed to non-performing assets amounting to PHP 113 billion (or about a fifth of the gross national product), and infusions into these bankrupt government banks amounted to 12 to 17 percent

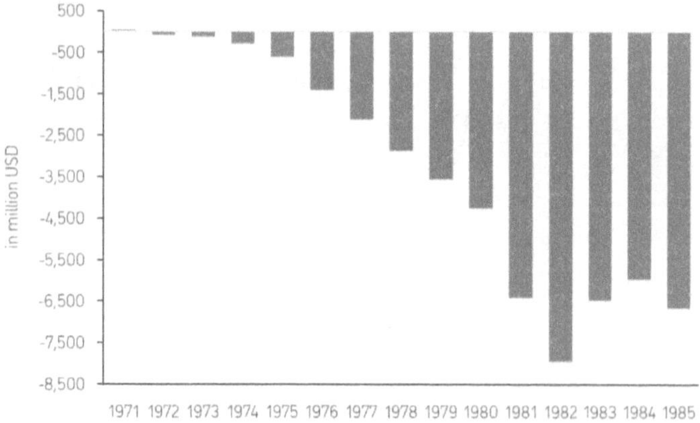

FIGURE 16.2 Exodus of capital, 1971–1985 (Note: Negative cumulative capital inflow denotes capital flight; source of data: Robert S. Dohner and Ponciano Intal Jr., "Debt Crisis and Adjustment in the Philippines," in *Developing Country Debt and the World Economy*, ed. Jeffrey Sachs [Chicago: University of Chicago Press, 1989], 169–92.)

of total government spending from 1984 to 1986.[69] As recounted by former finance secretary Jesus Estanislao, this meant a transfusion of fresh capital—taken straight from taxpayers' money—amounting to PHP 10 billion (in 1986 prices) for the DBP and another PHP 10 billion for the PNB. He elaborated:

> My first assignment in government was with DBP. It was a bankrupt bank. When I took over, more than 93 percent of the assets recorded in the books of DBP were non-performing assets [NPAs]. So when we had NPAs running around, the communist insurgents [in] the countryside, we

> had the worst kind of NPA in our banking system . . . . Eventually we had to foreclose those assets. And who were these? They were the cronies and the relatives of the people who were in power at that time.[70]

The stifling of competition due to crony capitalism alienated the rest of the business sector, turned would-be investors off, and planted in them a growing sense of economic deterioration. This all led to much capital flight (figure 16.2). From 1965 to 1986, a whopping USD 22.3 billion of capital (in real terms, or adjusted for inflation) fled the country, progressively worsening from 1973 until the declaration of the debt moratorium in 1983.[71] This lost money made up nearly 80 percent of the country's external debt then.

Some say that it was the assassination of Ninoy Aquino in 1983 that tipped over Philippine society and led to a sea of change. After Ninoy was killed, it was reported that capital left the country via the Manila International Airport at a rate of around USD 3 million a day.[72] Also, a number of prominent businessmen—after years of silence or even acquiescence to the state of affairs during much of the dictatorship—had enough, took to the streets, and became more vocal against the regime. Some prominent business leaders formed a "Monday Group" that led "yellow confetti rallies" in Makati City's Ayala Triangle in 1983 in protest of Ninoy's assassination. The events were called as such because protesters threw, from atop the surrounding buildings, yellow confetti made from "yellow pages" (business directories). Similar confetti rallies were since replicated in other parts of the country.[73]

But that is not what is seen from the data: capital was leaving the country many years before Aquino was assassinated in 1983. It so happened that the rate of capital flight peaked in 1981 and 1982.[74] By 1986, former finance secretary Jaime Ongpin was quoted telling bankers that "every successful businessman, lawyer, accountant, doctor, and dentist I know has some form of cash or assets which he began to squirrel abroad after Marcos declared martial law in 1972 and, in the process, frightened every Filipino who had anything to lose."[75] To a large extent this can also be explained by the drop in interest rates in the late 1970s, owing to the expansion of money supply. If you were an investor with extra money at the time, it did not make sense to put your money in Philippine securities. You would have earned more investing abroad. So, in a way, the Marcos regime "encouraged" capital flight.[76]

Capital flight came in a variety of ways: from smuggling cash personally, hiring couriers to carry dollars past airport customs officials, snail mail, interbank transfers, or even contracting the services of bankers in the "Binondo Central Bank." Meanwhile, exports were also underinvoiced and imports were overinvoiced, and the resulting gap between invoices and actual values were deposited abroad as well.[77]

The very fact that the Marcoses and cronies spirited away billions of pesos outside the country throughout martial law in itself represented capital flight. We already discussed the Swiss bank accounts and the pseudonyms used by the first couple in chapter 15.

Let us discuss here some of lesser-known instances of Marcosian capital flight. For example, investigations found out that the Marcos regime used telecommunications firms that they controlled—including the Philippine Communications Satellite Corporation or PHILCOMSAT—to "steadily" stash away "tens of millions of dollars" to the US over the course of ten to fifteen years.[78] PHILCOMSAT, a

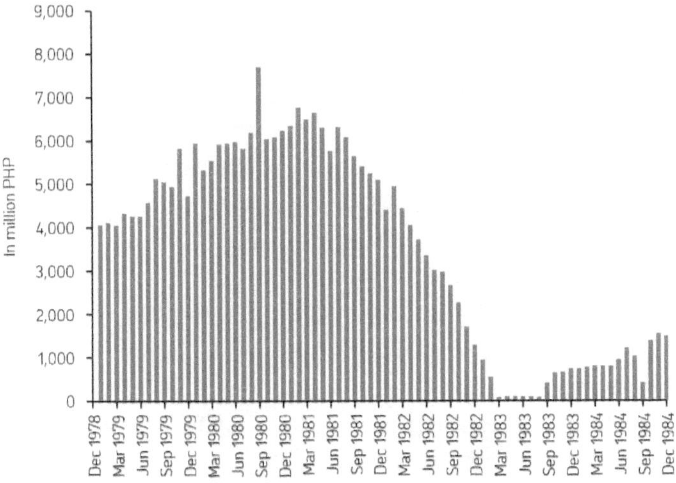

FIGURE 16.3 Commercial paper outstanding, 1979–1984 (Reprinted from Victoria S. Licuanan, *An Analysis of the Institutional Framework of the Philippine Short-Term Financial Markets* [Manila: Philippine Institute for Development Studies, 1986], 110.)

joint venture of the private sector and the government, was the Philippines' only link to the international satellite fleet called Intelsat. It was effectively owned by cronies like "Sugar King" Roberto Benedicto, while its board chairman was none other than Ferdinand Marcos Jr., who was appointed to the post in 1985 at the relatively tender age of 27. But accounts paint a picture of him as an absentee chairman. One report said, "[Bongbong] had been drawing a monthly salary of between USD 9,756 and USD 97,560 but rarely visited the office and apparently had no duties there."[79] The huge sums sent abroad through PHILCOMSAT and other telecom firms would be used to buy various assets in California worth more than USD 100 million. These properties included about 40 acres of land in Texas worth USD 1.3 million (different still from the thousands of hectares of land the Marcoses owned in Texas, which would later be used to pay off human rights victims[80]), 37 parcels of land in Los Angeles, San Diego, and San Francisco in California (totaling USD 11 million), "several lots" in Beverly Hills, and even a "30-room mansion" in the name of Marcos's alleged mistress, Dovie Beams.[81]

Meanwhile, in January 1981, one case of capital flight led to a full-blown financial crisis: a Filipino-Chinese businessman named Dewey Dee suddenly fled the country with his family, leaving in his wake about USD 80 million (about PHP 635 million) in debts that were unpaid by his textile company. Immediately, Dee's flight led to a string of defaults. The effects rippled throughout the financial sector. Dee owed money to several banks, and his disappearance generated a scare that other defaults might happen soon. Investors refused to continue investing in the money market, particularly in a type of security called "commercial paper," or short-term debt instruments where a borrower promises to pay a specific amount on a stated date with interest. This resulted in the steep decline of commerical paper, both issued and outstanding (figure 16.3). This drop would last for years, well beyond 1981: by 1983, the commercial paper market was virtually nonexistent.[82] At the same time, small depositors also withdrew their money hurriedly and deposited them in larger non-Chinese banks, which were deemed safer—a classic bank run, in short. The following is an account of how the contagion spread:

> Banks like Solidbank and Pacific Bank were hit by runs. The country's two biggest investment

> houses, Bancom and Atrium Capital, were forced to shut down, along with several others. The feedback loop created by the financial panic made predictions of bank runs a self-fulfilling prophecy—unless the government could step in to restore confidence.[83]

As it turns out, about forty banks, investment houses, financial companies, and other financial institutions were put at risk because of Dee's sudden disappearance. This included the financing firms of prominent Marcos cronies such as Herminio Disini (of the nuclear power plant fame) and Ricardo Silverio (of Delta Motors). Eventually, the Central Bank had to make assurances that they would offer financial support to the embattled financial institutions. Many non-financial corporations were also hit, including the businesses of Marcos's cronies—which turned out to be heavily indebted. For example, Disini's "corporate empire . . . fell apart as a result of the crisis," and soon after he left the Philippines to retire in Austria.[84] The Marcos government rescued these non-financial corporations by setting up a PHP 5-billion rescue fund. But among the first to get money out of this fund were—as expected—the crony businesses. In many other instances, firms' loans were converted to equity as they were bailed out by government. As a result of these bailouts, government financial institutions—such as the PNB, DBP, GSIS, and especially the NDC—suddenly had substantial equity positions or shares in these corporations worth several billions of pesos. The bailouts represented a huge fiscal sink for the government, but way worse was the fact that the huge corporate portfolio of government financial institutions would deteriorate, contributing to the fiscal crisis in the mid-1980s.

What happened to Dewey Dee? He became an international fugitive, traced by the Interpol in Haiti and Costa Rica, until he went to the US and in June 1983, entered Canada, where he applied and was successfully granted asylum in 1986.[85] Before he sought asylum, he admitted to being one of Ferdinand's front men in several multimillion deals,[86] notably in Marcos's purchase of Redwood Bank in San Francisco. This transaction was in direct contravention of Philippine and US laws and almost led to the bank's ruin because of spurious lending activities (the bank incurred losses amounting to USD 26 million from 1982 to 1984 as it made "insider loans" to Marcos associates like crony Rolando Gapud and even Ferdinand's alleged mistress, Dovie Beams[87]).

At any rate, the huge sums of capital that left the country throughout martial law—as exemplified by the PHILCOMSAT and Dewey Dee scandals—could have, in principle, mitigated or even prevented altogether the debt crisis in the mid-1980s. As posed by de Dios, Gochoco-Bautista, and Punongbayan: "The question must be asked: without capital flight, would the Philippines have suffered a debt crisis?"[88]

The Central Bank did try to stem capital outflow through the issuance of the so-called Jobo bills. But as discussed in chapter 14, this led to a monetary contraction that cut off credit to the private sector and induced the country's worst postwar recession in 1984 and 1985.

IN SUMMARY, IT IS NOT AT ALL TRUE THAT MARCOS fought the oligarchy. In fact, he perpetuated it by creating his own coterie of cronies that simply replaced the old elite. Even before that, Marcos was very much part of the political elite, engaging in run-of-the-mill corrupt acts as legislator. The crony capitalism that he put in place for decades would erode economic growth and culminate in the country's deepest economic crisis since World War II—it was still the worst even to this day.

Interestingly, right after the fall of the dictatorship, some of Marcos's cronies even entered into compromise agreements with the PCGG and gave testimony to the widescale corruption of the Marcoses (in exchange of immunity from lawsuits).[89] Among these former cronies were pharmaceuticals kingpin Jose Campos, who readily surrendered 197 titles of real estate properties located in Metro Manila, Rizal, Laguna, Cavite, Bataan, and Baguio that he held for Marcos. The combined price of the properties was about USD 52.5 million.[90] Other cronies who gave in and cooperated—although to varying degrees—with the PCGG were Rolando Gapud (Marcos's financial adviser), banana kingpin Antonio Floirendo,[91] Jesus Tanchanco (first administrator of the NFA), Baltazar Aquino (former public works minister), and Raymundo Feliciano.

Some cronies have been successfully convicted for their crimes and misdeeds. For instance, in 2021, the Supreme Court awarded more than a billion pesos in damages to the government for the fraudulent Bataan Nuclear Power Plant deal brokered by crony Herminio Disini. The decision will be enforced on Disini's estate, for he died in 2014.[92] In the same year, the Sandiganbayan ordered the transfer to the Philippine government of several parcels of land from a certain Alfonso Lim Sr., another Marcos associate.[93] Much earlier, in 2014, the Supreme Court decided unanimously that Danding Cojuangco's shares in the United Coconut Planters Bank (UCPB) were in fact owned by the government.[94]

But in many other instances, the Marcos cronies have prevailed after slugging it out in court battles for decades. Many have been acquitted or otherwise died without being convicted, mainly because of the unacceptably long time by which cases are resolved. In 2018, a case filed against the Marcoses and Rodolfo Cuenca (in pursuit of PHP 51 billion in damages) was dismissed by the Supreme Court for lack of sufficient evidence—assailing that the PCGG had presented mere photocopies of evidence, which are inadmissible in court.[95] Meanwhile, in 2020, another PHP 102-billion case against the behest loans received by Roberto Benedicto was also junked—again for lack of sufficient evidence.[96] In 2021, a case against the Marcoses and their cronies Ricardo Silverio and Pablo Carlos Jr. was dismissed after a whopping 34 years.[97] In other instances, trials were not even started: in 2021, the Supreme Court barred the Sandiganbayan from acting any further on cases filed against Danding Cojuangco in relation to the coco levy fund—these have unreasonably sat in court for about 32 years.[98]

Again, the snail's pace of the Philippine justice system is largely to blame for the fact that many of Marcos's cronies and associates have gone scot-free and managed to avoid the long arm of the law. Nevertheless, their complicity to the Marcos regime is well documented in various authoritative sources. Finally, the courts' failure to convict them in many cases does not make the cronies' contributions to the atrocities of martial law any less real.

17 Marcos plundered to protect the economy?

CLAIM
The Marcoses were only hiding the money of the Filipino people "to protect the economy."

VERDICT
FALSE

ON 29 AUGUST 2017, WEEKS BEFORE FERDINAND Marcos Sr.'s hundredth birth anniversary, then-President Rodrigo Duterte made before the media a singularly preposterous claim: that the Marcoses hid the money of the Filipino people "to protect the economy." This was supposedly an explanation allegedly intimated to him by a spokesman of the Marcoses, with whom he had been speaking. Duterte explained (in his usual incoherent language):

> The only reason, they said, their father was protecting the economy for the eventual—if he is exiled. But he thought of regaining Malacañang and that is why it looks like they hid it.[1]

He made this statement after the Marcoses allegedly offered to return part of their wealth (including "even a few gold bars" albeit "not as much as Fort Knox"), ostensibly to help Duterte finance some of his pet projects. Later, Duterte said that if he were the Marcoses he would surrender the money in exchange for immunity.[2]

Duterte's closeness to the Marcoses is no secret. To begin with, Duterte himself is self-admittedly a huge fan of Marcos—he even idolized the former dictator. As early as February 2016, while on the campaign trail for the presidency, Duterte said, "If I turn back time, before and now, if he did not stay long as president, if he did not become a dictator, the best president was Marcos."[3] Meanwhile, on November 2016, Duterte allowed the burial of Ferdinand Marcos in the Libingan ng mga Bayani,[4] despite much opposition from human rights victims, the Commission on Human Rights, and the National Historical Commission of the Philippines (which said in a pamphlet that, contrary to Duterte's claims, Marcos's record during World War II as a soldier was "fraught with myths, factual inconsistencies, and lies"[5]). In May 2017, Duterte praised Marcos's martial law as "very good."[6] Then on 26 July 2017, barely a year in office, Duterte wanted to abolish the Presidential Commission on Good Government (PCGG; though he was not the first president to suggest such a change).[7]

In the 2022 elections though, Bongbong sought the presidency while presidential daughter, Sara Duterte—with whom the older Duterte spars often—sought the vice presidency alongside the dictator's son. In November 2021, Rodrigo Duterte alluded that Bongbong takes cocaine and is a "weak leader."[8] Yet those remarks did not prevent Bongbong from snagging the presidency. In fact, one might say that one of Duterte's most lasting impacts is paving the way for the Marcoses' return to Malacañang.

Of course, the Marcoses themselves did not need Duterte's help to gaslight the people. For instance, Imelda once justified her extravagant shopping spree of real estate properties in New York by saying that her actions helped save the Philippine economy. She said:

> We were buying properties in New York to a place where we could anchor our economic development through free enterprise because it centered down for free enterprise in New York. And when it is 12 o'clock in New York, a.m., it is 12 o'clock p.m. in the Philippines. And the sun will never set on free enterprise. And so the grand plan was really to make the Philippines the trade center, the commercial center, the distribution center of the world.[9]

OF COURSE, IT IS NOT TRUE THAT THE MARCOSES plundered to protect the economy. Apart from being inherently bad and illegal, widespread corruption—facilitated by crony capitalism—led to chronic inefficiency in both the public and private sectors. Meanwhile, the stashing of billions of dollars in offshore accounts bled the public coffers dry of much-needed international reserves (in dollars), especially as the debt crisis came to a head by the early 1980s.

Recall, too, that the Marcoses continued to profligately spend the public's money on their personal lives—spending millions of dollars on food, clothes, and travel—even in the last few years of the regime, as poverty and prices and joblessness were already skyrocketing. As I wrote in one of my Rappler pieces in 2017:

> That billions of dollars' worth of Filipinos' money benefited a single family is already outrageous in itself. But the fact that the Marcoses siphoned such money at the time the country desperately needed it—to pay for our huge external debt and to finance our economic development—is just cruel and depraved. It's like stabbing the back of a person who was already suffering from a severe hemorrhage.[10]

It was a supreme act of economic treachery that—far from protecting our economy—undeniably brought the country to ruin. Further, the Marcosian plunder does not merit any kind of sugarcoating or compromise agreement. At the very least, we should not forget that such an atrocity happened—and that it was in fact an atrocity, as established by tons of court cases, legislation, and academic research, among others.

The problem with Duterte's statement—even though it is patently false—is that it is an example of government-spread lies that fuel disinformation in other places, including in social media. It is bad enough that there is a plethora of Marcos lies and myths online without top government officials mouthing—or even actively funding the spread of—similar lies, thereby lending any undeserved credence to them.

18 The Marcoses own a million tons of gold?

CLAIM 1 The Marcoses are rich because they own a million tons of gold (another claim puts it at two quadrillion tons).	**VERDICT** FALSE
CLAIM 2 The Marcoses are rich because Ferdinand inherited gold from Jose Rizal, with whom he founded the World Bank.	**VERDICT** FALSE
CLAIM 3 The Marcoses will distribute their gold and other riches if they win again.	**VERDICT** FALSE

FINALLY, WE TACKLE THE INFAMOUS GOLD-related "golden age" myths: myths designed to cover the mass plunder of the Marcoses with a fine sheen of gold and to dazzle the public seeking the truth. You would be surprised how many gold-related myths surrounding the Marcoses are there and just how ridiculous these can get.

At the most basic level, the Marcoses allegedly owned huge reserves of gold whose amounts vary, depending on the source. But rumor has it that they own at least a million tons of gold, worth anywhere from USD 987 billion[1] to USD 2 quadrillion.[2] (One YouTube video was even emphatically titled: "MARCOS GOLD CAN SAVE THE WORLD 987 BILLION DOLLARS AND MILLION TONS OF GOLD IN THE PHILIPPINES.")[3]

Then there is a ton of myths as well on how the Marcoses came to acquire such huge amounts of gold and where these currently are. One rumor says that Ferdinand Marcos owned 1.715 million tons of gold deposited with the People's Bank of China, allegedly proven by a "safekeeping receipt" co-signed by Marcos himself, Miguel Cuaderno of the Central Bank, and Chinese Communist Party chair Mao Zedong.[4] Another myth says that Marcos's million tons of gold are lodged with the World Bank.[5] Marcos also supposedly inherited in 1974 the "White Vatican Account" of national hero Jose Rizal.[6] An even crazier version of this myth says that Jose Rizal staged his death in 1896 and lived on to a ripe old age of 113 as a priest taking cover under the pseudonym Jose Antonio Diaz. Then in 1944, at age 83, Rizal co-founded with Marcos (who was only 27 at the time) the World Bank as a "global debt facility."[7] On short-form video platform TikTok, there is at least one video claiming that Marcos lent money to 170 countries in the 1950s, after World War II, and that such money has now appreciated to a mind-boggling amount of nearly PHP 136 quadrillion. (For scale, one quadrillion is one million billion—does that even make sense?)

Before the age of social media, the most widespread "golden age" myth is that Marcos discovered the fabled treasure left in the Philippines by Japanese general Tomoyuki Yamashita. As the myth goes,

> Legend has it that during World War II, the Japanese appropriated millions in war bullion from the territories they occupied. Since the Japanese command under General Yamashita assumed that the Philippines would never be recaptured, it was chosen as the safest place to conceal the loot. But at the close of the war, Allied and Filipino soldiers forced the Imperial Army to retreat in haste, leaving Yamashita's gold behind in several undisclosed locations.[8]

Marcos enters the picture as the person who is said to have stumbled on the widely sought Yamashita treasure trove, when Marcos was an erstwhile guerrilla commander during World War II.[9] It was not until 1992—shortly after the Marcoses returned to the Philippines and when Imelda set out to run for the presidency—that Imelda "confessed" that her husband's wealth came not from plunder during the dictatorship but from the Yamashita treasure. She added that such riches were used to tide over the Philippine government as it entered an economic crisis around 1970, and that parts of the wealth were hidden in various Marcos properties across the nation.[10] Later, in 2013, she gave an interview to renowned economist Winnie Monsod and mentioned that their family had 7,000 tons of gold kept in 170 banks.[11]

In the age of social media, another prominent story that came to light is that Marcos became a lawyer of the "Tallano royal family." Apart from supposedly owning the entire Philippines (known as "Maharlika") until the middle of the eighteenth century, the Tallanos also supposedly ruled over other jurisdictions like Brunei, South Borneo, Sabah, the Spratlys, and even Hawai'i.[12] Marcos allegedly became a lawyer of the Tallano family at one point, and in return for his services, was compensated with 192,000 tons of gold. That was how Marcos became incredibly rich, the story goes.

But the plot does not end there: there are also absurd allegations that about 3,500 metric tons of gold bars were stolen from the Marcoses by certain opposition leaders (headed by ex-president Noynoy Aquino) and deposited in Thailand.[13]

NEEDLESS TO SAY—AND AT THE RISK OF LENDING even an iota of credibility to these lies—the preposterous Marcos gold myths are false. To date, only about 244,000 metric tons of gold have ever been discovered around the world.[14] This is not even a fourth of the million tons of gold that the Marcoses alone purportedly own. Historians also say that there is not a shred of evidence to prove that Marcos owned any gold from the mythical Yamashita treasure, nor that he lawyered for the "Tallano royal family" and that he received tons of gold from them. Moreover, the "Tallano royal family" never existed and thus, never owned the Philippines at any point in time.

The gold myth is so crazy that some historians have resorted to lampooning it; for instance, a "Tallano Gold Soap" was being sold on online shopping platforms (like Shopee) and historian Xiao Chua satirized it on TikTok with a fake infomercial.

Moreover, there were no gold bars recovered from the Marcoses, as verified by the PCGG.[15] So there was nothing for anyone (including opposition figures) to spirit away to Thailand.

Crazy as these gold myths are, it is necessary to talk about them because so many people share (and worse, believe) such myths online—whether on Facebook, YouTube, or even the newer TikTok. And these posts often end up being viral. For instance, one YouTube post about the million tons of gold supposedly owned by the Marcoses was viewed at least a million times before being fact-checked by Rappler in February 2019.[16] Another TikTok video that made claims about the unlikely PHP 136-quadrillion Marcos gold got at least 44,000 likes when I bumped into it myself.

Another problem is that the Marcoses themselves have made no real effort to stop the myths outright. In rare occasions that they have been asked on media, the Marcos children have dismissed or diminished the gold myths. For instance, in an interview in the ONE News program *The Chiefs*, Imee replied when asked about the Tallano gold, "*Ano 'yun?* (What's that?)" and proceeded to say that it was nothing but an "urban legend."[17] However, she also did not deny—once and for all—that the myths are false. Imee elaborated: "I think it's fun to think of all the gold, and it continues to be urban legend. And people are always tantalized by the possibility . . . . I don't know, I've never seen any gold, I've heard about it being talked about constantly, *pero wala naman akong nakikita, wala naman kaming napapakinabangan, wala namang nabenta* (But I don't see any, we never benefited from any of it, none of it was sold)."

Bongbong and the people around him have also obfuscated the issue. In 2022, months before the pivotal presidential elections, Vic Rodriguez, Bongbong's spokesperson, was asked by Rappler to make a categorical statement denying or affirming the Tallano gold myth. But the spokesperson merely feigned ignorance: "Honestly, I don't have any social media account so *hindi ko alam ang sinabi mong* content (I don't know about the content you're talking about). To be candid with you, I have always been candid with all of you, *hindi ko alam* (I don't know)."[18] During the 2022 presidential interviews, Bongbong said when asked by ONE News about the veracity of their gold reserves, "Wala pa akong nakitang kahit anong gold na sinasabi nila. Baka may alam sila, sabihan ako (I haven't seen any of the purported gold. If they know anything about it, let me know.)"[19]

Although he now denies the existence of such gold, he sang a different tune more than three decades earlier. In a 1990 *Inquirer* interview, Bongbong said, "Only I know where it is and how to get it." (In 2022, he claimed he was joking in that 1990 interview.[20]) Moreover, in various court documents, he mentioned that "income from legitimately-owned property includes income from trading of precious metals from the years 1946 to 1954," and that his father had sought the assistance of a certain Constante Rubio "to assist [Marcos Sr.] in his business of trading metals, more specifically gold."[21] Is this what they call "strategic ambiguity"?

AT ANY RATE, ALLOWING THE GOLD MYTHS TO persist presents dangers in the real world. For instance, several people cling—desperately, in some instances—to the notion that one day, the Marcoses will share their immense wealth to the Filipino people.

On the one hand, there is a full-fledged Marcos cult wherein members (as they told on camera) utterly believe Marcos Sr. was a saint, that he did not steal money, that he just hid the country's wealth, and that the day will come that the Marcos riches will be shared with the nation and will be used for the "development of our country."[22]

Unfortunately, myths abound outside this cult. On 23 September 2017, about 100,000 Marcos loyalists trooped to the open grounds of the University of the Philippines Los Baños (UPLB) because a group called One Social Family Credit Cooperative had spread the rumor that the Marcoses were set to hand out cash (about PHP 10,000 a month) coming from their (ill-gotten) wealth.[23] During the event, a booklet published by a certain "Bullion Buyer Ltd." containing the supposed "golden" achievements by Ferdinand Marcos Sr. was handed out to the crowd. People bearing the booklet were, according to the organizers, to be prioritized for cash disbursement through their bank accounts. But the event bore the obvious signs of a scam, with people asked to shell out a nominal membership fee of PHP 10 to PHP 30 per person. Many went home disappointed. Although the Marcoses denied links to the UPLB event (Bongbong himself said that it was "clearly a scam"), other schemes centering on the distribution of Marcos wealth have been invented in the past, hoodwinking several people. Years before the UPLB incident, some boomers (including a friend's *lola* or grandmother) have dutifully held on to certificates that allegedly will grant them access to a portion of the Marcoses' wealth in an unspecified date in the future. But until the day she died, my friend's lola never got hold of any Marcos wealth she was promised.

This brings us to the final myth that we will tackle in this book: that the Marcoses will return to the Filipino people their wealth once they are back in Malacañang.

Such promises are nothing new. As early as 1998, when Imelda ran for president for the second time, she promised that she would give away USD 800 million of their wealth (kept in foreign banks) to the poor once she is elected president.[24] She withdrew from the presidential race shortly after, ostensibly "to save the Filipino people from the ultimate injustice of a possible bloody election." (But there were rumors that she did so in a bid to earn a presidential pardon from one of the frontrunners. At that time, she was already convicted of graft, punishable by 12 years of imprisonment, but was on bail.)[25]

The promise of Marcosian riches would evolve over time. These days, one myth goes that it is imperative for Bongbong to win as president because he will carry out one of the last instructions of his father: that is, to set up a "foundation" through which their family return the "Marcos treasures" to the Filipino masses.[26] Although Marcos did write in his diary in 1969 that he stood ready to give away his "worldly possessions" through a foundation, there was no stated plan on how Imelda or her children or any of their descendants will distribute the family's (ill-gotten) wealth to the Filipino people. At the same time, the government through the PCGG and various courts have had a difficult time wresting the billions of pesos worth of ill-gotten wealth from the Marcoses. To recap, the PCGG has recovered so far more than PHP 174 billion in ill-gotten wealth from the Marcoses and their cronies, and the government is still going after nearly PHP 126 billion more.

If the Marcoses are really willing to give away their billions, they would have done so long ago. And why bother defending themselves at all in the various court cases, both past and pending ones? Why resist the government's efforts at recovery and even hire top-notch lawyers in their defense of their (stolen) riches?

The 2022 elections might have given us a glimpse of a part of the remaining ill-gotten wealth that the Marcoses still have access to. In an interview for Bloomberg, Robert Swift, the lead counsel for the Hawai'i case against the Marcoses (which led to the first reparations for martial law victims), said, "I'm confident that some of the money that was acquired by Ferdinand Marcos and hidden is going to find its way in the 2022 elections in the Philippines."[27]

HOW I WISH MANY FILIPINOS WILL STOP PINNING their hopes on the mythical Marcos gold. First, the purported Marcos gold has been used to dupe people into investment scams. Apart from the 2017 incident at UPLB, the latest scam was revealed in November 2022 where an investor in Mindanao lost a total of PHP 5 million to octagenarians who had "offered him a cut of PHP 700 million from the sale of over PHP 17-trillion worth of 'Marcoses' gold'" kept supposedly inside the Bangko Sentral.[28] Said the businessman, "Because they were old, I felt assured that they could be trusted. In my thinking, they were old so it's impossible for them to do wrong."

Second, even supposing such gold hoards exist, the Marcoses have not given up on their ill-gotten wealth voluntarily in the past, and they would not do so any time in the future.

Third and most importantly, believing the gold myths only perpetuates the notion that the Marcoses are filthy rich, and this serves their political project. It adds to their mystique as some sort of a Filipino royal family. This is probably why even though the gold myths are often laughably ridiculous, the Marcoses have not denied them outright. Therein lies their cunning as a family: they can twist an endless web of lies but still get away with it. If there is one thing we know about the Marcoses, it is that image has long been key to their political success. Facts and data are nothing compared to the power of image and perception. This was succinctly but chillingly captured by Imelda herself, who said in Lauren Greenfield's 2019 documentary *The Kingmaker*: "Perception is real, the truth is not."

EPILOGUE

WHEN I WAS STILL WRITING THIS BOOK—MONTHS before the 2022 elections where Marcos Jr. emerged with a landslide win—some trolls had attacked my credibility to write about martial law economics, reasoning that I was not even alive during martial law. One troll said, "the best person who can correct the story of ML is the one who is not born that period? Yeah, right. Forget about JPE. Listen to one of [Maria] Ressa's tentacles."[1]

Amusingly, this reminds me of a presentation made by Dr. Maris Diokno, historian and former chair of the National Historical Commission of the Philippines. In one of her slides, she shared a meme: a conversation between two people where one said, "*Galit na galit ka, eh wala ka naman nung Martial Law* (Why are you so angry? You didn't even live during martial law.)" In reply, the other person said, "*Eh ikaw, tuwang-tuwa ka sa Pasko, wala ka naman dun sa Bethlehem* (But why are you so happy about Christmas, when you weren't even at Bethlehem)."

At the risk of belaboring the point, one need not experience an episode in our history to study and write about it. That is exactly the purpose of seeking out references and cross-checking facts across various sources—which we have meticulously done in this book. More generally, that is the very purpose of schooling and education: we do not need to reinvent algebra or rediscover the DNA in order to learn about them and even become experts in them. We can simply stand on the shoulders of giants by learning from books, articles, and other credible sources.

A similar charge is that I myself was not a victim of martial law, so I have no business writing about it. But for this, Dr. Diokno also had a handy retort in her presentation: she shared the following 2016 tweet by user @steelawake:

> Bes, ang Martial Law parang bagyo. May lugar na umuulan, may nasalanta, may namatayan. Sa iba, umaraw. So wala ka nang paki kasi naarawan ka?
>
> (Friend, martial law is like a typhoon. In some places it rained, with people affected or killed. In other places, the sun shone. So you don't care anymore because you were at a sunny place?)

Besides, one can very well argue that virtually all Filipinos who lived during and after martial law were victimized by it, in one way or another. Even if you or your family members were not imprisoned or tortured by soldiers during that time, you may very well be an *economic* victim of martial law: your parents' business may have folded around the 1970s or 1980s; your parents may have endured a dearth of good jobs, forcing them to leave you behind at a young age to seek greener pastures abroad; or fast-forward to today, you are not earning as much as you ought to because the Marcos regime pulled down the economic trajectory of the

Philippines permanently—after all, it is only recently that our economy has regained solid footing.

Here, let me reiterate the core message of this book: far from being a "golden age" for the economy, martial law was a period of gross economic mismanagement and economic suffering for millions of Filipinos and their descendants. One would think that the COVID-19 pandemic would present an even deeper economic crisis for the Philippines. But, as discussed in chapter 13, in 2021, we got back to positive growth after just five consecutive quarters of decline and a cumulative 10-percent decline. In contrast, the Marcosian crisis in the 1980s lasted nine consecutive quarters and garnered a cumulative 14-percent decline. In other words, the Marcosian economic crisis is still the Philippines' worst economic crisis after World War II. A dictator proved more damaging than a global pandemic.

UNFORTUNATELY, FACTS DO NOT ALWAYS WORK ON all people. A lot of research has shown that no matter how well-studied or carefully researched a statement is, often, it can be no match to people's cognitive biases (notably *confirmation bias* or people's tendency to "seek out or evaluate information in a way that fits with their existing thinking and preconceptions"[2]) and the rising tide of disinformation (which comes in many forms and from many fronts).

For instance, in a 2016 mobile survey by the Social Weather Stations, a mere fifth of the 1,200 respondents strongly agreed to the statement: "From the time of martial law in 1972 up to People Power in 1986, much oppression was done by the regime of President Ferdinand Marcos to the Filipino people." Meanwhile, 24 percent or close to a fourth "somewhat agreed," making for 44-percent agreement. In contrast, 19 percent (again close to a fifth) "strongly disagreed" about the oppression during martial law, and 11 percent somewhat disagreed (totaling a 30-percent disagreement). Astonishingly, a sizable 19 percent were undecided.[3]

What gives?

First, you have the Marcoses themselves, who for decades have fabricated their own lies, financed falsehoods made by supporters, or done nothing to suppress the myths deodorizing their family's bloody and corrupt past. The Marcoses have been planting the seeds of the "golden age" myths ever since their return to the country in the 1990s. For instance, right after returning in 1991, Imelda decided to run for president in the 1992 elections. Around that time, she criticized the administration of former president Corazon Aquino as "sick and misdirected." Imelda added: "Happy days are here again. If we are united, I am sure this nation will be great again."[4] Fast-forward to 2013, Imelda told the media that she wished that Bongbong would run for the presidency. This created buzz and, more importantly, an opportunity for the Marcoses to be relevant again and defend the record of their patriarch. At times, the Marcoses' messaging is aided and amplified by ranking government officials, like what former president Rodrigo Duterte did throughout much of his term. Such statements of support only serve to perpetuate the lies and give the Marcoses a veneer of legitimacy—no matter how feeble these are. The Marcoses have also reinforced the mythology around them in social media and even in art forms, such as films. In 2022, known Marcos propagandist and director Darryl Yap wrote and directed a film centering on the Marcoses titled *Maid in Malacañang*. Its poster was inspired by an old painting of the Marcoses by Ralph Wolfe Cowan but the faces in the original were replaced with those of the movie's actors like Cesar Montano as Ferdinand Sr., Ruffa Gutierrez as Imelda, and Cristine Reyes as Imee, to name a few.[5] With Marcos Jr.'s election as president, the mythmaking continues.

Second, you have, of course, the Marcos loyalists and apologists churning regular content on social media in disinformation networks and cascades. Studying the web of networks on Facebook, Rappler found out that in 2014 and 2015, there was a noticeable spike in the number of Facebook pages and groups peddling pro-Marcos content. Moreover, these pages and groups overlap significantly with other Facebook accounts that churned out pro-Duterte messages.[6] In recent years, new studies document the narratives in pro-Marcos content, such as the "us-versus-them" and the "light-darkness-light" messages (that is, the light of martial law, the darkness of post-EDSA Philippines, and the promised light of another Marcos government).[7]

Speaking of narratives, back in his inaugural speech in 1965, Ferdinand Marcos himself started using narratives of darkness to portray what he had inherited from his predecessors:

> We are in crisis. You know that the government treasury is empty . . . . Our government in the past few months has exhausted all available domestic and foreign sources of borrowing. Our public financial institutions have been burdened to the last loanable peso. The lending capacity of the Central Bank has been utilized to the full. Our national government is indebted to our local governments. There are no funds available for public works and little of the appropriations for

> our national government for the present fiscal year. Industry is at a standstill. Many corporations have declared bankruptcy. Local manufacturing firms have been compelled to close or reduce their capacity. Unemployment has increased. Prices of essential commodities and services remain unstable. The availability of rice remains uncertain . . . [8]

Listening to Marcos then, you might get the impression that the Philippines before his rule was nothing short of a medieval country riddled with nothing but despair and misery. My point is simply that the Marcoses have in fact been using light versus darkness narratives since day one. (Interestingly, Marcos would later cause even greater social, political, and economic problems than the ones he eloquently railed against at the beginning of his regime.)

Returning to present day, the manner of spreading Marcosian disinformation online has also attracted some scholars: some communications scholars unraveled a centralized effort to "broker" propaganda via YouTube through networks that appear to be a decentralized effort. Such "networked political brokerage" allows content creators to "construct new realities . . . and cement their political narratives without being subjected to the scrutiny of and by traditional gatekeepers."[9] Rappler calls this "networked propaganda."

Apart from online efforts on the part of the Marcoses and their loyalists, the online platforms themselves (Facebook, Twitter, YouTube, TikTok, etc.) are much to blame for the spread of Marcosian disinformation. Unfortunately, these platforms have massively failed to rid people's timelines and feeds of blatant pieces of disinformation. On the one hand, there are the devious algorithms that force-feed us with content that make us more hooked to our timelines and feeds than ever. But the bigger culprit would be the platforms' business models that generate profit from engagement more than anything else. At the same time, they have escaped legal responsibility because of the global nature of their businesses, as well as the inability of authorities in their home countries to hold them accountable (for instance, many American politicians do not even use the apps and cannot ask the right questions during hearings—frustrating their efforts at effective oversight). It is a sorry and dangerous state of affairs, one that creates an "infodemic" that can very well destroy democracies. In fact, it already has. As explained by Rappler CEO and Nobel Peace Prize winner Maria Ressa when she accepted her award at Oslo on 10 December 2021:

> So while the public debate is focused downstream on content moderation, the real sleight of hand, happens further upstream, where algorithms of distribution have been programmed by humans with their coded bias. Their editorial agenda is profit driven, carried out by machines at scale. The impact is global, with cheap armies on social media tearing down democracy in at least 81 countries around the world. That impunity must stop.[10]

For years, Maria Ressa bravely took to task social media companies—especially Facebook and its founder Mark Zuckerberg—not only for failing to do enough to combat disinformation on their platforms, but also compromising democracies worldwide. Her media organization, Rappler, already published many investigative pieces on how President Duterte weaponized social media during his election campaign in 2016 and well after he took office, perpetrating lie after lie—and even appointing friendly social media influencers and trolls to strategic government positions. Thankfully, Ressa has since drawn much international attention to the horrors of disinformation in the Philippines—and brought with her innumerable accolades in the process.[11]

To be fair, some platforms are responding to the spread of disinformation. YouTube, for instance, started to place "information panels" atop videos about martial law in the Philippines.[12] But how effective are these panels? And what about videos and other content that cross over to platforms without additional context? Meanwhile, in January 2022, Twitter also introduced a new way for people to report misleading tweets.[13] But why only then and only in select countries? Just a few months before this new Twitter policy, Rappler found out that in the last quarter of 2021, there was a boom in new Twitter users that initiated "Twitter parties" with hashtags like #LabanMarcos (Fight, Marcos) or #BringBackMarcos, or otherwise attacked people who have been critical of Marcos or even just retweeted stories about the Marcoses. Aside from new accounts, there was also an uptick in old or dormant accounts that were revived and that participated in similar activities.[14] All of these happened half a year before the pivotal 2022 national elections. Fast-forward to 2022, billionaire Elon Musk's takeover of Twitter does not bode well for the fight against disinformation.[15]

This problem with social media platforms is truly global, and coordination among countries and with giant tech companies will be difficult but necessary. In 2022, Ressa and fellow Nobel Peace Prize laureate Dmitry Muratov laid down a ten-pronged agenda to push back against the toxic rise of disinformation globally. They implored governments to respect data protection laws and hold tech companies accountable, as well as call on multilateral organizations such as the EU to ban "surveillance advertising" and cut off disinformation upstream.[16] Lawmakers in the US, where many of the tech companies are based, must also enact stronger regulations. One thing is certain: as long as the infodemic is not fixed, Filipinos can expect an ever rising tide of Marcosian lies (among many other lies) in the decades to come. Sure, an army of fact-checkers had emerged in recent years. In the case of Marcosian lies, notable fact-checkers include Rappler[17] and VERA Files.[18] But while necessary, fact-checks can only do so much against the even bigger tide of disinformation. Apart from fact-checking, journalism at large is facing steep competition from new storytellers, namely the bloggers—or more aptly *vloggers*. In the aftermath of the 2022 elections, Rappler reported in a documentary that many of the pro-Marcos vloggers are in fact independent storytellers not employed by any PR firm but instead make money from the platforms directly. They attended Marcos Jr.'s events armed with nothing but their own cameras, microphones, and tripods.[19] So numerous are these vloggers that, in fact, the Marcos Jr. administration promised to accredit them as media people authorized to tail the president alongside legitimate journalists (although in the first half year of Marcos Jr.'s presidency, this plan seems to have fallen apart).[20]

ARGUABLY, THE BIGGEST SOURCE OF PROBLEMS when it comes to Marcosian disinformation lies in our deeply flawed education system: textbooks that either make false statements about martial law or inadequately cover the topic, teachers themselves who display pro-Marcos bias to their students, and higher-ups in the Department of Education who have deliberately or unwittingly suppressed anti-Marcos statements in the curriculum. At the very least, the broken education system made Filipinos a lot more vulnerable to online disinformation.

In 2019, before the pandemic, I was invited by the Human Rights Violations Victims' Memorial Commission (MemCom for short, an agency created by Republic Act No. 10368 for the sole purpose of memorializing martial law and its victims) to join them in Iloilo City and deliver a lecture on martial law economics before Araling Panlipunan (AP; Social Studies) heads and regional coordinators from all over the Philippines. It was a whole-day event, with various speakers talking about different aspects of martial law—from the political milieu, the economy, and the ill-gotten wealth, to the human rights violations and reparations for victims, among others. There was even a film showing of *Liway*, a 2018 independent film based on the life of Marcos dissident Cecilia Flores-Oebanda and her detention during martial law. She even made a surprise appearance and gave a short talk. It was a chance for the AP teachers from all over the country to interact with a martial law human rights victim in the flesh.

Although most people in the event were receptive of the ideas presented before them, I think I have never witnessed a more vivid display of regionalism than what happened here in my entire life. Participants from the same region were understandably grouped in the same table, and I noticed that participants in some regions (most notably Region I—the Ilocos Region, Ferdinand Sr.'s home region and bailiwick of the Marcoses) were not paying close attention to the

FIGURE 0.2 "Kumander Liway" with Araling Panlipunan coordinators and teachers. After the film *Liway* was shown to AP teachers, Cecilia Flores-Oebanda (or "Kumander Liway") herself made a surprise appearance and gave a short talk. Not all were impressed or even interested. (Photo by the author)

proceedings: they were chatting among themselves and some were even listening to something else through their earphones as Flores-Oebanda was speaking in front of the audience. Teachers from the other regions, meanwhile, paid rapt attention to the program. Things escalated in the open forum, which was reserved at the very end of the whole-day program. At that point, only I and another speaker were left at the venue to answer questions, and we felt very much like we were on a firing line facing a congregation of around 200 or so. The first to queue at the microphone were those from Region I, who very clearly appeared to have been saving their misgivings the entire day—which they poured in one go, one impassioned (almost angry) statement after another. They said, "Why are you blaming everything on Marcos?" and "What about the misdeeds done by other presidents? Why not talk about them?" (Maybe not coincidentally, teachers from Region XI or the Davao Region chimed in with similar questions.) The other speaker and I tried our best to temper the situation by calmly replying with "We're not blaming everything on Marcos, but he was responsible for a lot of the bad things that happened," and "No president is perfect, but we're focusing today on the Marcos regime because it was arguably the most consequential in our history." We were supported by teachers from other regions, who themselves made statements countering their fellow participants when it was their turn at the microphone. This latter group of teachers also lamented the fact that there were not enough resources that they can use to teach their students about martial law and—more unsettlingly—that their previous attempts to introduce martial law topics in class have been thwarted or discouraged by higher-ups in the DepEd hierarchy.

Aside from regionalism among basic education teachers, another big issue in education is the fact that the teaching of Philippine history was removed from high school with the implementation of the K-12 Basic Education Curriculum since 2014.[21] The idea is that the new curriculum now employs a "spiral approach," wherein students get exposed first to basic ideas and then to more complex or expansive ideas as they progress through the grade levels. So, after learning Philippine history in Grades 5 and 6 (at elementary school), students need to move on to Asian history and world history in high school without even revisiting Philippine history—as was the case during previous generations (including mine)—to reinforce ideas.

At the same time, the teaching of Philippine history in high school was excised due to the apparent need to "decongest" the basic education curriculum.

What this means is that martial law is only covered in a few precious weeks in the last part of Grade 6 Araling Panlipunan. To be specific, the current Grade 6 AP curriculum covers in one year the entire period from the early 19th century and the Philippine Revolution to the present, and martial law is only allotted time in the fourth quarter, and only in its first three weeks.[22] Clearly, that is not enough time for students to understand martial law and its lessons. Also, the DepEd's "most essential learning competencies"—which students should, in principle, master—regarding martial law only involve examining the problems and challenges of martial law, as well as discussing the events that led to martial law's end and the rise of the People Power Revolution. After this brief brush with martial law history—which, of course, depends entirely on how well teachers taught it—students are no longer exposed to the subject again unless they take history classes in college. For most kids these days, Grade 6 Araling Panlipunan is their only chance of learning about martial law. Imagine that.

Former DepEd secretary Leonor Briones defended the removal of Philippine history in junior high school (a policy that was in fact put in place by her predecessors in the Aquino II administration—ironically) by saying that "discussions of events in Philippine history, especially on martial law, are 'naturally integrated' in several subjects, among them Southeast Asian political landscape in the fourth quarter of Grade 7."[23] But some history teachers who see the effects of such a policy beg to differ. As one intimated,

> Since 2014, I have worked in two different private schools. Whenever I ask young Grade 7 students about national heroes or historical events, I mostly get blank stares as a response. From my level, I can see the slow death of Philippine History at the secondary level becoming ever more inevitable. With the lack of appreciation for our nation's past at this age bracket, I worry for our nation's future.[24]

Petitions to bring back the teaching of Philippine history in high school—and give it more justice in the classroom by allotting more time for it—have cropped up, but so far with limited success. Hence, students still have little choice but to look up and learn about martial law from online sources of varying quality and credibility—and usually they fall prey to all manner of disinformation. (Throughout the pandemic, some use or refer to TikTok videos as if they were a more reliable reference than books and other traditional references. Does anybody still read these days?) Also, there are fears that historical distortion might worsen with vice president Sara Duterte—Marcos Jr.'s running mate—assigned at the start of her term to head the DepEd.[25]

Speaking of references, history textbooks are another big problem. Even in the middle of martial law, prominent history texts like Teodoro Agoncillo's *History of the Filipino People* faced pressure from government to excise in between editions certain portions that might put the regime in an unfavorable light.[26] Problems continue to plague history textbooks in the present. In 2018, during a budget hearing for the DepEd in the Senate, Senator Risa Hontiveros confronted DepEd Secretary Briones about history textbooks used in some schools that tended to "whitewash" martial law.[27] For instance, one textbook used in a school in

Valenzuela City, titled *Makabayan: Kasaysayang Pilipino*, extolled peace and order during martial law and made mention of some programs like land reform—and nothing else. Worse, some textbooks even fail to mention martial law at all. One textbook used in Bulacan, titled *Pilipinas: Bansang Papaunlad*, discussed Philippine history but abruptly ended in 1946, somehow managing to omit martial law entirely.

Sadly, there are still fewer good references on the *economic* aspects of martial law, which tend to be skipped in most references on the topic—a sad fact, even if economics is crucial for a fuller understanding of martial law and its effects, as I hope I have imparted in this book. Most good references on martial law economics are monographs or book chapters or journal articles that basic education teachers find too full of jargon and too inaccessible. Most teachers also have little time to pore over and incorporate such academic materials in their syllabi. (The lack of accessible references on this topic is precisely one of my motivations for writing this book.)

THANKFULLY, IN RECENT YEARS, THERE HAVE been stronger efforts at improving the way we educate the youth about martial law and at pushing back against the sea of lies in which we are drowning. For instance, the MemCom is in the process of building a permanent martial law museum, to be called the "Freedom Memorial Museum," within UP Diliman grounds. Its design, called "Fall of the Brutal," is a giant lopsided fist inspired by the brutalist design so favored by Ferdinand and Imelda.[28] Unfortunately, the museum, which was originally slated for a 2022 opening, was delayed by the COVID-19 pandemic. Worse, the MemCom itself risks having a much smaller budget—or even no budget at all—with Marcos Jr. now in office. The first and current head of the MemCom, Chuck Crisanto, asks, "Will the sitting president now allow a museum to be built which will house the narrative of how his father committed certain atrocities?"[29] Aside from the museum, the MemCom has been making the rounds nationwide since 2018—together with a pool of historians and other resource persons (including myself)—to educate students and teachers alike about various "essential truths" about martial law.

Meanwhile, at the University of the Philippines, there have been new course offerings on martial law, such as Philippine Studies 21 ("Wika, Panitikan, at Kultura sa Ilalim ng Batas Militar" [Language, Literature, and Culture under Martial Law]; first offered in 2019 by the Department of Filipino and Philippine Literature) and Economics 118 ("The Philippine Economy in the 1970s and 1980s"; offered by the School of Economics). Not only has Economics 118 proven to be one of the most popular courses at the UPSE—easily filling an auditorium—but it was also arguably the most eye-opening and revelatory, according to past students.[30] As one would expect, though, the teaching of new courses on martial law was met with some slight resistance from the Marcoses. Responding to the launch of Philippine Studies 21, Imee said in Filipino, "It's good that it will be studied. At least, hopefully, we would be given a chance to say our knowledge on what happened. It's important that there are different viewpoints and that everyone is heard."[31] But this goes against why precisely the courses were introduced: facts and truth cannot be debated. Rather than argue whether it is raining outside or not; one just need look outside to know for sure.

There's still plenty to be done, obviously. For one, to arm students wading daily through massive amounts of social

FIGURE 0.3 The proposed Freedom Memorial Museum. The planned construction of the museum at UP Diliman was delayed by the pandemic. Will this still push through with another Marcos in Malacañang? (Photo by the author)

media content, we need the DepEd to require the teaching of critical thinking skills online, as is done in other countries nowadays. In Finland, for example, fighting fake news online has been successfully incorporated in their basic education curriculum:

> In maths lessons . . . pupils learn how easy it is to lie with statistics. In art, they see how an image's meaning can be manipulated. In history, they analyse notable propaganda campaigns, while Finnish language teachers work with them on the many ways in which words can be used to confuse, mislead and deceive.[32]

There is no reason why a similar curriculum could not work in the Philippines, where the stakes are arguably higher, the youth are more vulnerable, and the spread of disinformation is much more pernicious. According to a 2021 online survey conducted by the Ateneo School of Government, a majority (63 percent) of students were overconfident in their ability to detect fake information. Yet they only scored an average of 6.9 out of 10.[33]

But even before teaching media and online literacy to our students, there is the bigger problem that they consistently fare poorly in international assessments on science, math, and—most relevant to us here—reading. In the 2018 Programme for International Student Assessment, the Philippines ranked dead last in reading among 79 countries, and a whopping 81 percent of our students had difficulty reading texts of moderate length. Meanwhile, in the 2019 Southeast Asia Primary Learning Metrics, an unsettling nine in every ten of our students were considered to have poor reading skills.[34] The World Bank said in a separate report that such harrowing extent of learning poverty in the Philippines was a whopping "56.4 percentage points higher than the average for the East Asia and Pacific region and 30.5 percentage points higher than the average for lower middle income countries."[35] How can we expect our students to be critical thinkers online if they cannot even understand what they read?

VERY QUICKLY, ONE REALIZES THAT THE TASK OF fighting Marcosian disinformation opens a Pandora's box of long-term issues and problems that will take years—perhaps even decades—to fix. Beyond fact-checking, there needs to be greater action on the part of social media platforms to fix their algorithms and curtail the spread of lies online. Beyond bringing back Philippine history in high school and revamping the materials used by teachers and learners in classrooms, there needs to be a culture change in the basic education system to promote critical thinking among teachers and administrators as well as a more conscious and aggressive incorporation of critical thinking subjects in the curriculum, explicitly addressing the tsunami of online content and disinformation.

It is going to be a long struggle. But what choice do we have? As the martial law declaration passed its fiftieth year in 2022, we simply cannot let the atrocities of martial law slip away from the collective memory of Filipinos, especially as the martial law babies become older while their children and grandchildren have no recollection of it at all. Bear in mind that the Marcoses spent *decades* rehabilitating their image. Their success in spreading lies nowadays was by no means the product of overnight effort. It is the product of numerous years of planning, strategy, and patience. But if they can be diligent and patient, I believe defenders of the truth can be even more so. At any rate, lies cannot live on forever. This calls to mind a memorable quote from the HBO miniseries *Chernobyl* (2020): "Every lie we tell incurs a debt to the truth. Sooner or later, that debt is paid." Luckily, we have the trump card: that the truth always prevails in the end. But we cannot rest on that fact. We have our work cut out for us. We just have to keep at it.

Never forget. Never again.

ACKNOWLEDGMENTS

THIS BOOK IS THE CULMINATION OF NEARLY SEVEN years' worth of research into martial law economics. Admittedly, even with everything I wrote in this book, I only barely scratched the surface. In fact, I am still learning new things about martial law economics to this day. And, of course, there is still so much more to write about. Here, I would like to thank the many people who pushed me to study this subject and from whom I have learned a great deal.

First and foremost, a million thanks go to University of the Philippines School of Economics (UPSE) Professor Emeritus Emmanuel "Noel" S. de Dios, who got me thinking about this topic in the first place. His 2015 op-ed in *BusinessWorld* about martial law economics, titled "The Truth about the Economy under the Marcos Regime,"[1] was extremely revelatory for me. Among other things, it opened my eyes to the fact that I was not properly exposed to or educated about this particular episode in our economic history—even after graduating with bachelor's and master's degrees in economics. His piece inspired me to organize my initial thoughts for my own article for Rappler published on 5

March 2016.[2] I have never stopped thinking and writing about martial law ever since. I also thank Sir Noel for the privilege of having me as a teaching fellow when he taught martial law economics at the UPSE in the first semester of academic year 2017–2018. I discovered that there was so much about this subject to last an entire semester of teaching. Thanks as well to my co-teaching fellow then, Miharu Kimwell, and the students with whom we had plenty of engaging and thought-provoking conversations. Finally, I thank Sir Noel for inviting me to co-author a paper on martial law economics, which was, in many ways, an update to the 1984 white paper by UPSE economists. When we presented the paper—together with our co-author Professor Emeritus Maria Socorro Gochoco-Bautista—on 21 September 2018,[3] it turned out to be the biggest Friday seminar at the UPSE in recent memory, packing the UPSE Auditorium to the brim.

Next, I thank friends and colleagues at the Human Rights Violations Victims' Memorial Commission (MemCom), led by its director Chuck Crisanto, for involving me in the past few years in their myriad efforts to disseminate "essential truths" about the martial law era. My engagements with them started in 2018, when their consultant Joel Sarmenta invited me to join their Discussion Group 7286, which brought together academics and educators who are knowledgeable in various aspects of martial law. Since then, we made the rounds all over the country and talked to students and educators nationwide. I have learned tons from my interactions with the people in the MemCom and its network of amazing people: Atty. Byron Bocar, Dr. Neil Santillan, Dr. Aurora Parong, Jess Pasibe, Ester Isberto, and many others. I also thank the wonderful staff of the MemCom, especially Patty Raymundo, who has very ably assisted me over the years.

I also thank Tina Bawagan—social science teacher and a dear friend and former colleague of my mom at the Philippine Science High School–Main Campus—for introducing me to another group of anti-martial law advocates. In 2017, Tita Tina invited me to speak at Pisay about martial law economics. At that talk, I met the amazing people behind the Martial Law Chronicles Project, Diwa ng Martial Law, and Pisay Never Again, including Susan Quimpo (whom we sorely miss), Mel Cardenas, and Floyd Gonda. There, I also met Reina Licauco, who has since generously supported my educational advocacies.

I also give thanks to my Rappler family, especially my editors Chay Hofileña and Glenda Gloria, for allowing me a column space where I have written a number of pieces on martial law economics. Some of those pieces have gone viral and inspired a number of my readers to take notice and even take action on this subject. This book also benefited a lot from Rappler's various fact-checks on martial law and the Marcoses. I also appreciate the support I got from the other Rappler *manangs*, including Marites Dañguilan Vitug, Beth Frondoso, and Maria Ressa herself.

Thanks as well to Jojo Abinales and Leia Castañeda Anastacio for inviting me to write a short chapter on martial law economics for the anthology they edited, *The Marcos Era: A Reader*, published by the Ateneo de Manila University Press in 2022. As a young academic, I felt humbled to see my name alongside many of my academic and journalistic idols in one hefty and timely volume.

I am also very thankful to my Usapang Econ and PumaPodcast families for granting my wish in 2019 to create a podcast episode on martial law economics (you can listen to it on Spotify or wherever you listen to podcasts).

A ton of hugs and kisses go to my mom, Aurora, who, with her lawyerly attention to detail, painstakingly combed through the several drafts of this book to identify several and hard-to-spot typographical errors. She also imparted to me stories about how martial law impacted our family back in the day. I also thank my dad, Henry, who peacefully passed away in 2021 on the anniversary of the declaration of martial law, for gifting me his interest in history and politics. Much love goes to my boyfriend, Menjelle, who supported this effort all the way despite having to put up with my many late nights as I finished the drafts. And thanks as well to Ate Jo for sharing her stories about the Negros Island famine.

And then of course, let me thank Karina Bolasco, director of the Ateneo de Manila University Press, as well as her efficient and amazing team for taking a chance on this book. Working with them has been a blast, and I consider it a privilege of a lifetime to be publishing my first ever book with them. A special shoutout to Ace Vincent Molo and Julian Dela Cerna of the editorial team, Almira Manduriao and Jerome Punzal of the marketing team, and Albert Raqueño, who did the cover art splendidly.

Finally, I thank the countless people with whom I have exchanged ideas and views about martial law economics over the years, whether online or offline, but especially the multitude of students, teachers, human rights advocates, and casual history buffs I met in various fora and seminars. I have no doubt that in the coming years, more and more individuals—forming larger communities—will learn the truth about martial law and spread its lessons—even though it sounds like a lot more work, and even if it must proceed one lecture, one chat group, or one afternoon coffee meetup at a time.

APPENDIX

THE MARCOS SR. ECONOMY IN NUMBERS

14%	Total decline of Philippine gross domestic product (GDP) in 1984 and 1985, during the Philippines' worst economic crisis since World War II; in contrast, the economy contracted by only 9.6 percent in 2020 during the COVID-19 pandemic (and returned to positive growth soon after)
21 years	The time it took for the Philippines to regain its income per person in 1982; every Filipino in 2003 had as much income as every Filipino in 1982
50%	Highest annual postwar inflation rate of the Philippines, recorded in 1984
12.6%	Peak unemployment rate in 1985, at the height of the economic crisis
32.9%	Peak underemployment rate in 1984, at the height of the economic crisis
60.6%	Proportion of poor Filipinos in 1983

50%	Increase in the number of poor families from 1971 to 1985
92%	Decline of peso's purchasing power from 1965 to 1985
PHP 8.1	In 1985, this was the real value of your PHP 100 from 1965
71% and 76%	Decline in the real value of wages from 1969 to 1985 for skilled and unskilled labor, respectively
1/5	Fraction of children found to be "seriously malnourished" during the Negros Island famine of 1985
9.33	Factor by which the percent share of overseas Filipino workers (OFWs) in the population increased from 1975 to 1983
0	Number of years that the Philippines became the world's top rice exporter
PHP 3.90 = USD 1	Exchange rate in December 1965, when Marcos first took office as president
PHP 19.50 = USD 1	Exchange rate in February 1986, when the Marcoses were ousted from Malacañang and fled to Hawai'i
USD 30 million	Estimated commissions gained by Marcos from the Bataan Nuclear Power Plant (BNPP)
0	Kilowatts of electricity produced by the BNPP
21 years	The time it took Filipinos to pay for the BNPP (the payments ended only in April 2007)

USD 25.45 billion	Amount of external debt accumulated by Marcos from 1965 to 1985
90.55%	Ratio of external debt to gross national income (GNI) in 1985, Marcos's last full year in office
3.76	Factor by which the debt-to-GDP ratio increased from 1974 to 1985
2018	The year when Marcosian debts were all paid off (32 years after EDSA)
USD 22.3 billion	Amount of capital that fled the country from 1965 to 1986
PHP 300 billion	Estimated losses of the Central Bank because of Marcos's economic mismanagement and crony capitalism
USD 600 million to 1.1 billion	Estimated amount by which former Central Bank governor Jaime Laya overstated the Philippines' international reserves to hide the fact that it was fast being depleted
USD 174.23 billion	Amount of the Marcoses' ill-gotten wealth recovered by the Presidential Commission on Good Government (PCGG) from 1986 to December 2020
USD 125.98 billion	Estimated amount of the Marcoses' ill-gotten wealth yet to be recovered by the PCGG
USD 8 million	Total estimated value of Imelda's three jewelry collections forfeited in favor of the Philippine government

USD 68 million	Amount of ill-gotten wealth spent by the Marcoses for personal consumption (e.g., food, clothes, hotels, transportation, shopping, antiques, etc.) in their last two years in power—even as the economy was already tanking
2,860	Number of pairs of Imelda's shoes recovered in Malacañang and Tacloban City
1	Number of Imelda's swan feather gown (from a lot more) recovered from Malacañang after their ouster
3,240	Estimated number of people killed during martial law according to Amnesty International
34,000	Estimated number of people tortured during martial law according to Amnesty International
11,103	Total number of confirmed martial law victims who received compensation from the Human Rights Victims' Claims Board in 2018
312,000	Hectares of forest land lost each year from 1968 to 1984 due to timber concessions granted by Marcos to his cronies
244,000	Total metric tons of gold ever mined around the world to date
0	Number of true statements about the Marcoses' Yamashita or Tallano gold

NOTES

Foreword

1 The original quote from US Senator Daniel Patrick Moynihan is: "You are entitled to your opinion. But you are not entitled to your own facts."

2 "Facts are like beads; they require a string to hold them, to connect them. But if there is no string, if there is no unifying idea, then even the most distinguished authorities cannot help producing unsatisfactory work. No theory, no history." Werner Sombart, "Economic Theory and Economic History," *The Economic History Review* 2, no. 1 (January 1929): 5, https://doi.org/10.2307/2589870.

3 See, for example, Maria Serena I. Diokno, Kerby C. Alvarez, Francisco Jayme Paolo A. Guiang, Dondy Pepito G. Ramos II, and Aaron F. Viernes, "The Dilemma of Philippine History Textbooks," Far Eastern University Public Policy Center, accessed 4 January 2023, https://publicpolicy.feu.org.ph/the-dilemma-of-philippine-history-textbooks-a-review-of-select-grades-5-and-6-araling-panlipunan-textbooks/.

4 It should be said, however, that the resort to social media for political campaigns and disinformation is not confined

to the Duterte or Marcos camps, although the latter have exploited it earlier and more effectively.

5 See, for example, Jonathan Corpus Ong and Jason Vincent A. Cabañes, *Architects of Networked Disinformation: Behind the Scenes of Troll Accounts and Fake News Production in the Philippines* (Leicester: Newton Tech4Dev Network, 2018), 53, 57–60.

Introduction

1 Maria Leonor "Leni" Robredo is the wife of Jesse Robredo, the interior and local government secretary during the term of former president Benigno Aquino III. Aquino III was the only son of former president Corazon Aquino, who fought against Marcos Sr. in the 1986 snap election and replaced him as president after the EDSA People Power Revolution.

2 Though this is by no means the biggest presidential mandate in Philippine history, which is typically measured by percentage share of the votes. That distinction goes to former president Ramon Magsaysay who got 68.9 percent of the votes in the 1953 polls. Marcos Jr. only got the third largest mandate in history, although he repeatedly claims he got the largest one. "VERA Files Fact Check: Marcos Jr's 'Biggest Electoral Mandate' Statement Needs Context," VERA Files, 2 July 2022, https://verafiles.org/articles/vera-files-fact-check-marcos-jrs-biggest-electoral-mandate-statement-needs-context.

3 I met one of these closeted BBM (Marcos Jr.'s election branding) supporters: a neighbor in Cavite. He said that he supported presidential candidate former Manila mayor Isko Moreno, but when I asked his wife, he was actually supporting BBM.

4 Dean Dulay, Allen Hicken, Ronald Holmes, and Anil Menon, "Who's Voting for 'Bongbong' Marcos to Be the Next Filipino President?," *The Washington Post*, 6 May 2022,

https://www.washingtonpost.com/politics/2022/05/06/bongbong-marcos-duterte-philippines-election-may9/.

5 Originally, Sara Duterte wanted to run for reelection as Davao City mayor, but later changed her mind and decided to run for vice president alongside Marcos Jr.

6 Marco Sumayao, "Painting the Marcos Myth with Ferdinand as Malakas, Imelda as Maganda," Esquire Philippines, 24 September 2018, https://www.esquiremag.ph/culture/lifestyle/marcos-malakas-maganda-a2239-20180924-lfrm.

7 Beatriz Romualdez Francia, *Imelda and the Clans: A Story of the Philippines* (Mandaluyong City: Solar Publishing Corporation, 1988), 38.

8 Francia, *Imelda and the Clans.*

9 After a few years serving under Marcos, Mijares fled to the United States and wrote a tell-all book called *The Conjugal Dictatorship*. He then mysteriously disappeared in 1976, and later, his son Boyet was tortured and found dead in the mountains of Antipolo—allegedly thrown off a helicopter, according to eyewitnesses. Raissa Robles, *Marcos Martial Law: Never Again*, ed. Alan Robles (Manila: Filipinos for a Better Future, 2016), 1.

10 "The Bogus Anniversary," Editorial, *Philippine Daily Inquirer*, 21 September 2021, https://opinion.inquirer.net/144418/the-bogus-anniversary. Incidentally, when Marcos Jr. won the presidency in 2022, he was number seven on the ballot. Meanwhile, in October 2015, he was quoted as saying, "I was told that I was the seventh person to file certificate of candidacy [for Vice President]. I guess the lucky 7 for us Marcoses is still here. I think it's a good omen." He lost in that race. Tina G. Santos, "Bongbong Marcos Believes in Numerology, Too," *Philippine Daily Inquirer*, 14 October 2015, https://newsinfo.inquirer.net/730724/bongbong-marcos-believes-in-numerology-too.

11 Manuel L. Quezon III, "September 23, Not 21," The Long View, *Philippine Daily Inquirer*, 19 September 2018, https://opinion.inquirer.net/116178/september-23-not-21.

12 In response to the Wikipedia edits, there has been a growing movement of "Wiki warriors" expunging disinformation on Wikipedia articles or otherwise writing new articles to spread truths about martial law. For example, the 2021 "edit-a-thon" organized by the Human Rights Violations Victims' Memorial Commission involved 34 editors, created four new Wikipedia articles, and edited 40 articles in a span of four days. Wikipedia, s.v. "First People Power Wikipedia Editathon—February 2021," last modified 4 March 2021, 09:29, https://en.wikipedia.org/wiki/Wikipedia:First_People_Power_Wikipedia_Editathon_-_February_2021.

13 See Appendix 3.2 of Miguel Paolo P. Reyes and Ricardo T. Jose, eds., "Marcos Pa Rin! The Legacy and the Curse of the Marcos Regime," *Kasarinlan: Philippine Journal of Third World Studies* 27, nos. 1–2 and 28, nos. 1–2 (2012–2013): 433–36.

14 Mark Vincent Tolibao, "Hindi Totoo: Proyekto ni Bongbong Marcos ang Bangui Wind Farm sa Ilocos Norte," Rappler, 15 October 2021, https://www.rappler.com/newsbreak/fact-check/bangui-wind-farm-ilocos-norte-project-bongbong-marcos/.

15 Lian Buan, "Marcos Jr. in Ilocos Norte: Absentee Governor Who 'Could Have Done Better'," Rappler, 22 January 2022, https://www.rappler.com/newsbreak/in-depth/ferdinand-bongbong-marcos-jr-ilocos-norte-absentee-governor/.

16 World Bank, "Philippines: Northwind Bangui Bay Project," accessed 2 December 2021, https://projects.worldbank.org/en/projects-operations/project-detail/P087464.

17 Sofia Tomacruz, "Bongbong Marcos Asked Cambridge Analytica to 'Rebrand' Family Image," Rappler, 15 July 2020, https://www.rappler.com/nation/bongbong-marcos-cambridge-analytica-rebrand-family-image/.

18 Gemma B. Mendoza, "Networked Propaganda: How the Marcoses Are Using Social Media to Reclaim Malacañang," Rappler, 20 November 2019, https://www.rappler.com/news

break/investigative/marcos-networked-propaganda-social-media/.

19 Sofia Tomacruz, "Robredo Widens Lead over Marcos in Recount in 3 Pilot Provinces," Rappler, 18 October 2019, https://www.rappler.com/nation/robredo-widens-lead-over-marcos-results-pet-recount-pilot-provinces/.

20 Carmela Fonbuena, "Marcoses Take Seats in Senate, Congress, Province and City," Rappler, 14 May 2019, https://www.rappler.com/nation/elections/230629-marcoses-take-seat-senate-congress-province-city-ilocos/.

21 Lian Buan, "Dictator's Son Bongbong Marcos to Run for President in 2022," Rappler, 5 October 2021, https://www.rappler.com/nation/elections/bongbong-marcos-to-run-president-2022/.

22 In fact, this is backed by preliminary research by political scientist Yuko Kasuya of Keio University.

23 Floyd Whaley, "30 Years After Revolution, Some Filipinos Yearn for 'Golden Age' of Marcos," *The New York Times*, 26 February 2016, https://www.nytimes.com/2016/02/24/world/asia/30-years-after-revolution-some-filipinos-yearn-for-golden-age-of-marcos.html.

24 Howard Johnson (@Howardrjohnson), "BBC NEWS: Philippine dictator's son runs for the presidency," Twitter, 15 January 2022, 11:57 a.m., https://twitter.com/Howardrjohnson/status/1482200203230777345.

25 Dharel Placido, "Marcos Era Best Time PH Ever Had: Imelda," ABS-CBN News, 13 October 2015, https://news.abs-cbn.com/nation/10/13/15/marcos-era-best-time-ph-ever-had-imelda.

26 Maria Ressa (@mariaressa), Twitter, 9 December 2019, 8:50 a.m., https://twitter.com/mariaressa/status/1203839355250335744.

27 Emmanuel S. de Dios, Maria Socorro Gochoco-Bautista, and Jan Carlo Punongbayan, "Martial Law and the Philippine Economy," University of the Philippines School of Economics Discussion Paper no. 2021-07, November 2021.

01: The Philippines was the richest country in Asia?

1 Tatiana Maligro, "False: Philippines Was Richest Country Next to Japan during Marcos' Term," Rappler, 29 September 2021, https://www.rappler.com/newsbreak/fact-check/philippines-richest-country-next-japan-marcos-term.

2 "VERA Files Fact Check: PH Not Richest Country in Asia during Marcos Era," VERA Files, 27 May 2021, https://verafiles.org/articles/vera-files-fact-check-ph-not-richest-country-asia-during-mar.

3 This comparison of countries takes into account the varied costs of living across countries; in other words, this uses GDP in purchasing power parity or PPP terms. See Esteban Ortiz-Ospina and Marco Molteni, "What Are PPP Adjustments and Why Do We Need Them?," Our World in Data, 16 March 2017, https://ourworldindata.org/what-are-ppps/.

4 Data from the Penn World Table 10.0. We exclude here countries in the Middle East and North Africa (MENA).

5 The ASEAN was formally established on 8 August 1967, originally comprising just the Philippines, Indonesia, Malaysia, Singapore, and Thailand.

6 Ian Nicolas Cigaral, "Vietnamese Set to Get Richer than Filipinos This Year—IMF," Philstar.com, 14 October 2020, https://www.philstar.com/business/2020/10/14/2049564/vietnamese-set-get-richer-filipinos-year-imf.

7 This is a phrase I first heard from another University of the Philippines School of Economics professor, the renowned Solita "Winnie" Monsod, who also served as socioeconomic planning secretary of former president Corazon Aquino.

8 JC Punongbayan and Manuel Leonard Albis, "Were It Not for Marcos, Filipinos Today Would Have Been Richer," Rappler, 24 November 2016, https://www.rappler.com/voices/thought-leaders/marcos-philippine-economy.

02: The exchange rate was PHP 1.5 or PHP 2 per US dollar?

1 Pauline Macaraeg, "False: Forex at P1.50 to P2 per Dollar during Marcos Years," Rappler, 17 September 2019, https://www.rappler.com/newsbreak/fact-check/forex-philippine-peso-dollar-rate-marcos-years.

2 Edwin W. Kemmerer, "The Establishment of the Gold Standard in the Philippines," *Quarterly Journal of Economics* 19, no. 4 (August 1905): 585–609, https://doi.org/10.2307/1885290.

3 Committee on Finance, United States Senate, *Philippine Trade Act of 1946: Hearings before the Committee on Finance, United States Senate, Seventy-ninth Congress, Second Session on H.R. 5856* (Washington: United States Government Printing Office, 1946), 38, https://www.finance.senate.gov/imo/media/doc/79Hrg.Philippine.pdf.

4 Committee on Finance, *Philippine Trade Act of 1946*, 40.

5 Robert F. Emery, "The Successful Philippine Decontrol and Devaluation," *Asian Survey* 3, no. 6 (1963): 274–84, https://doi.org/10.2307/3023519.

6 The Bell Trade Act is more famous (or infamous?) for essentially giving the Americans equal or "parity" rights to use our natural resources. Again, this went against the spirit of the law. This parity rights provision went against the 1935 Constitution and required a plebiscite among Filipinos: 78.89 percent of Filipinos agreed to it.

7 Emery, "The Successful Philippine Decontrol," 275.

8 Emmanuel S. de Dios, "Pre-Martial Law Political Economy: Import Substitution" (Economics 198 lecture, School of Economics, University of the Philippines Diliman, Quezon City, 26 August 2017).

9 More accurately, a balance-of-payments shortage.

10 Manuel F. Montes, "Stabilization and Adjustment Policies and Programmes—Country Study 12: The Philippines" (working paper, World Institute for Development Economics Research, United Nations University, Helsinki, 1987).

11 Robert S. Dohner and Ponciano Intal Jr., "The Marcos Legacy: Economic Policy and Foreign Debt in the Philippines," in *Developing Country Debt and Economic Performance*, vol. 3, *Country Studies—Indonesia, Korea, Philippines, Turkey*, eds. Jeffrey D. Sachs and Susan M. Collins (Chicago: University of Chicago Press, 1989), 433.
12 Emery, "The Successful Philippine Decontrol," 276–77.
13 Emery, 276.
14 Emery.
15 Emery, 280.
16 Emery, 282.
17 Quijano de Manila [Nick Joaquin], *Reportage on the Marcoses* (Mandaluyong City: Anvil Publishing, 2013), 3.
18 Montes, "Stabilization and Adjustment Policies and Programmes," 2.
19 These were the "twin" budget and current account deficits.
20 De Dios, Gochoco-Bautista, and Punongbayan, "Martial Law and the Philippine Economy," 7.
21 The Left has repeatedly charged Marcos as a proponent of neoliberal policies of the West (avoidance of overvalued currencies, for instance, is part of the Washington Consensus, which, to many, epitomizes neoliberalism). De Dios, Gochoco-Bautista, and Punongbayan, "Martial Law and the Philippine Economy," 22. But his refusal to devalue the peso for the sake of export development and trade liberalization is but one manifestation of the fact that he was not as neoliberal as he was painted to be by some critics from the Left.

03: "Golden age" of agriculture?

1 Kristine Joy Patag, "Fact Check: Who Established IRRI?," Philstar.com, 14 October 2021, https://www.philstar.com/headlines/2021/10/14/2134105/fact-check-who-established-irri.

2 Percival Bueser, "False: Tilapia Was Introduced to Philippines during Marcos Presidency," Rappler, 16 December 2020, https://www.rappler.com/newsbreak/fact-check/tilapia-introduced-philippines-marcos-presidency/.

3 Executive Order No. 1061, s. 1985, signed 5 November 1985, *Official Gazette*, https://www.officialgazette.gov.ph/1985/11/05/executive-order-no-1061-s-1985/. In November 1986, through another executive order, president Corazon Aquino later expanded PhilRice's board membership to ensure "broader representation from all sectors in the rice industry." Executive Order No. 60, s. 1986, signed 7 November 1986, *Official Gazette*, https://www.officialgazette.gov.ph/1986/11/07/executive-order-no-60-s-1986/.

4 Patag, "Fact Check: Who Established IRRI?"

5 Tom Hargrove and W. Ronnie Coffman, "Breeding History," *Rice Today*, November 2016, 10.

6 Except in 1982, during which the Philippines was neither a net rice importer nor exporter.

7 "The Marcos Agrarian Reform Program: Promises and Contradictions," Martial Law Museum, accessed 25 October 2021, https://martiallawmuseum.ph/fl/magaral/the-marcos-agrarian-reform-program-promises-and-contradictions/.

8 "Agrarian Reform History," Department of Agrarian Reform, accessed 25 October 2021, https://www.dar.gov.ph/about-us/agrarian-reform-history/.

9 Eduardo Climaco Tadem, "Technocracy and the Peasantry: Martial Law Development Paradigms and Philippine Agrarian Reform," *Journal of Contemporary Asia* 45, no. 3 (2015): 394–419, https://doi.org/10.1080/00472336.2014.93538.

10 Previous land reform programs even had much higher retention limits (ranging from 300 to 1,024 hectares), which favored corporate farms and individual landholders of large tracts of land. Marife M. Ballesteros, Jenica Ancheta, and Tatum Ramos, "The Comprehensive Agrarian Reform Program after 30 Years: Accomplishments and Forward

Options," Philippine Institute for Development Studies Discussion Paper Series, no. 2017-34, December 2017.

11 "Ferdinand E. Marcos, Third State of the Nation Address, January 22, 1968," *Official Gazette*, https://www.officialgazette.gov.ph/1968/01/22/ferdinand-e-marcos-third-state-of-the-nation-address-january-22-1968/.

12 See, for example, Ponciano S. Intal Jr., Leah Francine Cu, and Jo Anne Illescas, "Rice Prices and the National Food Authority," Philippine Institute for Development Studies Discussion Paper Series, no. 2012-27, October 2012.

13 "Marcos Acts to End a Shortage of Rice," *The New York Times*, 9 August 1973, https://www.nytimes.com/1973/08/09/archives/marcos-acts-to-end-a-shortage-of-rice.html.

14 Alice Villadolid, "Philippines Facing Rice Famine," *The New York Times*, 10 August 1973, https://www.nytimes.com/1973/08/10/archives/philippines-facing-rice-famine-white-rice-disappears.html.

15 JC Punongbayan, "[Analysis] Will Rice Tariffication Live Up to Its Promise?," Rappler, 7 December 2018, https://www.rappler.com/voices/thought-leaders/analysis-will-rice-tariffication-live-up-to-promise.

16 "The Marcos Agrarian Reform Program."

17 "The Marcos Agrarian Reform Program."

18 "The Marcos Agrarian Reform Program."

19 Tadem, "Technocracy and the Peasantry," 406.

20 Letter of Instruction No. 143, s. 1973, signed 31 October 1973, *Official Gazette*, https://www.officialgazette.gov.ph/1973/10/31/letter-of-instructions-no-143-s-1973/.

21 Cristina C. David and Arsenio Balisacan, "Philippine Rice Supply Demand: Prospects and Policy Implications," Philippine Institute for Development Studies Discussion Paper Series, no. 95-28, October 1995.

22 Katrina Hallare, "Dominguez Rebuts Marcos on Masagana 99 Feat: 'I Cleaned up the Mess'," Inquirer.net, 20 May 2020, https://newsinfo.inquirer.net/1278265/dominguez-rebuts-marcos-on-masagana-99-feat-i-cleaned-up-the-mess.

23 Hallare, "Dominguez Rebuts Marcos."

24 Emmanuel F. Esguerra, "Some Notes on the Masagana 99 Program," *Philippine Sociological Review* 29, no. 1 (1981): 35–43.

25 Miguel Paolo P. Reyes, Joel F. Ariate Jr., and Larah Vinda del Mundo, "'Success' of Masagana 99 All in Imee's Head—UP Researchers," VERA Files, 24 May 2020, https://www.verafiles.org/articles/success-masagana-99-all-imees-head-researchers.

26 Esguerra, "Some Notes on the Masagana 99 Program."

27 Esguerra.

28 Operations Evaluation Department, Asian Development Bank, *An Evaluation of Small-scale Freshwater Rural Aquaculture Development for Poverty Reduction* (Mandaluyong City: Asian Development Bank, 2005), 75.

29 Cielito F. Habito, "Wild Promises and P20 Rice," No Free Lunch, *Philippine Daily Inquirer*, 3 May 2022, https://opinion.inquirer.net/152594/wild-promises-and-p20-rice.

30 Llanesca T. Panti, "Marcos on P20/kg Rice: It's an Aspiration Hinging on Fixing Value Chain," GMA News Online, 26 May 2022, https://www.gmanetwork.com/news/money/economy/832926/marcos-jr-on-p20-kg-rice-it-s-an-aspiration-hinging-on-fixing-value-chain/story/.

31 Daphne Galvez, "Look: Marcos Jr. Recreates Father's Iconic Photo at IRRI," Inquirer.net, 29 November 2022, https://newsinfo.inquirer.net/1699321/look-marcos-jr-recreates-fathers-photo-at-irri.

32 JC Punongbayan, "[Analysis] Pinakamataas ang Inflation sa Loob ng Halos 14 Taon. Pa'no Na?" Rappler, 5 November 2022, https://www.rappler.com/voices/thought-leaders/analysis-what-happens-now-philippine-inflation-october-2022/.

04: Marcos invented the Nutribun? No one went hungry?

1 Mark Vincent Tolibao, "Hindi Totoo: Proyekto ni Marcos ang Nutribun Noong Dekada '70," Rappler, 5 October 2021, https://www.rappler.com/newsbreak/fact-check/project-ferdinand-marcos-nutribun-noong-1970s.

2 Percival Bueser, "Hindi Totoo: Binigyan ni Marcos ng Nutribuns ang Batang Michael Jordan Noong 1969," Rappler, 11 October 2021, https://www.rappler.com/newsbreak/fact-check/ferdinand-marcos-gave-michael-jordan-nutribuns-1969/.

3 "Nutribuns Featuring Imee Marcos' Name Spotted Being Distributed as Part of Social Aid Program," Yahoo! News, 9 June 2022, https://ph.news.yahoo.com/nutribuns-featuring-imee-marcos-name-031814954.html.

4 "VERA Files Fact Check: Imee Marcos Falsely Claims No Child Went Hungry during Her Father's Rule Because of Nutribun," VERA Files, 13 June 2022, https://verafiles.org/articles/vera-files-fact-check-imee-marcos-falsely-claims-no-child-went-hungry-during-her-fathers-rule-because-of-nutribun.

5 Jenny B. Orillos, "A History of the Nutribun, the Well-Intentioned Bread from the '70s," Esquire Philippines, 21 September 2018, https://www.esquiremag.ph/culture/lifestyle/nutribun-history-a1623-20180921-lfrm.

6 John D. Nystuen et al., *Assessment of the P.L. 480 Title II Program Phaseout for the Philippines: Final Report* (Ann Arbor, MI: Community Systems Foundation and United States Agency for International Development, 1985), https://pdf.usaid.gov/pdf_docs/pdaaz379.pdf.

7 Denison Rey A. Dalupang, "Bun Fight: Was the Nutribun a Marcos Project?," Philstar.com NewsLab, accessed 30 October 2021, https://newslab.philstar.com/31-years-of-amnesia/nutribun.

8 Joel F. Ariate Jr. and Miguel Paolo P. Reyes, "Marcos Propaganda in a Time of Plague," VERA Files, 22 April 2020,

https://verafiles.org/articles/marcos-propaganda-time-plague.

9 Orillos, "A History of the Nutribun."

10 Nystuen et al., *Assessment of the P.L. 480 Title II Program Phaseout*, iv.

11 James K. Boyce, *The Philippines: The Political Economy of Growth and Impoverishment in the Marcos Era* (Hampshire: The Macmillan Press Ltd., 1993).

12 Fe del Mundo, Thaddeus Evangelista, and Mario Arciaga, "Trends in the Health and Nutrition of Filipino Children (0–19 Years) in the Decade 1973 to 1983," *Transactions of the National Academy of Science and Technology (Philippines)* 9 (1987): 461–94.

13 Nystuen et al., *Assessment of the P.L. 480 Title II Program Phaseout*, 66.

14 United Nations Children's Fund (UNICEF) Philippines, "Addressing Stunting and Malnutrition Should Go beyond Nutrition Month Celebration," 3 August 2020, https://www.unicef.org/philippines/press-releases/addressing-stunting-and-malnutrition-should-go-beyond-nutrition-month-celebration/.

15 Nicai de Guzman, "History of Street Food in the Philippines," Esquire Philippines, 26 May 2017, https://www.esquiremag.ph/food-and-drink/food/filipino-street-food-a1729-20170526-lfrm/.

16 George H. Ropes, "The Nutri-Pak: Experience with an Indigenous Supplementary Feeding Intervention in the Philippines," in *Nutrition Policy Implementation: Issues and Experience*, eds. Nevin S. Scrimshaw and Mitchel B. Wallerstein (New York: Plenum Press, 1982), 131–39.

17 "Masagana 99, Nutribun, and Imelda's 'Edifice Complex' of Hospitals," GMA News Online, 20 September 2012, https://www.gmanetwork.com/news/lifestyle/healthandwellness/274389/masagana-99-nutribun-and-imelda-s-edifice-complex-of-hospitals/story/.

18 R. C. Joshi et al., "Current Status of the Golden Apple Snail in the Ifugao Rice Terraces, Philippines," *Journal of Sustainable Agriculture* 18, nos. 2–3 (2001): 71–90, https://doi.org/10.1300/J064v18n02_07.

19 I. M. Revilla, G. F. Estoy Jr., and F. V. Salazar, "State of Golden Kuhol (Snail) Infestation in Selected Rice Farming Villages of Nueva Ecija (Philippines)," in *Rice Integrated Pest Management Network Program Report* (Los Baños: International Rice Research Institute, 1992), 40–64.

20 Sol Jose Vanzi, "Bongbong Uses Duck vs. Golden Snail," Philippine Headline News Online, 5 November 2000, http://www.newsflash.org/2000/11/ht/ht001321.htm.

21 "Never Forget the Famine in Negros," Bantayog ng mga Bayani, accessed 30 October 2021, https://www.bantayog.org/never-forget-the-famine-in-negros/.

22 Michael F. Scott, "On Negros, Sugar and Famine, Prawns and Hope," *Los Angeles Times*, 15 February 1987, https://www.latimes.com/archives/la-xpm-1987-02-15-op-3420-story.html.

23 Committee on Appropriations, House of Representatives (United States), One Hundredth Congress, *Foreign Assistance and Related Programs Appropriations for 1988*, pt. 4 (Washington: United States Government Printing Office, 1987), 78.

24 Anika Burgess, "Stark Photos of the 1986 Philippine Revolution that Took Down a Dictator," Atlas Obscura, 26 February 2016, https://www.atlasobscura.com/articles/stark-photos-of-the-philippine-revolution-that-took-down-a-dictator.

25 AlterMidya, "ALAB Alternatibong Balita (Marcos Years: Golden Age?) | Setyembre 16, 2022," YouTube video, 40:50, 16 September 2022, https://youtu.be/MG_5Z4jOKqU.

26 Inday Espina-Varona, "Under Marcos, the Lush Sugar Lands of Negros Island Turned Red," LiCAS.news, 22 September 2020, https://www.licas.news/2020/09/22/under-marcos-the-lush-sugar-lands-of-negros-island-turned-red/.

27 "Never Forget the Famine in Negros."

28 Steve Lohr, "Rebels and Hunger Stalk Province in Philippines," *New York Times*, 6 May 1985, https://timesmachine.nytimes.com/timesmachine/1985/05/06/218634.html?pageNumber=2.

29 This was the subject of the 2018 independent film *Liway* (dir. Kip Oebanda, Cinemalaya Foundation).

30 Benedict J. Tria Kerkvliet, "Contemporary Philippine Leftist Politics in Historical Perspective," in *The Revolution Falters: The Left in Philippine Politics after 1986*, ed. Patricio N. Abinales (Ithaca, NY: Southeast Asia Program Publications, Cornell University, 1996), 9–27. Others have estimated a smaller but still sizable number of 12,000, as noted in de Dios, Gochoco-Bautista, and Punongbayan, "Martial Law and the Philippine Economy," 33.

31 "Lookback: Sea Tragedies in the Philippines," CNN Philippines, 3 July 2015, https://www.cnnphilippines.com/news/2015/07/03/sea-tragedies-philippines.html.

32 Inday Espina-Varona, "Marcos' MassKara Speech Ignores Roots of Sugar Industry Crisis," Rappler, 23 October 2022, https://www.rappler.com/nation/visayas/ferdinand-marcos-jr-speech-masskara-festival-2022-ignores-sugar-industry-crisis-roots/.

33 Paul John Caña, "Sugar Wars: Looking Back at the Negros Famine of the 1980s," Esquire Philippines, 15 April 2021, https://www.esquiremag.ph/long-reads/features/negros-famine-of-the-1980s-a00289-20210415-lfrm2.

34 Technically, *sakadas* (coming from the Spanish *los sacadas* or "imported ones") refers to migrant sugarcane farmers brought in do manual work in haciendas. These days, most of them come from Antique province in Panay Island.

35 Among the lasting manifestations of the Negros elite's wealth are the grandiose heritage houses in places like Silay City and Talisay City. Vanessa Hidalgo, "Heritage Homes of Negros," *Philippine Daily Inquirer*, 29 July 2017, https://business.inquirer.net/234013/heritage-homes-negros/.

36 Dohner and Intal, "The Marcos Legacy," 461.
37 Dohner and Intal, 462.
38 Caña, "Sugar Wars."
39 Scott, "On Negros."
40 I am indebted to the seminal work of Dohner and Intal (1989b) for this section.
41 Ricardo Manapat, *Some Are Smarter than Others: The History of Marcos' Crony Capitalism*, annotated ed. (Quezon City: Bughaw, an imprint of the Ateneo de Manila University Press, 2020).
42 "Presidential Decree No. 388, s. 1974," *Official Gazette*, signed 2 February 1974, https://www.officialgazette.gov.ph/1974/02/02/presidential-decree-no-388-s-1974/.
43 Dohner and Intal, "The Marcos Legacy," 463.
44 William Branigin, "Marcos Circle Said to Skim $1 Billion From Sugar Sales," *The Washington Post*, 28 March 1986, https://www.washingtonpost.com/archive/politics/1986/03/28/marcos-circle-said-to-skim-1-billion-from-sugar-sales/b0ae096b-12a5-44b1-94ac-27ec0a9452c5/.
45 Dianne Sampang, "Missing Context: Cory Aquino Stopped FTI's Operations after 1986 EDSA Revolution," Rappler, 30 September 2021, https://www.rappler.com/newsbreak/fact-check/cory-aquino-stopped-food-terminal-inc-operations-after-1986-edsa-revolution.
46 "The History," Food Terminal Incorporated, accessed 10 November 2021, http://www.fti.gov.ph/history.
47 Presidential Decree No. 2030, s. 1986, signed 4 February 1986, *Official Gazette*, https://www.officialgazette.gov.ph/1986/02/04/presidential-decree-no-2030-s-1986/.
48 Ponciano S. Intal Jr. and Luis Osman Ranit, "Literature Review of the Agricultural Distribution Services Sector: Performance, Efficiency and Research Issues," in *Special Issues in Agriculture*, ed. Eliseo R. Ponce (Makati City: Philippine Institute for Development Studies, 2004), 46.
49 Ramon L. Clarete, "Options for National Food Authority Reforms in the Philippines," in *From Parastatals to Private*

Trade: Lessons from Asian Agriculture, eds. Shahidur Rashid, Ashok Gulati, and Ralph Cummings Jr. (Baltimore: Published for the International Food Policy Research Institute by The Johns Hopkins University Press, 2008), 179.

50 Celia M. Reyes, "An Initial Verdict on Our Fight against Poverty," Philippine Institute for Development Studies Discussion Paper Series, no. 2004-48, December 2004.

51 UP Third World Studies Center and VERA Files, "Analysis: Imee's Win to Boost Efforts to Restore Marcos Name in History," ABS-CBN News, 26 May 2019, https://news.abs-cbn.com/spotlight/05/26/19/opinion-imees-win-to-boost-efforts-to-restore-marcos-name-in-history.

52 JC Punongbayan, "[Analysis] No, Mr. President, Malayo Pa Tayo sa P20/Kilo ng Bigas," Rappler, 18 November 2022, https://www.rappler.com/voices/thought-leaders/analysis-no-mr-president-marcos-jr-philippines-still-far-away-price-rice-per-kilo-20-pesos/.

05: No public funds were spent for Imelda's hospitals?

1 "Supporters Suffer from Food Poisoning at Imelda Marcos' Birthday Party," Rappler, 3 July 2019, https://www.rappler.com/nation/234509-supporters-suffer-food-poisoning-imelda-marcos-birthday-party-july-2019/.

2 Jason Gutierrez, "Hundreds Get Food Poisoning at Imelda Marcos's 90th Birthday Party," *The New York Times*, 3 July 2019, https://www.nytimes.com/2019/07/03/world/asia/imelda-marcos-food-poisoning.html.

3 Carmen Pedrosa, *The Rise and Fall of Imelda Marcos* (Makati City: Bookmark, 1987).

4 Allegedly, there were other hospitals planned but aborted, including a Brain Center, a Blood Center, and an Orthopedic and Trauma Center. Michael Tan, "Heart Center at 32," Pinoy Kasi, *Philippine Daily Inquirer*, 7 May 2007.

5 Percival Bueser, "False: No Gov't Funds Spent Building Imelda Marcos' Pet Infrastructure Projects," Rappler, 19 August 2021, https://www.rappler.com/newsbreak/fact-check/no-government-funds-spent-build-imelda-marcos-pet-infrastructure-projects/.

6 "DOH Flags 'Philippine Heart Center' Page Posting Marcos Content as Fake," Philstar.com, 10 November 2021, https://www.philstar.com/headlines/2021/11/10/2140321/doh-flags-philippine-heart-center-page-posting-marcos-content-fake.

7 Batasang Pambansa, *Record of the Batasan: Proceedings and Debates; First Session, 1984–1985*, vol. 5 (Quezon City: Batasang Pambansa, 1985), 993–94.

8 Dohner and Intal, "The Marcos Legacy," 401. This is precisely why a proper reckoning of the public deficit at the time must include the deficits of both government agencies as well as government corporations, in what is called the "consolidated public sector deficit."

9 De Dios, Gochoco-Bautista, and Punongbayan, "Martial Law and the Philippine Economy," 32.

10 Mark Fineman, "Nation Takes Holiday to Heart: Filipinos in Love With Valentine's Day," *Los Angeles Times*, 13 February 1988, https://www.latimes.com/archives/la-xpm-1988-02-13-mn-10867-story.html.

11 Fineman, "Nation Takes Holiday to Heart."

12 Batasang Pambansa, *Record of the Batasan*, 994.

13 Boyce, *The Philippines*.

14 Boyce.

15 John F. Doherty, "The Philippine Urban Poor," Philippine Studies Occasional Paper no. 8, Philippine Studies Program, Center for Asian and Pacific Studies, University of Hawai'i, 1985, 34.

16 Doherty, "The Philippine Urban Poor," 33.

17 But admittedly, these were "rough estimates." Emmanuel S. de Dios, ed., *An Analysis of the Philippine Economic*

Crisis: A Workshop Report (Quezon City: University of the Philippines Press, 1984).

18 Boyce, *The Philippines*.

19 Del Mundo, Evangelista, and Arciaga, "Trends in the Health and Nutrition of Filipino Children," 461.

20 De Dios, *An Analysis of the Philippine Economic Crisis*, 28.

21 "Systemic Lupus Erythematosus (SLE)," United States Centers for Disease Control and Prevention, updated 5 July 2022, https://www.cdc.gov/lupus/facts/detailed.html/.

22 Jodesz Gavilan, "When Ferdinand Marcos Hid His Illness from Filipinos," Rappler, 23 September 2020, https://www.rappler.com/newsbreak/in-depth/ferdinand-marcos-hidden-illness-philippines/.

23 Gavilan, "When Ferdinand Marcos Hid His Illness from Filipinos."

24 Interestingly, the next president to establish strong population policy was Noynoy Aquino, who also faced much opposition from the Church but managed to pass in 2013 the Reproductive Health Act, after decades of languishing in Congress. "History," Commission on Population and Development, accessed 10 November 2021, https://popcom.gov.ph/history/.

25 Alejandro N. Herrin, "Population Policy in the Philippines: 1969–2002," Philippine Institute for Development Studies Discussion Paper Series, no. 2002-08, September 2002, 18.

26 For more on poverty and hunger, see chapters 4 and 6.

06: Nobody was poor?

1 Edita A. Tan and Virginia Holazo, "Measuring Poverty Incidence in a Segmented Market: The Philippine Case," *Philippine Economic Journal* 18, no. 4 (1979): 450–90.

2 This was noted as well by Carmelita Ericta and Emma Fabian in "A Documentation of the Philippines' Family Income and Expenditure Survey," Philippine Institute for

Development Studies Discussion Paper Series, no. 2009-18, July 2009.

3 The most relevant for data on poverty is the Family Income and Expenditure Survey (FIES).

4 Arsenio M. Balisacan, "The Human Face of Poverty During a Period of Macroeconomic Adjustment," in *Perspectives on Philippine Poverty* (Quezon City: University of the Philippines Center for Integrative and Development Studies, University of the Philippines Press, and Yale University Council on Southeast Asian Studies, 1993), 17–46.

5 Nobuhiko Fuwa, "Evolution of Rural Poverty in Indonesia, the Philippines and Thailand" (unpublished manuscript. 2002), https://www.h.chiba-u.jp/lab/mkt/Poverty3.pdf.

6 Clyde Haberman, "Manila after Marcos: Managing a Frail Economy; A Daunting Task: Crippled Economy," *The New York Times*, 28 February 1986, https://www.nytimes.com/1986/02/28/world/manila-after-marcos-managing-a-frail-economy-a-daunting-task-crippled-economy.html.

7 Emmanuel S. de Dios, "Poverty, Growth, and the Fiscal Crisis," in *Poverty, Growth, and the Fiscal Crisis* (Makati City: Philippine Institute for Development Studies, 1993), 4.

8 Boyce, *The Philippines.* The phrase was originally used by international economist Jagdish Bhagwati in a different context.

9 Boyce, 4.

10 Boyce, 5.

11 Boyce.

12 Raul V. Fabella, "Investment Grade: Boon or Bane?," Per SE, 6 April 2013, https://econ.upd.edu.ph/perse/?p=2324. Originally published in *BusinessWorld*, 3 April 2013.

13 "Philippine Standard Geographic Code (PSGC)," Philippine Statistics Authority, accessed 15 December 2021, https://psa.gov.ph/classification/psgc/?q=psgc/municipalities.

14 "Philippine Standard Geographic Code."

15 Fat dynasties refer to "those officials who have relatives that simultaneously hold office," in contrast to thin dynasties

or "officials whose relative(s) used to hold elected office—they follow each other sequentially." Ronald U. Mendoza, Leonardo M. Jaminola III, and Jurel K. Yap, "From Fat to Obese: Political Dynasties after the 2019 Midterm Elections," Ateneo School of Government Working Paper no. 19-013, September 2019, 3.

16 Henry Kamm, "Manila Beautifies Slum for the Pope," *The New York Times*, 8 February 1981, https://www.nytimes.com/1981/02/08/world/manila-beautifies-slum-for-the-pope.html.

17 Pamela G. Hollie, "Manila Squatters Are an Eyesore for Mrs. Marcos," *The New York Times*, 30 June 1982, https://www.nytimes.com/1982/06/30/world/manila-squatters-are-an-eyesore-for-mrs-marcos.html.

18 See chapter 4.

19 Boyce, *The Philippines*, 347.

20 Of course, the pandemic resulted in a huge rise in poverty by 2021 (the next FIES year after 2018). Philippine Statistics Authority, "Updated 2015 and 2018 Full Year Official Poverty Statistics," 4 June 2020, https://psa.gov.ph/poverty-press-releases/nid/162559.

21 Note that the poverty thresholds have changed over time.

07: Most literate country in Asia?

1 Placido, "Marcos Era Best Time PH Ever Had: Imelda."

2 Whaley, "30 Years After Revolution."

3 Pauline Macaraeg, "False: PH Most Literate Asian Country under Marcos, Literacy Rate Dropped after His Ouster," Rappler, 21 October 2020, https://www.rappler.com/newsbreak/fact-check/philippines-most-literate-country-asia-marcos-administration-literacy-rate-dropped-after-ouster/.

4 "Ferdinand E. Marcos, Fifteenth State of the Nation Address, July 28, 1980," *Official Gazette*, https://www.official

gazette.gov.ph/1980/07/28/ferdinand-e-marcos-fifteenth-state-of-the-nation-address-july-28-1980/.

5 The assumption of a logistic trend is based on the government's formulation of literacy rate targets in the past. Michael Alba, "Estimating Literacy Rate: A Study Relating Literacy Rate with Combined Gross Elementary and Secondary Schools Enrollment Rate," *Philippine Journal of Development* 8, no. 1 (1981): 71–87.

6 Pernia puts it at 82.6 percent, based on United Nations Educational, Scientific and Cultural Organization (UNESCO) data. Ernesto Pernia, "Economic Growth Performance of Indonesia, the Philippines and Thailand: The Human Resource Dimension," Asian Development Bank Technical Report no. 48, January 1990, 10.

7 Education minister Jaime Laya cited these figures from a 1979 study by the United Nations Children's Fund (UNICEF) and the National Economic and Development Authority (NEDA). Ministry of Education, Culture, and Sports, *Philippine Education Indicators, 1965–1985* (Manila: Ministry of Education, Culture, and Sports, 1986).

8 Rappler used the same data in their own fact-check in October 2020. Macaraeg, "False: PH Most Literate Asian Country under Marcos."

9 Pernia, "Economic Growth Performance of Indonesia, the Philippines and Thailand."

10 Mark Fineman, "Literacy Declining: Philippines: New Crisis in Education," *Los Angeles Times*, 21 November 1987, https://www.latimes.com/archives/la-xpm-1987-11-21-mn-5465-story.html.

11 Fineman, "Literacy Declining."

12 Fineman.

13 De Dios, *An Analysis of the Philippine Economic Crisis*.

14 Pernia, "Economic Growth Performance of Indonesia, the Philippines and Thailand."

15 Fineman, "Literacy Declining."

16 Michael David Sy, "Marcos the Plagiarist: A Pictorial Bibliography," The Martial Law Chronicles Project, 4 December 2020, https://www.martiallawchroniclesproject.com/marcos-the-plagiarist-a-pictorial-bibliography/.

17 John A. Lent, The Philippine Press under Martial Law, *Index on Censorship* 3, no. 1 (March 1974): 57, https://doi.org/10.1080/03064227408532297.

18 Mark Maca, "Education in the 'New Society' and the Philippine Labour Export Policy (1972–1986)," *Journal of International and Comparative Education* 7, no. 1 (April 2018): 8, https://doi.org/10.14425/jice.2018.7.1.1.

19 Filomeno V. Aguilar Jr., "Political Conjuncture and Scholarly Disjunctures: Reflections on Studies of the Philippine State under Marcos," *Philippine Studies: Historical and Ethnographic Viewpoints* 67, no. 1 (March 2019): 17.

20 Vernon R. Totanes, "*History of the Filipino People* and Martial Law: A Forgotten Chapter in the History of a History Book, 1960–2010," *Philippine Studies* 58, no. 3 (September 2010): 313–48.

08: Golden age of infrastructure?

1 ABS-CBN News (@ABSCBNNews), "TINGNAN: Bida sa birthday cakes sa ika-90 kaarawan ni dating First Lady Imelda Marcos ang mga imprastrukturang ipinatayo noong rehimeng Marcos. (Grace Alba, ABS-CBN News)," Twitter, 3 July 2019, 7:27 a.m., https://twitter.com/ABSCBNNews/status/1146198806213455872.

2 As discussed in chapter 5, the ninetieth birthday celebration of Imelda was also memorable for the food poisoning of guests at the party held on 3 July 2019 at the Ynares Sports Complex in Pasig City. The party continued even as more than 200 people were rushed to hospitals. "Supporters Suffer from Food Poisoning."

3 Imelda, also called the "Rose of Tacloban," was allegedly the one who requested that San Juanico Bridge be built in the first place. Manapat, *Some Are Smarter than Others*.

4 Sofia Guanzon, "False: Former South Korean President Visited NLEX in 1960s," Rappler, 29 March 2021, https://www.rappler.com/newsbreak/fact-check/former-south-korean-president-visited-nlex-1960/.

5 As discussed in chapter 3.

6 Percival Bueser, "False: More than 50,000 Bridges Built during the Marcos Administration," Rappler, 18 May 2021, https://www.rappler.com/newsbreak/fact-check/more-than-50000-bridges-built-during-marcos-administration/.

7 "Full Text: President Marcos' Inaugural Speech," Rappler, 30 June 2022, https://www.rappler.com/nation/full-text-philippine-president-marcos-jr-inaugural-speech/.

8 Bueser, "False: More than 50,000 Bridges Built."

9 *Philippine Statistical Yearbook 1986* (Manila: National Economic and Development Authority, 1986).

10 Angelica Flores Juan, "Hindi Totoo: Proyekto ni Ferdinand Marcos ang NAIA," Rappler, 15 October 2021, https://www.rappler.com/newsbreak/fact-check/naia-project-ferdinand-marcos/.

11 See architect Gerard Lico's book, *Edifice Complex: Power, Myth, and Marcos State Architecture* (Quezon City: Ateneo de Manila University Press, 2003).

12 Lico, *Edifice Complex*.

13 Kathleen de Villa, "Imelda Marcos and Her 'Edifice Complex'," *Philippine Daily Inquirer*, 16 September 2017, https://business.inquirer.net/236962/imelda-marcos-edifice-complex.

14 Pedrosa, *The Rise and Fall of Imelda Marcos*, 155.

15 Presidential Communications Development and Strategic Planning Office, *Philippine Electoral Almanac*, rev. and expanded ed. (Manila: Presidential Communications Development and Strategic Planning Office, 2015), 109.

16 Marcos would be the second and the last president, as of writing, to be reelected.
17 Pedrosa, *The Rise and Fall of Imelda Marcos*.
18 Gilda Cordero-Fernando, "The Guardians of Splendor," *Philippine Daily Inquirer*, 13 January 2013, https://lifestyle.inquirer.net/85155/the-guardians-of-splendor/.
19 David A. Andelman, "Manila's Hotel Boom May Turn Into Bust," *The New York Times*, 29 September 1976, https://www.nytimes.com/1976/09/29/archives/manilas-hotel-boom-may-turn-into-bust-manilas-spectacular-hotel.html.
20 "Edifice Complex: Building on the Backs of the Filipino People," Martial Law Museum, accessed 5 December 2021, https://martiallawmuseum.ph/magaral/edifice-complex-building-on-the-backs-of-the-filipino-people/.
21 "A Peek Inside the Coconut Palace, A Reminder of Imelda Marcos' Edifice Complex," Esquire Philippines, 22 April 2020, https://www.esquiremag.ph/long-reads/features/inside-the-famed-coconut-palace-a00293-20200422-lfrm/.
22 Janet Cawley, "Marcos' Mountain Palace Is the House That Arrogance Built," *Chicago Tribune*, 30 March 1986, https://www.chicagotribune.com/news/ct-xpm-1986-03-30-8601230361-story.html.
23 Lico, *Edifice Complex*, 121.
24 Fernando del Mundo, "26 Dead in Philippines Movie Theater Collapse," United Press International, 17 November 1981, https://www.upi.com/Archives/1981/11/17/26-dead-in-Philippines-movie-theater-collapse/8733374821200/.
25 Nicai de Guzman, "The Mysterious Curse of the Manila Film Center," Esquire Philippines, 7 November 2019, https://www.esquiremag.ph/long-reads/features/manila-film-center-haunted-a1729-20191107-lfrm2; Gelo Gonzales, "Viral: Clip of Lino Brocka Talking about the Manila Film Center Tragedy," Rappler, 17 May 2022, https://www.rappler.com/technology/internet-culture/lino-brocka-signed-documentary-manila-film-center.

26 After the accident, exorcisms at the site were also conducted, which lasted for about a week. Gonzales, "Viral: Clip of Lino Brocka."

27 Robles, *Marcos Martial Law*, 161.

28 Jose V. Beltran Jr., "The Concept of Urban Renewal in Metropolitan Manila: An Analysis" (master's thesis, University of Tasmania, 1982).

29 "Edifice Complex: Building on the Backs."

30 Pedrosa, *The Rise and Fall of Imelda Marcos*, 156.

31 "Slum Evictions in Manila Embarrass the World Bank," *The New York Times*, 7 October 1976, https://www.nytimes.com/1976/10/07/archives/slam-evictions-in-manila-embarrass-the-world-bank-evictions-from.html.

32 As discussed in chapter 6.

33 Michael Charleston B. Chua, "Ang Imeldific: Representasyon at Kapangyarihan sa Sto. Niño Shrine sa Lungsod ng Tacloban," *Philippine Social Sciences Review* 60, no. 1 (January 2008–December 2009): 75.

34 De Dios, *An Analysis of the Philippine Economic Crisis*, 35.

35 We will discuss how this happened in chapter 13.

36 De Dios, *An Analysis of the Philippine Economic Crisis*, 14.

37 Tatiana Maligro, "Kulang sa Konteksto: Ginaya ng South Korea ang Disenyo ng Bataan Nuclear Power Plant," Rappler, 30 October 2021, https://www.rappler.com/newsbreak/fact-check/south-korea-copied-design-bataan-nuclear-power-plant/.

38 "Mothballed Plant Cost $2.3 Billion," *Philippine Daily Inquirer*, 17 September 2016, https://technology.inquirer.net/52355/mothballed-plant-cost-2-3-billion.

39 See chapter 5 for more on the designer hospitals.

40 Dohner and Intal, "Debt Crisis and Adjustment in the Philippines," 176.

41 Boyce, *The Philippines*.

42 "JICA to Help Philippines Ease Traffic Congestion in Metro Manila," Japan International Cooperation Agency,

20 September 2018, https://www.jica.go.jp/philippine/english/office/topics/news/180920.html.

43 De Dios, *An Analysis of the Philippine Economic Crisis*, 15.

44 De Dios, 14.

45 This section draws heavily from the accounts of Ricardo Manapat in *Some Are Smarter than Others* (2020).

46 Manapat, 292.

47 The overpricing of contracts, like this one, can in fact be considered, at the time, a form of capital flight.

48 Boyce, *The Philippines*, 284.

49 Reiniel Pawid, "Panukalang Pagbubukas ng BNPP Delikado, Ayon sa Geologist," ABS-CBN News, 18 June 2022, https://news.abs-cbn.com/spotlight/06/18/22/panukalang-pagbubukas-ng-bnpp-delikado-ayon-sa-geologist.

50 Lian Buan, "SC Awards over P1 Billion to Government for Marcos Crony Power Plant Mess," Rappler, 15 June 2021, https://www.rappler.com/nation/supreme-court-awards-billions-government-marcos-crony-bataan-power-plant-mess.

51 Manapat, *Some Are Smarter than Others*, 247.

52 Manapat.

53 Manapat.

54 Manapat, 251.

55 Manapat, 258–60.

56 Dohner and Intal, "The Marcos Legacy," 477.

57 Charles W. Lindsey, "Economic Crisis in the Philippines," *Far Eastern Survey* 24, no. 12 (December 1984): 1187, https://doi.org/10.2307/2644357.

58 "Friends in Need," *Time*, 24 August 1981, http://content.time.com/time/subscriber/article/0,33009,949392,00.html.

59 This is an example of a phenomenon known in economics as "moral hazard."

60 John Crewdson, "Marcos Graft Staggering," *Chicago Tribune*, 23 March 1986, https://www.chicagotribune.com/news/ct-xpm-1986-03-23-8601210600-story.html.

61 *Republic of the Philippines v. Rodolfo M. Cuenca et al.*, G.R. No. 198393, 829 Phil. 139, 4 April 2018.
62 Ina Reformina, "Supreme Court Junks Ill-Gotten Wealth Case vs Marcos, Cronies," ABS-CBN News, 19 June 2018, https://news.abs-cbn.com/news/06/19/18/supreme-court-junks-ill-gotten-wealth-case-vs-marcos-cronies.
63 *Republic of the Philippines v. Cuenca et al.*
64 Marlon Ramos and Vince F. Nonato, "SC Clears Marcoses, Cronies on Behest Loans," *Philippine Daily Inquirer*, 20 June 2018, https://newsinfo.inquirer.net/1002394/sc-clears-marcoses-cronies-on-behest-loans.
65 Pauline Macaraeg, "False: No President after Marcos Built Mass Transit Projects," Rappler, 16 October 2019, https://www.rappler.com/newsbreak/fact-check/242590-no-president-after-marcos-developed-mass-transit-projects/.
66 Percival Bueser, "False: Former President Marcos Planned Skyway Stage 3," Rappler, 21 January 2021, https://www.rappler.com/newsbreak/fact-check/former-president-marcos-planned-skyway-stage-3/.
67 The New People's Army (NPA) later took credit for blasting it. "VERA Files Fact Check: Marcos Bust in Benguet Not Ordered Destroyed by Noynoy Aquino Admin," VERA Files, 31 May 2019, https://verafiles.org/articles/vera-files-fact-check-marcos-bust-benguet-not-ordered-destro.
68 Mark Fineman, "Government Spares Huge Marcos Bust," *Los Angeles Times*, 8 March 1986, https://www.latimes.com/archives/la-xpm-1986-03-08-mn-16561-story.html.
69 Fineman, "Government Spares Huge Marcos Bust."
70 Sherwin de Vera, "'The North Resists': Groups Recall 'True Legacy' of Marcos at Defaced Bust in Benguet," Rappler, 20 November 2021, https://www.rappler.com/nation/defaced-marcos-bust-benguet-remains-site-of-protest/.
71 Kimberlie Quitasol and Mariejo S. Ramos, "Faceless Marcos Bust Back at Center Stage of Protest," *Philippine Daily Inquirer*,

19 November 2021, https://newsinfo.inquirer.net/1517066/faceless-marcos-bust-back-at-center-stage-of-protest.

09: Marcos signed the 13th-month pay law? Contractualization did not exist?

1 Presidential Decree No. 851, s. 1975, signed 16 December 1975, *Official Gazette*, https://www.officialgazette.gov.ph/1975/12/16/presidential-decree-no-851-s-1975/.

2 Memorandum Order No. 28, s. 1986, signed 13 August 1986, *Official Gazette*, https://www.officialgazette.gov.ph/1986/08/13/memorandum-order-no-28-s-1986/.

3 Joel F. Ariate Jr. and Miguel Paolo P. Reyes, "Who Should Filipino Workers Thank for the 13th Month Pay," VERA Files, 24 December 2020, https://verafiles.org/articles/who-should-filipino-workers-thank-the13th-month-pay.

4 Boyce, *The Philippines*.

5 Boyce, 29.

6 Jonna P. Estudillo, "Income Inequality in the Philippines, 1961–91," *The Developing Economies* 35, no. 1 (1997): 70.

7 See, for example, Carmelita Ericta and Emma Fabian, "A Documentation of the Philippines' Family Income and Expenditure Survey," Philippine Institute for Development Studies Discussion Paper Series, no. 2009-18, July 2009.

8 Boyce, *The Philippines*, 43.

9 Boyce, 44.

10 Interestingly, this is also the venue of Marcos Jr.'s inauguration as the seventeenth president of the Philippines on 30 June 2022.

11 These labor organizations include the National Association of Trade Unions and the Malayang Samahang Magsasaka. "Appendix: A History of the Philippine Political Protest," *Official Gazette*, accessed 25 November 2021, https://mirror.officialgazette.gov.ph/edsa/the-ph-protest-appendix/.

12 Miguel Paolo P. Reyes and Joel F. Ariate Jr., "Marcos and the First Quarter Storm Part I: Paranoia and Pretense," VERA Files, 10 March 2020, https://verafiles.org/articles/marcos-and-first-quarter-storm-part-i-paranoia-and-pretense.

13 Barbara Mae Naredo Dacanay, "The 7 Deadly Protests of the First Quarter Storm," ANCX, 24 February 2020, https://news.abs-cbn.com/ancx/culture/spotlight/02/24/20/the-7-deadly-protests-of-the-first-quarter-storm.

14 Student activists, church activists, journalists, and human rights workers were also frequently at the receiving end of military and police abuses during martial law. Diane Orentlicher, Marvin E. Frankel, and Jack Greenberg, "The Philippines: A Country in Crisis—A Report by Lawyers Committee for International Human Rights Committee for International Human Rights," *Columbia Human Rights Law Review* 15 (1983): 69–129.

15 See chapter 12.

16 Lorenz Dantes Pasion, "False: Labor Contractualization Did Not Exist during Marcos Era," Rappler, 14 July 2021, https://www.rappler.com/newsbreak/fact-check/labor-contractualization-did-not-exist-ferdinand-marcos-era-administration/.

17 Presidential Decree No. 442, s. 1974, signed 1 May 1974, *Official Gazette*, https://www.officialgazette.gov.ph/1974/05/01/presidential-decree-no-442-s-1974/.

18 "VERA Files Fact Check: Marcos, Not Cory, Signed 'Endo' Law," VERA Files, 31 August 2018, https://verafiles.org/articles/vera-files-fact-check-marcos-not-cory-signed-endo-law.

10: Crime went down? Only one person was executed by the regime?

1 Mara Cepeda, "List: False Claims of Juan Ponce Enrile on Martial Law," Rappler, 21 September 2018, https://www.rappler.com/newsbreak/iq/212460-list-false-claims-juan-ponce-enrile-martial-law/.

2 Michael Bueza, "False: 'No Massacres' during Martial Law," Rappler, 21 September 2018, https://www.rappler.com/newsbreak/fact-check/212458-false-no-massacres-during-martial-law/.

3 Miguel Imperial, Vernise L. Tantuco, and Michael Bueza, "False: 'Only One Executed,' 'None Arrested' under Marcos' Martial Law—Enrile," Rappler, 21 September 2018, https://www.rappler.com/newsbreak/fact-check/212456-false-only-one-executed-none-arrested-criticizing-marcos-martial-law/.

4 De Dios, *An Analysis of the Philippine Economic Crisis.*

5 "Philippine Aide Reports Big Drop in Crime Rate," *The New York Times*, 10 October 1972, https://www.nytimes.com/1972/10/10/archives/philippine-aide-reports-big-drop-in-crime-rate.html.

6 De Dios, *An Analysis of the Philippine Economic Crisis*, 28.

7 De Dios, 29.

8 De Dios, 29. Tangentially, while the military was also deployed for peacekeeping, some also claim that Marcos successfully developed the Philippines' military to become Asia's best and most modern at the time. In addition, so the myth goes, Marcos also developed a missile system even before China did. Both have been debunked by media. Owen Cinco and Pauline Macaraeg, "False: Military under Marcos Was Most Advanced in Asia," Rappler, 17 November 2020, https://www.rappler.com/newsbreak/fact-check/philippine-military-under-ferdinand-marcos-most-advanced-asia/. There is likewise a myth going around that Marcos was able to develop an "anti-typhoon missile" that

uses silver iodide. Again, bonkers. Rochel Ellen Bernido, "Hindi Totoo: Matagumpay ang 'Anti-typhoon Missile' ni Marcos," Rappler, 7 May 2022, https://www.rappler.com/newsbreak/fact-check/anti-typhoon-missile-marcos-was-successful/.

9 Michael Bueza, "Fast Facts: Jovito Salonga," Rappler, 22 June 2014, https://www.rappler.com/newsbreak/iq/61263-fast-facts-jovito-salonga/.

10 Proclamation No. 1081, s. 1972, signed 21 September 1972, *Official Gazette*, https://www.officialgazette.gov.ph/1972/09/21/proclamation-no-1081/.

11 Human Rights Watch, *The Philippines: Violations of the Laws of War by Both Sides* (New York: Human Rights Watch, 1990).

12 Rachel A.G. Reyes, "3,257: Fact Checking the Marcos Killings, 1975–1985," *The Manila Times*, 12 April 2016, https://www.manilatimes.net/2016/04/12/featured-columns/columnists/3257-fact-checking-the-marcos-killings-1975-1985/255735.

13 Katerina Francisco, "Martial Law, the Dark Chapter in Philippine History," Rappler, 22 September 2016, https://www.rappler.com/newsbreak/iq/146939-martial-law-explainer-victims-stories/.

14 Ellen-Rae Cachola, "The Haunting of Martial Law: Records from the Marcos Regime," University of Hawai'i at Mānoa Law Library, 7 September 2017, https://library.law.hawaii.edu/2017/09/07/the-haunting-of-martial-law-records-from-the-marcos-regime/.

15 Jodesz Gavilan, "11,103 Victims of Human Rights Violations under Martial Law to Get Compensation," Rappler, 10 May 2018, https://www.rappler.com/nation/202033-human-rights-victims-claims-board-final-list-eligible-claimants-released/.

16 S. Sothi Rachagan and Richard F. Dorall, "The Conflict in Mindanao: Perspectives from South of the Border," *Aghamtao* 4 (1981): 61.

17 A good place to start would be Raissa Robles's *Marcos Martial Law: Never Again* (Manila: Filipinos for a Better Future, 2016) and Susan and Nathan Quimpo's *Subversive Lives: A Family Memoir of the Marcos Years* (Mandaluyong City: Anvil Publishing, 2012).

18 Popular wisdom says that Aquino's return and assassination marked the start of the political and economic crisis that brought down the Marcoses. But the fact is that the Marcos regime was already in danger even before Aquino's return. A power vacuum was looming because of Marcos's ill health, questions surrounding the legitimacy of his leadership, and the lack of an "heir apparent." Hence, as University of the Philippines School of Economics Professor Emeritus Emmanuel de Dios would say, the political and economic crisis caused Aquino's return, not the other way around.

19 Bueza, "False: 'No Massacres' during Martial Law."

20 Quoted in Carolyn O. Arguillas, "1974 Malisbong Massacre Memorialized in 'Forbidden Memory' Film," *MindaNews*, 17 November 2016, https://www.mindanews.com/top-stories/2016/11/1974-malisbong-massacre-memorialized-in-forbidden-memory-film/.

21 Arguillas, "1974 Malisbong Massacre Memorialized."

22 Arguillas. The Palimbang Massacre was the subject of the 2016 film *Forbidden Memory* (dir. Gutierrez "Teng" Mangansakan II, Cinema One Originals).

23 "Jabidah and Merdeka: The Inside Story," Rappler, 18 March 2018, https://www.rappler.com/newsbreak/24025-jabidah-massacre-merdeka-sabah/.

24 The gripping stories of martial law survivors, especially those in the regions, were captured in the 2022 documentary *11,103*, produced by Kara Magsanoc-Alikpala and directed by Miguel Alcazaren and Jeanette Ifurung. To know more, visit https://11103film.ph.

11: Filipinos' purchasing power fell after martial law?

1 Dexter Doria, "Golden Era Ang Martial Law??!! Ang Katotohanan, Ibinunyag! | #DidiSerye | Episode 2," YouTube video, 3:26, 18 January 2022, https://youtu.be/qciUzS6oqPk.

2 Using 1978 as base year. The overall price level actually started to rise precipitously near the tail end of 1983. *Philippine Statistical Yearbook 1984* (Manila: National Economic and Development Authority, 1984), 156; *Philippine Statistical Yearbook 1985* (Manila: National Economic and Development Authority, 1985), 136.

3 There are earlier price data but these are not comparable to the base or reference year used nowadays.

4 "Oil Embargo, 1973–1974," Office of the Historian, Foreign Service Institute, United States Department of State, accessed 6 November 2021, https://history.state.gov/milestones/1969-1976/oil-embargo.

5 According to Dohner and Intal, there were actually two devaluations in 1983, in June and October. Dohner and Intal, "The Marcos Legacy," 527.

6 Section 8, Presidential Decree No. 1956, s. 1984, signed 10 October 1984, *Official Gazette*, https://www.officialgazette.gov.ph/1984/10/10/presidential-decree-no-1956-s-1984/.

7 Maria Nimfa Mendoza, "Lessons Learned: Fossil Fuel Subsidies and Energy Sector Reform in the Philippines," Global Subsidies Initiative Report, International Institute for Sustainable Development, March 2014.

8 Manapat, *Some Are Smarter than Others*, 348.

9 A. V. H. Hartendorp, *History of Industry and Trade of the Philippines: From Pre-Spanish Times to the End of the Quirino Administration* (Manila: American Chamber of Commerce of the Philippines, 1958).

10 See, for example, Rappler, "Basagan ng Trip with Leloy Claudio: Inflation, Deflation, and Hyperinflation," YouTube video, 17:32, 14 September 2018, https://youtu.be/vobd9eDtjqc.

11 JC Punongbayan, "[Analysis] Why Is Philippine Inflation Now the Highest in ASEAN?," Rappler, 6 September 2018, https://www.rappler.com/voices/thought-leaders/analysis-reasons-philippine-inflation-now-highest-asean.

12 Ralf Rivas, "Consumers' Pain Worsens as Inflation Climbs to 8.1% in December 2022," Rappler, 5 January 2023, https://www.rappler.com/business/inflation-rate-philippines-december-2022/.

13 JC Punongbayan, "[Analysis] Mga Palpak na Proyekto ng Tatay na Marcos, Bakit Ibabalik ni Junior?," Rappler, 11 March 2022, https://www.rappler.com/voices/thought-leaders/analysis-why-would-ferdinand-bongbong-marcos-jr-bring-back-father-failed-projects/.

12: Unemployment rate was 66 percent because of EDSA? EDSA led to more OFWs?

1 Percival Bueser, "Hindi Totoo: 66% ang Unemployment Rate ng Filipinas Noong 1986," Rappler, 5 November 2021, https://www.rappler.com/newsbreak/fact-check/unemployment-rate-philippines-1986.

2 Emmanuel S. de Dios and Katrina Dinglasan, "Just How Good Is Unemployment as a Measure of Welfare? A Note," *Philippine Review of Economics* 52, no. 2 (December 2015): 242.

3 See chapter 11.

4 Glenda Marie Castro, "False: EDSA Revolution 'Removed' Regularization, Led to 'Increase' in OFWs," Rappler, 24 June 2019, https://www.rappler.com/newsbreak/fact-check/232783-ofws-spike-numbers-edsa-revolution/.

5 Presidential Decree No. 442, s. 1974, signed 1 May 1974, *Official Gazette*, https://www.officialgazette.gov.ph/1974/05/01/presidential-decree-no-442-s-1974/.

6 Andrei Medina and Veronica Pulumbarit, "How Martial Law Helped Create the OFW Phenomenon," GMA News

Online, 21 September 2012, https://www.gmanetwork.com/news/news/pinoyabroad/275011/how-martial-law-helped-create-the-ofw-phenomenon/story/.

7 Neil G. Ruiz, "Made for Export: Labor Migration, State Power, and Higher Education in a Developing Philippine Economy" (PhD diss., Massachusetts Institute of Technology, 2014).

8 Notable balance-of-payments (BOP) crises occurred in 1962 and 1970. An earlier BOP crisis happened in 1949 when the Philippine government used up its war rehabilitation funds to finance a huge trade deficit at the time. Montes, "Stabilization and Adjustment Policies and Programmes," 1.

9 Much later, in the 2000s and 2010s, remittances would prove to be a robust source of dollars—leading to several years of current account surpluses, rather than deficits.

10 Executive Order 857, s. 1982, signed 13 December 1982, *Official Gazette*, https://www.officialgazette.gov.ph/1982/12/13/executive-order-no-857-s-1982/.

11 Executive Order 1021, s. 1985, signed 1 May 1985, *Official Gazette*, https://www.officialgazette.gov.ph/1985/05/01/executive-order-no-1021-s-1985/.

12 My dad admitted, however, to a sense of adventurism that prevailed at the time, which helped him nudge in his decision to emigrate.

13 Ruth Francisco, "Essays on the Socioeconomic Consequences of Parental Migration for Children Left Behind" (PhD diss., University of the Philippines School of Economics, 2016).

14 JC Punongbayan, "[Analysis] The Paper Tiger That Was the Anti-Endo Bill," Rappler, 5 August 2019, https://www.rappler.com/voices/thought-leaders/237071-analysis-paper-tiger-that-was-anti-endo-bill/.

13: The economy tanked after the Marcoses were ousted?

1 Tatiana Maligro, "False: PH Economy Crashed in 1983 Due to US Sanctions," Rappler, 20 September 2021, https://www.rappler.com/newsbreak/fact-check/philippine-economy-crashed-1983-due-united-states-sanctions/.

2 In 2021, we were projected to have positive growth again and, indeed, we grew by 5.6 percent, exceeding expectations. Ralf Rivas, "Philippines' GDP Grows 5.6% in 2021, Beating Revised Target," Rappler, 27 January 2022, https://www.rappler.com/business/gross-domestic-product-philippines-q4-2021.

3 In the twenty-first century, semiconductors would still dominate the country's exports and imports (indicating that it still mainly involves assembly of components). In contrast, neighboring countries like Vietnam are now able to produce entire gadgets such as smartphones.

4 De Dios, Gochoco-Bautista, and Punongbayan, "Martial Law and the Philippine Economy." Protectionism worked in favor of other Asian economies (think of the Korean *chaebols*, or family-run conglomerates, and the Japanese *zaibatsus*) because they were decidedly export-oriented.

5 This happened again in 2022, as risks of global stagflation reaching an all-time high became imminent, owing largely to pandemic recovery and the Russian invasion of Ukraine.

14: Marcos added just USD 1 billion to the national debt?

1 JC Punongbayan, "[Analysis] Marcos Debt: Ano ang Katotohanan?," Rappler, 10 December 2021, https://www.rappler.com/voices/thought-leaders/analysis-what-is-the-truth-about-marcos-administration-debt/.

2 Percival Bueser, "False: National Debt during Cory Aquino's Term Reached P1 Trillion," Rappler, 17 June 2021, https://

www.rappler.com/newsbreak/fact-check/national-debt-cory-aquino-term-reached-p1-trillion/.

3 Percival Bueser, "False: World Bank's Interest Rate When Loaning to the Philippines Is 0%," Rappler, 17 July 2021, https://www.rappler.com/newsbreak/fact-check/world-bank-interest-rate-loan-philippines/.

4 JC Punongbayan, "[Analysis] We Never Defaulted on Our Loans? That's Historical Revisionism," Rappler, 11 April 2019, https://www.rappler.com/voices/thought-leaders/227938-analysis-philippines-never-defaulted-loans-historical-revisionism/.

5 James K. Boyce and Lyuba Zarsky, "Capital Flight from the Philippines, 1962–1986," *Journal of Philippine Development* 15, no. 2 (1988): 191–222.

6 "National Government Outstanding Debt Stock (In Million Pesos)," document downloaded from the Bureau of the Treasury website on 5 January 2022, https://www.treasury.gov.ph/wp-content/uploads/2022/02/Annual-Debt-1986-2021_web.pdf.

7 Dohner and Intal, "The Marcos Legacy," 503.

8 De Dios, Gochoco-Bautista, and Punongbayan, "Martial Law and the Philippine Economy," 19.

9 Dohner and Intal, "The Marcos Legacy," 389.

10 In 2022, yet another spell of interest rate hikes by the US Fed, headed by Jerome Powell, would spell doom to many countries around the world, especially those with huge dollar debts. But the Philippine economy was in a better position to weather this, with external debts just about 30 percent of its total debts—a far cry from levels during martial law.

11 ABS-CBN News, "After the Fact | ANC (25 February 2022)," YouTube video, 53:25, 25 February 2022, https://youtu.be/yUdWu95rxR4.

12 Dohner and Intal, "The Marcos Legacy," 390.

13 Dohner and Intal, 382.

14 Jovito R. Salonga, *Presidential Plunder: The Quest for the Marcos Ill-Gotten Wealth* (Quezon City: University of the Philippines Center for Leadership, Citizenship, and Democracy, 2000).

15 Jovito R. Salonga, *A Journey of Struggle and Hope* (Quezon City: University of the Philippines Center for Leadership, Citizenship, and Democracy and Regina Publishing, 2001), 140.

16 Salonga, *Presidential Plunder*, 6.

17 Dohner and Intal, "The Marcos Legacy," 382.

18 Percival Bueser, "False: AP YouTube Video Shows Marcos Ordering Banks to Release His Gold Wealth," Rappler, 30 April 2021, https://www.rappler.com/newsbreak/fact-check/associated-press-youtube-video-shows-marcos-ordering-banks-release-gold-wealth/.

19 De Dios, Gochoco-Bautista, and Punongbayan, "Martial Law and the Philippine Economy," 10.

20 Saleh M. Nsouli, "Petrodollar Recycling and Global Imbalances," International Monetary Fund, 23 March 2006, https://www.imf.org/en/News/Articles/2015/09/28/04/53/sp032306a.

21 That is, when inflation is deducted from the nominal interest rates to get the *real* interest rates.

22 De Dios, Gochoco-Bautista, and Punongbayan, "Martial Law and the Philippine Economy," 11. If nominal interest rates were fixed and inflation rose for one reason or another, creditors would receive the same interest despite the higher costs of living, so the real payments that they get from borrowers become smaller in effect.

23 Walden Bello and John Feffer, "Robert McNamara's Second Vietnam," Foreign Policy in Focus, 13 July 2009, https://fpif.org/robert_mcnamaras_second_vietnam/.

24 Indeed, the hotel was built precisely for the meeting, as discussed in chapter 8. See also Eric Toussaint, "The World Bank and the Philippines," Committee for the Abolition of Illegitimate Debt, 17 April 2020, https://www.cadtm

.org/The-World-Bank-and-the-Philippines. The idea that multilateral agencies, such as the World Bank, end up aiding dictators or authoritarian leaders is explored by William Easterly in *The Tyranny of Experts: Economists, Dictators, and the Forgotten Rights of the Poor* (New York: Basic Books, 2015).

25 He was also the first director-general of the National Economic and Development Authority (NEDA).

26 Sicat obtained his PhD from the Massachusetts Institute of Technology (MIT), Laya from Stanford (PhD), Ongpin from Harvard (MBA), Alba from Northwestern (PhD), and Paterno and Mapa from Harvard (MBA and PhD, respectively).

27 Teresa S. Encarnacion Tadem, "Philippine Technocracy and the Politics of Economic Decision Making during the Martial Law Period (1972–1986)," *Social Science Diliman* 9, no. 2 (July–December 2013): 1–25.

28 Quoted in Boyce, *The Philippines*, 350.

29 Dohner and Intal, "The Marcos Legacy," 390.

30 Dohner and Intal, 383.

31 Dohner and Intal.

32 Dohner and Intal.

33 Punongbayan, "We Never Defaulted on Our Loans?"

34 Kenneth N. Gilpin, "Philippine Debt Delay is Granted," *The New York Times*, 15 October 1983, https://www.nytimes.com/1983/10/15/business/philippine-debt-delay-is-granted.html.

35 Punongbayan, "We Never Defaulted on Our Loans?"

36 For further discussion on IMF's stabilization programs, see Anne O. Krueger, Stanley Fischer, and Jeffrey D. Sachs, "IMF Stabilization Programs," in *Economic and Financial Crises in Emerging Market Economies*, ed. Martin Feldstein (Chicago: University of Chicago Press, 2003), 297–362.

37 ABS-CBN News, "After the Fact | ANC (25 February 2022)."

38 Dohner and Intal, "The Marcos Legacy," 525.

39 "Executive Order 857, s. 1982." See chapter 12 for a broader discussion.

40 Executive Order No. 934, s. 1984, signed 13 February 1984, *Official Gazette*, https://www.officialgazette.gov.ph/1984/02/13/executive-order-no-934-s-1984/.

41 See chapter 15.

42 Dohner and Intal, "The Marcos Legacy," 526.

43 Dohner and Intal, 525.

44 Dohner and Intal, 528.

45 These projects were a copper smelter, a phosphate fertilizer plant, an aluminum smelter, a diesel engine manufacturing plant, the expansion of the cement industry, coconut industry rationalization, an integrated pulp and paper mill, petrochemical plants, projects for heavy engineering industries, an integrated steel mill, and the alcogas program. "A Range of 11 Big Industrial Projects Is in the Works," The Christian Science Monitor, 19 September 1980, https://www.csmonitor.com/1980/0919/091972.html.

46 Dohner and Intal, "The Marcos Legacy," 529.

47 Dohner and Intal, 531.

48 Dohner and Intal.

49 De Dios, Gochoco-Bautista, and Punongbayan, "Martial Law and the Philippine Economy."

50 ABS-CBN News, "After the Fact | ANC (25 February 2022)."

51 Maria Socorro Gochoco-Bautista, "The Past Performance of the Philippine Banking Sector and Challenges in the Postcrisis Period," in *Rising to the Challenge in Asia: A Study of Financial Markets*, vol. 10, *Philippines* (Manila: Asian Development Bank, 1999), 29–78; Josef T. Yap, Mario B. Lamberte, Teodoro S. Untalan, and Ma. Socorro V. Zingapan, "Central Bank Policies and the Behavior of the Money Market: The Case of the Philippines," Philippine Institute for Development Studies Working Paper Series, no. 90-24, November 1990.

52 Dohner and Intal, "The Marcos Legacy," 536.

53 Dohner and Intal, 533.

54 ABS-CBN News, "After the Fact | ANC (25 February 2022)."

55 ABS-CBN News.

56 Iris Gonzales, "The 1984 Confidential Report on Our Bloated Dollar Reserves," Eyes Wide Open, *The Philippine Star*, 6 May 2019, https://www.philstar.com/business/2019/05/06/1915265/1984-confidential-report-our-bloated-dollar-reserves.

57 Laya offered to resign in the wake of such revelation, but Marcos initially declined his resignation. In January 1984, Marcos "promoted" Laya to become minister for education, culture, and sports. James L. Rowe Jr., "Marcos Ousts Philippine Central Banker," *The Washington Post*, 12 January 1984, https://www.washingtonpost.com/archive/business/1984/01/12/marcos-ousts-philippine-central-banker/dbcc9815-d4aa-49b9-8002-0821b4ea8480/.

58 Gerardo Sicat, *Cesar Virata: Life and Times* (Quezon City: University of the Philippines Press, 2014), 505

59 Dohner and Intal, "The Marcos Legacy," 544–45.

60 ABS-CBN News, "After the Fact | ANC (25 February 2022)."

61 Dohner and Intal, "The Marcos Legacy," 554.

62 Montes, "Stabilization and Adjustment Policies and Programmes," 44–45.

63 Florian A. Alburo et al., *Economic Recovery and Long Run Growth: Agenda for Reforms*, vol. 1, *Main Report* (Manila: Philippine Institute for Development Studies, 1986), 16.

64 Richard Weintraub, "Biggest Aquino Challenge May Be IMF, Debt Relief," *The Washington Post*, 27 July 1986, https://www.washingtonpost.com/archive/business/1986/07/27/biggest-aquino-challenge-may-be-imf-debt-relief/d0044f5f-90ac-465b-84ee-ae80013e0b2d/.

15: Marcos riches came from hard work, not from large-scale plunder?

1 Uli Schmetzer, "The Legend of the Marcoses' Gold Treasure: Conflicting Tales Swirl around Claims over Dictator's Reputed Hoard. Some Believe Billions Were Bundled Out of the Philippines, While Skeptics Insist the Story Is Only a Fairy Tale," *The Baltimore Sun*, 22 November 1997, https://www.baltimoresun.com/news/bs-xpm-1997-11-22-1997326006-story.html.

2 ONE News, "'No Big Mystery'," Facebook video, 5:53, 13 December 2018, https://www.facebook.com/watch/?v=582760348844622.

3 Vernise L. Tantuco and Michael Bueza, "False: 'No Proof' That Marcos Couple Stole Billions from Filipinos," Rappler, 15 November 2018, https://www.rappler.com/newsbreak/fact-check/216792-false-no-proof-ferdinand-imelda-marcos-stole-billions-filipinos/.

4 He became president in 1965 at the relatively young age of 48.

5 Manapat, *Some Are Smarter than Others*, 69.

6 Conrado de Quiros, *Dead Aim: How Marcos Ambushed Philippine Democracy* (Pasig City: Foundation for Worldwide People's Power, 1997), 56.

7 Jose "Pepe" Diokno is the father of human rights lawyer Jose Manuel Tadeo "Chel" Diokno, who ran for senator in 2022 under the Leni Robredo-Kiko Pangilinan ticket, and historian Maria Serena "Maris" Diokno.

8 Dante C. Simbulan, *The Modern Principalia: The Historical Evolution of the Philippine Ruling Oligarchy* (Quezon City: University of the Philippines Press, 2005).

9 Salonga, *A Journey of Struggle and Hope*, 133.

10 Manapat, *Some Are Smarter than Others*, 398.

11 Myles A. Garcia, "The Ilusorio Family Inheritance Wars," Positively Filipino, 10 March 2015, http://www.positively

filipino.com/magazine/the-ilusorio-family-inheritance-wars.

12 Potenciano Ilusorio was a lawyer and businessman who would later introduce Marcos to actress Dovie Beams, with whom Marcos infamously had an affair and allegedly made an infamous audio sex tape. Eric S. Caruncho, "The Ilusorios, before the Fall," *Philippine Daily Inquirer*, 6 March 2016, https://lifestyle.inquirer.net/224185/the-ilusorios-before-the-fall/.

13 Manapat, *Some Are Smarter than Others*, 188.

14 Manapat, *Some Are Smarter than Others*; United States Securities and Exchange Commission, SEC Docket 11, no. 8 (1 February 1977).

15 *Republic of the Philippines v. Sandiganbayan, Ferdinand E. Marcos, and Imelda Romualdez Marcos*, G.R. No. 152154, 453 Phil. 1059, 15 July 2003.

16 "Imeldific," Wikitionary, last edited 20 August 2022, https://en.wiktionary.org/wiki/Imeldific.

17 Roger Wolmuth, "The Imelda Marcos Shopping Guide: A Cache 'n' Carry Way to Spend the Fortunes of a Nation," *People*, 7 April 1986, https://people.com/archive/the-imelda-marcos-shopping-guide-a-cache-n-carry-way-to-spend-the-fortunes-of-a-nation-vol-25-no-14/.

18 Manapat, *Some Are Smarter than Others*, 24.

19 "Imelda's Jewelry Collection Belongs to Gov't—Court," Rappler, 13 January 2014, https://www.rappler.com/nation/47862-court-forfeits-imelda-jewels-for-ph/.

20 Mark Barnes, "The Value of Marcos Jewels According to the Philippine Government," Rappler, 6 May 2016, https://www.rappler.com/moveph/132012-value-marcos-jewels-government/.

21 Presidential Commission on Good Government, "Marcos Ill-Gotten Jewels Worth More than a Billion Pesos," *Official Gazette*, 12 February 2016, https://www.officialgazette.gov.ph/2016/02/12/marcos-ill-gotten-jewels-appraisal/.

22 Janvic Mateo, "Kris Not Wearing Imelda's Jewelry – PCGG," *The Philippine Star*, 30 December 2015, https://www.philstar.com/headlines/2015/12/30/1537916/kris-not-wearing-imeldas-jewelry-pcgg.

23 Jam Pascual, "Remember Calauit? The New Imelda Docu Takes Us Back to One of the Marcoses' Absurd Legacies," *ANCX*, 31 January 2020, https://news.abs-cbn.com/ancx/culture/spotlight/01/31/20/remember-calauit-the-new-imelda-docu-takes-us-back-to-one-of-the-marcoses-absurd-legacies.

24 Bob Drogin, "'Animal Island' Fights to Survive: Philippines: A Wildlife Sanctuary Is under Attack by Squatters Who Lay Claim to the Land; The Dispute Is a Strange Legacy of Ex-President Ferdinand Marcos," *Los Angeles Times*, 24 November 1989, https://www.latimes.com/archives/la-xpm-1989-11-24-mn-184-story.html.

25 As shown in Lauren Greenfield's documentary film *The Kingmaker* (2019).

26 Drogin, "'Animal Island' Fights to Survive."

27 Nikki Alfonso-Gregorio, "Imelda Marcos: The Ex-First Lady Known for More than Just Her Shoes," *SBS Filipino*, 12 November 2018, https://www.sbs.com.au/language/english/imelda-marcos-the-ex-first-lady-known-for-more-than-just-her-shoes.

28 Allegedly, however, despite the extreme grandness of the occasion, there were reports of food poisoning among some high-profile guests. Pedrosa, *The Rise and Fall of Imelda Marcos*.

29 Robles, *Marcos Martial Law: Never Again*.

30 Maureen O'Connor, "5 Shopping Sprees So Wild, They Made History," *The Cut*, 15 April 2013, https://www.thecut.com/2013/04/5-shopping-sprees-so-wild-they-made-history.html.

31 O'Connor, "5 Shopping Sprees So Wild."

32 Antonio J. Montalvan II, "A Vignette of Marcos Profligacy," VERA Files, 26 November 2021, https://verafiles.org/articles/vignette-marcos-profligacy.

33 Manapat, *Some Are Smarter than Others*, 21.

34 Manapat, 23.

35 Manapat, 28.

36 *Republic of the Philippines v. Sandiganbayan.*

37 Jose Rodel Clapano, "Marcos Wealth in Escrow Now $676-M," *The Philippine Star*, 17 January 2003, https://www.philstar.com/headlines/2003/01/17/191798/marcos-wealth-escrow-now-676-m.

38 Elizabeth Olson, "Ferdinand Marcos's Swiss Bank Legacy: Tighter Rules for Despots and Criminals," *The New York Times*, 23 October 1998, https://www.nytimes.com/1998/10/23/world/ferdinand-marcos-s-swiss-bank-legacy-tighter-rules-for-despots-and-criminals.html.

39 "Imelda's Jewelry Collection Belongs to Gov't."

40 "[Podcast] Law of Duterte Land: Marcos Ill-Gotten Loot and Where to Find It," Rappler, 5 October 2021, https://www.rappler.com/newsbreak/podcasts-videos/law-duterte-land-episode-ruben-carranza-finding-marcos-ill-gotten-wealth/.

41 Glenda Marie Castro, "False: Wealth of Marcos Family from 'Hard Work,' and 'Not from Public Funds,'" Rappler, 30 September 2019, https://www.rappler.com/newsbreak/fact-check/240528-wealth-marcos-family-accumulated-filipino-taxes/.

42 Lian Buan, "Sandiganbayan: Imelda Marcos Stays Free While Appealing Conviction," Rappler, 30 November 2018, https://www.rappler.com/nation/217873-sandiganbayan-rules-imelda-marcos-free-while-appealing-conviction/.

43 Trisha Macas, "Duterte: Marcos Family Willing to Return 'Ill-Gotten' Wealth," GMA News Online, 29 August 2017, https://www.gmanetwork.com/news/news/nation/623714/duterte-marcos-family-willing-to-return-ill-gotten-wealth/story/.

44 Ina Reformina, "SC: It's Final, CIIF Block of SMC Shares Owned by Gov't," ABS-CBN News, 27 September 2012, https://news.abs-cbn.com/business/09/27/12/sc-upholds-ruling-affirming-24-govt-shares-smc.

45 Lian Buan, "Breakdown: P174B Recovered from Marcos Loot, P125B More to Get," Rappler, 29 September 2021, https://www.rappler.com/newsbreak/iq/breakdown-billions-recovered-marcos-ill-gotten-wealth-by-pcgg-more-to-get/.

46 Sofia Tomacruz, "Former Marcos Mansion in New York to Be Auctioned Off," Rappler, 5 September 2018, https://www.rappler.com/nation/211253-marcos-mansion-long-island-new-york-to-be-auctioned/.

47 Philip M. Lustre Jr., "Recovering Marcos' Ill-Gotten Wealth: After 30 Years, What?," Rappler, 25 February 2016, https://www.rappler.com/newsbreak/in-depth/123664-recovering-marcos-ill-gotten-wealth-30-years/.

48 JC Punongbayan, "[Analysis] Gusto Mo Ba na Tax Evader at 'Certified Convict' ang Maupo sa Malacañang?," Rappler, 21 January 2022, https://www.rappler.com/nation/analysis-do-you-want-tax-evader-certified-convict-preside-malacanang/.

49 Republic Act No. 10368, "An Act Providing for Reparation and Recognition of Victims of Human Rights Violations during the Marcos Regime, Documentation of Said Violations, Appropriating Funds Therefor and for Other Purposes," approved 25 February 2013, *Official Gazette*, https://www.officialgazette.gov.ph/2013/02/25/republic-act-no-10368/.

50 Aside from providing reparations for human rights victims, the law also mandates the memorialization of martial law through a memorial, library, or museum.

51 Jodesz Gavilan, "11,103 Victims of Human Rights Violations under Martial Law to Get Compensation," Rappler, 10 May 2018, https://www.rappler.com/nation/202033-human

-rights-victims-claims-board-final-list-eligible-claimants-released/.

52 Lian Buan, "Breakdown: P174B Recovered from Marcos Loot, P125B More to Get," Rappler, 29 September 2021, https://www.rappler.com/newsbreak/iq/breakdown-billions-recovered-marcos-ill-gotten-wealth-by-pcgg-more-to-get/.

53 "Mrs. Marcos Says Family Has $800M," Associated Press, 27 March 1998, https://apnews.com/article/ab033829d6fa1286b5097dc27314753d.

54 Manapat, *Some Are Smarter than Others*, 479.

55 Data from Freedom of Information (FOI) request to the Presidential Commission on Good Government (PCGG) for list of "guilty" verdicts against the Marcoses by A. De Jesus, 3 December 2021, https://www.foi.gov.ph/requests/aglzfmVmb2ktcGhyHgsSB0NvbnRlbnQiEVBDR0ctNjA0NjIwOTYyODY0DA.

56 *Francisco I. Chavez v. Imelda R. Marcos*, G.R. No. 185484, 834 Phil. 219, 27 June 2018.

57 "[Podcast] Law of Duterte Land: Marcos Ill-Gotten Loot and Where to Find It."

16: Marcos fought the oligarchy?

1 *Merriam-Webster*, s.v. "oligarchy (*n.*)," accessed 15 November 2021, https://www.merriam-webster.com/dictionary/oligarchy.

2 Ferdinand E. Marcos, "The True Filipino Ideology," *Official Gazette*, 12 May 1982, https://www.officialgazette.gov.ph/1982/05/12/essay-by-president-marcos-entitled-the-true-filipino-ideology/,

3 Christine Herrera, "Imelda to File P500-B Suit vs Marcos Cronies," *Philippine Daily Inquirer*, 5 December 1998.

4 ABS-CBN News, "After the Fact | ANC (25 February 2022)."

5 The same octopus was featured in Manapat's regular newsletter he published himself on the Marcos's corruption and excesses, which would be the basis of his authoritative book.

6 George M. Taber, "The Night I Invented Crony Capitalism," Knowledge at Wharton, 3 November 2015, https://knowledge.wharton.upenn.edu/article/the-night-i-invented-crony-capitalism/.

7 "Greatest Robbery of a Government," Guinness World Records, accessed 15 November 2021, https://www.guinnessworldrecords.com/world-records/65607-greatest-robbery-of-a-government. See chapter 15 for a discussion of the Marcoses' ill-gotten wealth.

8 Percival Bueser, "False: Guinness World Records Names Marcos Best President of All Time," Rappler, 16 February 2021, https://www.rappler.com/newsbreak/fact-check/guinness-world-records-names-marcos-best-president-of-all-time/.

9 Christa Escudero, "Marcos' 'Greatest Robbery of a Government' Guinness Record Suddenly Inaccessible" Rappler, 11 March 2022, https://www.rappler.com/nation/guinness-record-ferdinand-marcos-greatest-robbery-of-government-suddenly-inaccessible-march-2022/.

10 De Dios, *An Analysis of the Philippine Economic Crisis*, 10.

11 The data on inequality measures were discussed in chapter 9.

12 He was also famously one of the Liberal Party members injured in the Plaza Miranda Bombing on 21 August 1971.

13 Salonga, *Presidential Plunder*, 30–31.

14 This rings a bell in the 2019 closure of ABS-CBN by president Rodrigo Duterte and associates in Congress.

15 A new edition of this book was published by the Ateneo de Manila University Press in 2020. Interestingly, in this annotated edition, Manapat's sister Maria Cristina revealed that his brother was pursuing a PhD in Economics in New York before returning to the Philippines after EDSA I (Ricardo lived in involuntary exile in the US for six years).

16 ABS-CBN News, "After the Fact | ANC (25 February 2022)."

17 In a bid to break the telecommunications company duopoly, a new entrant, Dito Telecommunity, was introduced by Davao-based tycoon Dennis Uy (who was quite close to former president Rodrigo Duterte). Aika Rey, "Dito Telecommunity Now in Metro Manila," Rappler, 17 May 2021, https://www.rappler.com/business/dito-telecommunity-services-available-metro-manila-may-17-2021/.

18 JC Punongbayan, "[Analysis] FVR's Legacy: Reforms na Naglinis sa Kalat ng Batas Militar," Rappler, 5 August 2022, https://www.rappler.com/voices/thought-leaders/analysis-fidel-valdez-ramos-legacy-reforms-cleaned-martial-law-mess/.

19 See chapter 4 for a full discussion of the sugar monopoly and how it helped bring about the Negros Island famine in the mid-1980s.

20 This section benefited greatly from the discussion of Dohner and Intal (1989b).

21 De Dios, Gochoco-Bautista, and Punongbayan, "Martial Law and the Philippine Economy."

22 This hybrid coconut was a new high-yielding coconut variety that figured largely in the industry's replanting program.

23 Dohner and Intal, "The Marcos Legacy," 468.

24 Ramon L. Clarete and James A. Roumasset, "An Analysis of the Economic Policies Affecting the Philippine Coconut Industry," Philippine Institute for Development Studies Working Paper no. 83-08, 1983.

25 *Philippine Coconut Farmers Federation, Inc. (COCOFED) v. Republic of the Philippines*, G.R. Nos. 177857–58, 24 January 2012.

26 *Presidential Ad Hoc Fact-Finding Committee on Behest Loans v. Aniano A. Desierto et al.*, G.R. No. 130140, October 25, 1999.

27 Boyce, *The Philippines*, 321.

28 Boyce, 319.

29 Raul Rodrigo and Nancy Pe Rodrigo, "A Time of Troubles, 1981–1989," in *100 Years of Trust: The China Bank Story*, ed. Jose Dalisay (Makati City: China Banking Corporation, 2021), 157.

30 Gochoco-Bautista, "The Past Performance of the Philippine Banking Sector."

31 de Dios, Gochoco-Bautista, and Punongbayan, "Martial Law and the Philippine Economy."

32 Paul Krugman, James Alm, Susan M. Collins, and Eli Remolona, *Transforming the Philippine Economy* (Quezon City: APO Production Unit Inc., 1992).

33 ABS-CBN News, "After the Fact | ANC (25 February 2022)."

34 Florian Alburo and Dante Canlas, "Balance of Payments, Output, and the IMF," *Philippine Review of Economics and Business* 23, nos. 3–4 (September–December 1986): 287.

35 Republic Act No. 7653, "The New Central Bank Act" approved 14 June 1993, https://www.bsp.gov.ph/Pages/AboutTheBank/SealCharterAndHistory/BSPCharter/New_Central_Bank_Act.pdf.

36 Lee C. Chipongian, "CB-BOL Folded Up This Year; Assets Transferred to Treasury," *Manila Bulletin*, 25 February 2018, https://mb.com.ph/2018/02/25/cb-bol-folded-up-this-year-assets-transferred-to-treasury/. Starting in 2019, under the amended Bangko Sentral ng Pilipinas Charter, the BSP remitted half (rather than 75 percent) of its net profits to the national government—but no longer for the purpose of paying the debts of the old Central Bank. Bangko Sentral ng Pilipinas, "Notes to the Financial Statements," accessed 15 December 2022, https://www.bsp.gov.ph/Pages/AboutTheBank/AuditedFinancialStatements/2021FS/Notes.pdf.

37 Manuel L. Quezon III, "A Timeline of Martial Law," The Philippine Diary Project, 27 August 2021, https://philippinediaryproject.com/2021/08/27/a-timeline-of-martial-law/.

38 Joseph Lelyveld, "Rich Family Loses Power in Bitter Feud With Marcos," *The New York Times*, 22 April 1975, https://www.nytimes.com/1975/04/22/archives/rich-family-loses-power-in-bitter-feud-with-marcos.html.

39 Prior to running with Marcos, Fernando Lopez served as Iloilo City mayor, senator, and vice president to Elpidio Quirino in 1949.

40 Camille Elemia, "Fast Facts: How Marcos Silenced, Controlled the Media during Martial Law," Rappler, 19 September 2020, https://www.rappler.com/newsbreak/iq/how-marcos-silenced-media-press-freedom-martial-law/.

41 Eerily, this would presage another closure of ABS-CBN during the term of president Rodrigo Duterte.

42 Lelyveld, "Rich Family Loses Power."

43 Raul Rodrigo, "The Incredible Story of How Geny Lopez and Serge Osmeña Escaped from Prison in 1977," ANCX, 23 June 2020, https://news.abs-cbn.com/ancx/culture/spotlight/06/23/20/the-incredible-story-of-how-geny-lopez-and-serge-osmea-escaped-from-prison-in-1976.

44 Manapat, *Some Are Smarter than Others*, 347.

45 "Imee Marcos' UP Law 'Grad' a 'PR' Stunt, Late UP Law Dean's Account Shows," ABS-CBN News, 2 March 2019, https://news.abs-cbn.com/news/03/02/19/imee-marcos-up-law-grad-a-pr-stunt-late-up-law-deans-account-shows.

46 Salonga, *Presidential Plunder*, 6.

47 Mark Fineman, "Marcos-Era Gold Reported Missing: Philippines Tracing Flow of Millions in Bullion, Cash and Illegal Profits," *Los Angeles Times*, 16 March 1986, https://www.latimes.com/archives/la-xpm-1986-03-16-mn-26520-story.html.

48 Mark Fineman, "A 'Personal Piggy Bank': N.Y. Branch Helped Fund Marcos Spending Sprees," *Los Angeles Times*, 12 April 1986, https://www.latimes.com/archives/la-xpm-1986-04-12-mn-3498-story.html.

49 Salonga, *Presidential Plunder*, 90.

50 "PCGG Statement on the Indictment of Vilma Bautista," Presidential Commission on Good Government, 4 December 2012, https://thenewcommission.wordpress.com/2012/12/04/pcgg-statement-on-the-indictment-of-vilma-bautista/.

51 Rebecca Rosenberg, "Former Philippine First Lady's Aide Guilty in $32M Monet Theft," *New York Post*, 18 November 2013, https://nypost.com/2013/11/18/former-philippine-first-ladys-aide-guilty-in-32m-monet-theft/.

52 Bruce Golding and Kenneth Garger, "New York's No. 2 Tax Cheat Is Former Aide to Ex-First Lady of Philippines," *New York Post*, 15 January 2020, https://nypost.com/2020/01/15/new-yorks-no-2-tax-cheat-is-former-aide-to-ex-first-lady-of-philippines/.

53 Hannah Lazatin, "Did You Know Rustan's Was Supposed to Be Called Tanrus?," *Spot.ph*, 14 October 2017, https://www.spot.ph/newsfeatures/the-latest-news-features/71766/7-rustan-s-milestones-that-might-have-changed-the-country-s-retail-industry-entirely-lfrm-sa00184-20171014-src-tcph-lfrm.

54 Manapat, *Some Are Smarter than Others*, 340.

55 Letter as shown in Pedrosa, *The Rise and Fall of Imelda Marcos*.

56 Francia, *Imelda and the Clans*, 370.

57 Jose Dalisay Jr. and Antonette Reyes, *Builder of Bridges: The Rudy Cuenca Story* (Mandaluyong City: Anvil Publishing, 2010), 113.

58 Marites Dañguilan Vitug, *Power from the Forest: Politics of Logging in the Philippines* (Manila: Philippine Center for Investigative Journalism, 1993).

59 Karol Ilagan, "Timeline: Losing, Saving Philippine Forests," Philippine Center for Investigative Journalism, 12 May 2021, https://pcij.org/article/6886/losing-saving-philippine-forests.

60 Amador A. Remigio Jr., "Philippine Forest Resource Policy in the Marcos and Aquino Governments: A Comparative

Assessment," *Global Ecology and Biogeography Letters* 3 (1993): 192–212.

61 "The Cordillera Resistance against Chico Dam and Cellophil," Bantayog ng mga Bayani, accessed 10 December 2021, https://www.bantayog.org/the-cordillera-resistance-against-chico-dam-and-cellophil/.

62 TLAs would later figure prominently in landmark Supreme Court cases on environmental rights and protection, including the landmark case *Oposa v. Factoran* (G.R. No. 101803, 224 SCRA 792, 30 July 1993).

63 William Branigin, "'Crony Capitalism' Blamed for Economic Crisis," *The Washington Post*, 16 August 1984, https://www.washingtonpost.com/archive/politics/1984/08/16/crony-capitalism-blamed-for-economic-crisis/d99e8760-087d-4d25-ad66-3d324150dc4d/.

64 Remigio, "Philippine Forest Resource Policy."

65 Vitug, *Power from the Forest*.

66 Remigio, "Philippine Forest Resource Policy."

67 Presidential Decree No. 705, s. 1975, signed 19 May 1975, *Official Gazette*, https://www.officialgazette.gov.ph/1975/05/19/presidential-decree-no-705-s-1975/.

68 Dohner and Intal, "The Marcos Legacy," 479.

69 Dohner and Intal, 501–2.

70 ABS-CBN News, "After the Fact | ANC (25 February 2022)."

71 Boyce and Zarsky, "Capital Flight from the Philippines."

72 Boyce, *The Philippines*.

73 Rafael A. Evangelista, "Who Were Really behind Makati's Yellow Confetti Rallies?," Rappler, 24 September 2015, https://www.rappler.com/voices/ispeak/makati-confetti-rallies-marcos.

74 De Dios, Gochoco-Bautista, and Punongbayan, "Martial Law and the Philippine Economy."

75 Boyce, *The Philippines*.

76 Alburo and Canlas, "Balance of Payments," 288.

77 Boyce, *The Philippines*.

78 Ann Scott, "U.S. Auditors to Examine Documents Related to Philippines' Alleged Diverted Funds," United Press International, 17 March 1986, https://www.upi.com/Archives/1986/03/17/US-auditors-to-examine-documents-related-to-Philippines-alleged-diverted-funds/5918511419600/.

79 Scott, "U.S. Auditors to Examine Documents."

80 Haley Gilliland, "Where Did Ferdinand Marcos Hide His $14B Fortune?," *Australian Financial Review*, 21 July 2021, https://www.afr.com/world/asia/where-did-ferdinand-marcos-hide-his-14b-fortune-20210720-p58ba8.

81 Jack Reed, "Government Gathers Evidence on Marcos' Wealth," United Press International, 17 March 1986, https://www.upi.com/Archives/1986/03/17/Government-gathers-evidence-on-Marcos-wealth/7489511419600/.

82 Victoria S. Licuanan, *An Analysis of the Institutional Framework of the Philippine Short-Term Financial Markets* (Makati City: Philippine Institute for Development Studies, 1986).

83 Rodrigo and Pe Rodrigo, "A Time of Troubles," 155.

84 Dohner and Intal, "The Marcos Legacy," 478.

85 "A Business Tycoon Accused of Fleeing the Philippines After . . . ," United Press International, 28 July 1983, https://www.upi.com/Archives/1983/07/28/A-business-tycoon-accused-of-fleeing-the-Philippines-after/2150428212800/.

86 "Fugitive Tycoon: I Was Marcos Front Man," Associated Press, 31 January 1986, https://apnews.com/7f5cc3272eb7a39095c5632e6d1703f3.

87 John Crewdson, "Marcos Graft Staggering," *Chicago Tribune*, 23 March 1986, https://www.chicagotribune.com/news/ct-xpm-1986-03-23-8601210599-story.html.

88 De Dios, Gochoco-Bautista, and Punongbayan, "Martial Law and the Philippine Economy," 18

89 *Marcos: A Malignant Spirit*, dir. Rolly Reyes (1986, ABS-CBN News and Public Affairs).

90 Philip M. Lustre Jr., "Search for Marcos' Wealth: Compromising with Cronies," Rappler, 25 February 2016, https://www.rappler.com/newsbreak/in-depth/123667-marcos-cronies-compromise/.

91 In 1969, the Bureau of Corrections allowed Floirendo's Tagum Agricultural Development Company Inc. (TADECO) to "lease 3,000 hectares of land in the Davao Penal Colony for a banana plantation." In 2020, his son Antonio Floirendo Jr. was convicted of graft by the Sandiganbayan for remaining as a board member of TADECO while serving as a congressman. Elizabeth Marcelo, "Floirendo Gets 8 Years for Graft," *The Philippine Star*, 27 August 2020, https://www.philstar.com/nation/2020/08/27/2038061/floirendo-gets-8-years-graft.

92 Buan, "SC Awards over P1 Billion to Government for Marcos Crony Power Plant Mess."

93 "Sandiganbayan Orders Transfer of Properties under Marcos-Linked Businessman to Gov't," Rappler, 28 November 2021, https://www.rappler.com/nation/sandiganbayan-orders-transfer-properties-marcos-linked-businessman-government/.

94 "Gov't Owns Cojuangco's UCPB Shares—SC," Rappler, 10 July 2013, https://www.rappler.com/nation/33419-sc-cojuangco-ucpb-shares-belong-to-govt/.

95 "SC Junks P51-B PCGG Claim vs Marcoses, Cronies," Rappler, 19 June 2018, https://www.rappler.com/nation/205240-supreme-court-decision-pcgg-claim-vs-estate-ferdinand-marcos-cronies/.

96 Lian Buan, "PCGG Loses Appeal, P102-Billion Case vs Marcos Crony Still Junked," Rappler, 19 February 2020, https://www.rappler.com/nation/252237-pcgg-loses-appeal-sandiganbayan-cases-vs-marcos-crony-still-junked/.

97 Adrian Ayalin, "Sandiganbayan Junks Marcos Civil Case Involving Estate of Late Businessman Ricardo Silverio," ABS-CBN News, 16 July 2021, https://news.abs-cbn.com

/news/07/16/21/sandiganbayan-marcoses-ill-gotten-wealth -case-silverio-dismissed/.

98 Lian Buan, "Too Long in Court: SC Clears the Late Danding Cojuangco of Coco Levy Civil Suits," Rappler, 12 November 2021, https://www.rappler.com/nation/supreme -court-clears-late-danding-cojuangco-coco-levy-suits/.

17: Marcos plundered to protect the economy?

1 Pia Ranada, "Duterte: Marcos Family to Return Some Wealth to Gov't," Rappler, 29 August 2017, https://www .rappler.com/nation/180488-duterte-marcos-family-return -wealth/.

2 Pia Ranada, "Duterte: If I Were Marcoses, I'd Return Wealth for Immunity," Rappler, 5 September 2017, https:// www.rappler.com/nation/181242-duterte-marcos-wealth -immunity/.

3 Pia Ranada, "Marcos Best President If Not for Dictatorship—Duterte," Rappler, 10 February 2016, https:// www.rappler.com/nation/elections/121919-duterte-marcos -best-president/.

4 Pia Ranada, "Duterte Gives Go Signal for Marcos Hero's Burial," Rappler, 9 November 2016, https://www.rappler.com /nation/151801-duterte-go-signal-bury-marcos-supreme -court-ruling/.

5 Michael Bueza, "NHCP Objects to Marcos Burial at Libingan ng Mga Bayani," Rappler, 6 August 2016, https:// www.rappler.com/nation/142145-nhcp-objects-marcos -burial-libingan-bayani/.

6 Rappler, "Duterte: Marcos' Martial Law Was Very Good," YouTube video, 3:52, 25 May 2017, https://youtu.be/aXX5N 1sbK_A.

7 Agence France-Presse, "Duterte Gov't to Abolish Agency Hunting Marcos Plunder," Rappler, 26 July 2017, https://

www.rappler.com/nation/176824-philippines-abolish-pcgg-marcos-plunder/.

8 Pia Ranada, "Duterte Claims Presidential Bet into Cocaine, Calls Him 'Weak Leader'," Rappler, 18 November 2021, https://www.rappler.com/nation/elections/duterte-claims-presidential-bet-into-cocaine-weak-leader/.

9 Quoted in *Imelda*, dir. Ramona S. Diaz (2003; Los Angeles: Big Swing Productions).

10 JC Punongbayan, "Marcos Plundered to 'Protect' the Economy? Makes No Economic Sense," Rappler, 11 September 2017, https://www.rappler.com/voices/thought-leaders/181743-ferdinand-marcos-plunder-philippine-economy-no-economic-sense/.

18: The Marcoses own a million tons of gold?

1 Vernise L. Tantuco and Percival Bueser, "Hindi Totoo: Nagmamay-ari ng 'Milyong Tonelada ng Ginto' ang Pamilyang Marcos," Rappler, 7 December 2021, https://www.rappler.com/newsbreak/fact-check/marcos-family-owns-millions-tons-gold/.

2 Lorenz Dantes Pasion, "False: Marcos Family Owns '$2 Quadrillion' Worth of Gold," Rappler, 24 November 2021, https://www.rappler.com/newsbreak/fact-check/marcos-family-owns-quadrillion-worth-gold-treaty-versailles/.

3 Tantuco and Bueser, "Hindi Totoo: Nagmamay-Ari ng 'Milyong Tonelada ng Ginto' ang Pamilyang Marcos."

4 Percival Bueser, "False: People's Bank of China Safekeeping Receipt of Marcos Gold," Rappler, 19 June 2021, https://www.rappler.com/newsbreak/fact-check/certificate-peoples-bank-of-china-safekeeping-receipt-marcos-gold-certificate/.

5 Pauline Macaraeg, "False: Philippines Is Country with Highest Gold Reserves," Rappler, 29 June 2020, https://www

.rappler.com/newsbreak/fact-check/265133-philippines-country-with-highest-gold-reserves/.

6 Sofia Guanzon, "False: Ferdinand Marcos Inherits Jose Rizal's Gold in Vatican Bank," Rappler, 28 April 2021, https://www.rappler.com/newsbreak/fact-check/ferdinand-marcos-inherits-gold-jose-rizal-vatican-bank/.

7 Pauline Macaraeg, "False: Ferdinand Marcos, Jose Rizal Established World Bank," Rappler, 19 March 2021, https://www.rappler.com/newsbreak/fact-check/ferdinand-marcos-jose-rizal-established-world-bank/.

8 Piers Kelly, "Yamashita's Gold Has Been Found and It's Not What You Think," Rappler, 7 August 2016, https://www.rappler.com/voices/thought-leaders/142197-general-yamashita-treasure/.

9 Marcos Sr.'s guerilla unit was supposedly called "Maharlika," but historians had already debunked its veracity. Fast-forward to 2022 and early 2023, Marcos Jr. proposed a sovereign wealth fund called the Maharlika Investment Fund.

10 Robert H. Reid, "Imelda Marcos Says Family Had Japanese Gold, Not Embezzled Funds," Associated Press, 4 February 1992, https://apnews.com/article/3150d17a15a4324ef73aa9a5ab26b8ab.

11 Lian Buan, "If Marcos Never Saw Gold, Why Tell Court Gold Was Their Source of Wealth?," Rappler, 7 March 2022, https://www.rappler.com/nation/elections/ferdinand-bongbong-marcos-jr-never-saw-gold-told-court-source-wealth/.

12 "False: Filipino 'Royal Family' Ruled over Pre-colonial 'Maharlika Kingdom'," Rappler, 15 February 2019, https://www.rappler.com/newsbreak/fact-check/223032-false-filipino-royal-family-ruled-over-pre-colonial-maharlika-kingdom/.

13 Vernise L. Tantuco, "Hoax: Marcos Gold Bars, Jewelry 'Taken by Aquinos,' Opposition," Rappler, 7 December 2018, https://www.rappler.com/newsbreak/fact-check/218276

-hoax-marcos-gold-bars-jewelry-taken-by-aquinos-opposition/.

14 "How Much Gold Has Been Found in the World?," United States Geological Survey, accessed 15 December 2021, https://www.usgs.gov/faqs/how-much-gold-has-been-found-world.

15 Lian Buan, "5 Reasons the Gold Shipment Complaint vs Aquino Is a Joke," Rappler, 7 January 2017, https://www.rappler.com/newsbreak/inside-track/157567-reasons-gold-shipment-complaint-against-aquino-joke/.

16 Vernise L. Tantuco, "False: Marcos Family Owns a 'Million Tons of Gold'," Rappler, 19 February 2019, https://www.rappler.com/newsbreak/fact-check/223461-false-marcos-family-own-million-tons-gold/.

17 ONE News, "'No Big Mystery'."

18 Lian Buan, "[Watch] Tallano Gold? 'Hindi Ko Alam Iyan,' Says Marcos Jr. Spokesman," Rappler, 17 January 2022, https://www.rappler.com/nation/elections/video-ferdinand-bongbong-marcos-jr-spokesperson-vic-rodriguez-response-tallano-gold/.

19 Rambo Talabong, "Gold for Filipinos? 'I've Never Seen It,' Says Marcos Jr.," Rappler, 25 January 2022, https://www.rappler.com/nation/elections/ferdinand-bongbong-marcos-jr-response-tallano-gold-for-filipinos/.

20 One PH, "Tallano Gold ng mga Marcos?" Facebook video, 2:16, 16 March 2022, https://www.facebook.com/OnePHonCignal/videos/1358452734632826/.

21 Buan, "If Marcos Never Saw Gold."

22 Associated Press Archive, "Philippines: Ferdinand Marcos Cult Worship," YouTube video, 2:57, 23 July 2015, https://youtu.be/eWH9Mz5QwR4.

23 "Thousands Flock UPLB for 'Promised Cash' from Marcos Wealth," Rappler, 23 September 2017, https://www.rappler.com/moveph/183112-thousands-flock-up-los-banos-marcos-wealth/.

24 "Mrs. Marcos Says Family Has $800M."

25 "Imelda Marcos Withdraws from Philippine Presidential Race," CNN, 29 April 1998, http://edition.cnn.com/WORLD/asiapcf/9804/29/philippines.marcos/.

26 Jose Atienza, "Missing Context: Bongbong to Set up Foundation, Give Away 'Marcos Treasure' If Elected President," Rappler, 4 June 2021, https://www.rappler.com/newsbreak/fact-check/bongbong-marcos-set-up-marcos-foundation-elected-president/.

27 Catalina Ricci S. Madarang, "Marcos Hidden Wealth May Show Up for 2022, Says US Litigator," *Interaksyon*, 6 August 2021, https://interaksyon.philstar.com/politics-issues/2021/08/06/197654/us-litigator-looking-for-marcos-wealth-says-it-may-show-up-for-2022/.

28 Abby Boiser, "Trader Duped by Seniors in 'Marcos Gold' Investment," *Philippine Daily Inquirer*, 29 November 2022, https://newsinfo.inquirer.net/1699013/trader-duped-by-seniors-in-marcos-gold-investment.

Epilogue

1 This refers, of course, to my stint as longtime Rappler columnist.

2 Alain Samson, ed., *Behavioral Economics Guide 2022* (London: Behavioral Science Solutions Ltd., 2022), 146.

3 Patricia Lourdes Viray, "Survey: 44% of Filipinos Agree There Was Oppression under Marcos," Philstar.com, 20 March 2016, https://www.philstar.com/headlines/2016/03/20/1564889/survey-44-filipinos-agree-there-was-oppression-under-marcos.

4 Cathrine Gonzales and Addie Pobre, "Timeline: How the Marcoses Made Their Political Comeback," Rappler, 25 February 2017, https://www.rappler.com/newsbreak/iq/162459-timeline-marcos-political-comeback/.

5 Kevin Conley, "Ralph Wolfe Cowan's Portraits of Leaders and Kings," *Town & Country*, 19 April 2016, https://www

.townandcountrymag.com/leisure/arts-and-culture/g2236/ralph-wolfe-cowan-portraits/.

6 Gemma B. Mendoza, "Networked Propaganda: How the Marcoses Are Using Social Media to Reclaim Malacañang," Rappler, 20 November 2019, https://www.rappler.com/newsbreak/investigative/245290-marcos-networked-propaganda-social-media/.

7 Fernan Tamalayan, "The Politics of Nostalgia and the Marcos Golden Age in the Philippines," *Asia Review* 11, no. 3 (December 2021): 273–304.

8 "Inaugural Address of President Marcos, December 30, 1965," *Official Gazette*, https://www.officialgazette.gov.ph/1965/12/30/inaugural-address-of-president-marcos-december-30-1965/.

9 Cheryll Ruth R. Soriano and Fatima Gaw, "Platforms, Alternative Influence, and Networked Political Brokerage on YouTube," *Convergence: The International Journal of Research into New Media Technologies* 28, no. 3 (June 2022): 781–803, https://doi.org/10.1177/13548565211029769.

10 Maria Ressa, "Nobel Lecture," The Nobel Prize, accessed 5 January 2022, https://www.nobelprize.org/prizes/peace/2021/ressa/lecture/.

11 Apart from being awarded the 2021 Nobel Peace Prize together with Russian journalist Dmitry Muratov "for their efforts to safeguard freedom of expression, which is a precondition for democracy and lasting peace," she was also named one of *Time*'s Persons of the Year for 2018, along with other journalists from around the world, collectively called "The Guardians" at the frontlines of the "war on truth."

12 "YouTube Rolls Out Information Panels on 'Martial Law in the Philippines,'" Rappler, 9 December 2021, https://www.rappler.com/technology/social-media/youtube-rolls-out-information-panels-martial-law-philippines/.

13 Gelo Gonzales, "Twitter Tests Option for Reporting Misleading Tweets in PH, Brazil, Spain," Rappler, 18

January 2022, https://www.rappler.com/technology/social-media/twitter-test-report-misleading-tweets-philippines-brazil-spain/.

14 Gaby Baizas, Pauline Macaraeg, and Dylan Salcedo, "Marcos Network Tries to Take Over Twitter with Freshly-Made Accounts," Rappler, 18 January 2022, https://www.rappler.com/nation/elections/ferdinand-bongbong-marcos-jr-tries-take-over-twitter-freshly-made-accounts/.

15 Vittoria Elliot, "Elon Musk Has Put Twitter's Free Speech in Danger," *WIRED*, 7 November 2022, https://www.wired.com/story/twitter-free-speech-musk-takeover/.

16 "Full Text: Maria Ressa, Dmitry Muratov's 10-Point Plan to Address the Information Crisis," Rappler, 3 September 2022, https://www.rappler.com/technology/social-media/full-text-maria-ressa-dmitry-muratov-10-point-plan-address-information-crisis/.

17 "Fact Check: Lies about EDSA, Martial Law, Marcoses," Rappler, 25 February 2020, https://www.rappler.com/newsbreak/fact-check/252652-lies-about-edsa-revolution-martial-law/.

18 Enrico Berdos, "VERA Files Fact Check Yearender: Marcos Jr.'s Presidential Bid Props up Pro-Marcos Propaganda," VERA Files, 18 December 2021, https://verafiles.org/articles/vera-files-fact-check-yearender-marcos-jrs-presidential-bid.

19 "Documentary: Ang Bagong Media ng Bagong Lipunan," Rappler, 22 June 2022, https://www.rappler.com/newsbreak/podcasts-videos/documentary-new-media-society-vloggers-by-rambo-talabong/.

20 Rambo Talabong, "For Malacañang Access, Marcos Vloggers Are Going Pro," Rappler, 20 June 2022, https://www.rappler.com/newsbreak/in-depth/for-malacanang-access-marcos-vloggers-going-professional/; Rambo Talabong, "Marcos Vloggers are Fighting. Here's Why," Rappler, 1 September 2022, https://www.rappler.com/newsbreak/in-depth/reasons-why-marcos-jr-vloggers-fighting/.

21 Jamaico D. Ignacio, "[Opinion] The Slow Death of Philippine History in High School," Rappler, 26 October 2019, https://www.rappler.com/moveph/243058-opinion-slow-death-philippine-history-high-school/.

22 Department of Education, "K to 12 Most Essential Learning Competencies with Corresponding CG Codes," accessed 10 December 2021, 45, https://commons.deped.gov.ph/K-to-12-MELCS-with-CG-Codes.pdf.

23 Ignacio, "The Slow Death of Philippine History in High School."

24 Ignacio.

25 Rather reluctantly, though, since she first eyed the Department of National Defense. Lian Buan, "Sara Duterte Will Be Education Secretary – Marcos Jr.," Rappler, 11 May 2022, https://www.rappler.com/nation/elections/marcos-jr-says-sara-duterte-education-secretary/.

26 Totanes, "*History of the Filipino People* and Martial Law."

27 "Hontiveros Slams Textbooks 'Whitewashing' Martial Law," ABS-CBN News, 20 September 2018, https://news.abs-cbn.com/focus/09/20/18/hontiveros-slams-textbooks-whitewashing-martial-law.

28 Jodesz Gavilan, "Martial Law Museum Set to Open by 2022," Rappler, 23 September 2019, https://www.rappler.com/nation/240809-martial-law-museum-set-opening-2022/.

29 "Under Bongbong Marcos Admin, Martial Law Museum Faces Uncertain Future," *CNN Philippines*, 24 June 2022, https://www.cnnphilippines.com/news/2022/6/24/martial-law-museum-marcos-admin.html.

30 In the first semester of academic year 2017–2018, I had the chance of co-teaching this course as a teaching fellow alongside Professor Emeritus Emmanuel de Dios and Miharu Kimwell (also a teaching fellow). In fact, a lot of the materials cited in this book came from the syllabus and other assigned readings in that course. Some of our students said it was their favorite course ever.

31 Aika Rey, "U.P. Martial Law Subject Should Show Marcos Side Too, Says Imee," Rappler, 18 September 2019, https://www.rappler.com/nation/240431-imee-marcos-says-up-martial-law-class-should-hear-their-side/.

32 Jon Henley, "How Finland Starts Its Fight against Fake News in Primary Schools," *The Guardian*, 29 January 2020, https://www.theguardian.com/world/2020/jan/28/fact-from-fiction-finlands-new-lessons-in-combating-fake-news.

33 Dwight de Leon, "Study Says Duterte Supporters Less Likely to Spot 'Fake News.' But Why?," Rappler, 17 November 2021, https://www.rappler.com/nation/ateneo-research-findings-duterte-supporters-likely-believe-fake-news-november-2021/.

34 JC Punongbayan, "[Analysis] 8 Facts from WB Education Report They Don't Want You to Read," Rappler, 16 July 2021, https://www.rappler.com/voices/thought-leaders/analysis-facts-what-government-does-not-want-you-read-world-bank-education-report/.

35 World Bank, "Philippines: Learning Poverty Brief," June 2022, 1.

Acknowledgments

1 Accessed via the Per SE website of the UP School of Economics, https://econ.upd.edu.ph/perse/?p=5058.

2 JC Punongbayan and Kevin Mandrilla, "Marcos Years Marked 'Golden Age' of PH Economy? Look at the Data," Rappler, 5 March 2016, https://www.rappler.com/voices/imho/marcos-economy-golden-age-philippines.

3 Maybe it should have been held on 23 September instead.

SELECTED REFERENCES

Alba, Michael. 1981. "Estimating Literacy Rate: A Study Relating Literacy Rate with Combined Gross Elementary and Secondary Schools Enrollment Rate." *Philippine Journal of Development* 8, no. 1: 71–87.

Alburo, Florian A., Romeo M. Bautista, Dante B. Canlas, Benjamin E. Diokno, Emmanuel S. de Dios, Raul V. Fabella, Mario C. Feranil, Gabriel U. Iglesias, Ponciano S. Intal Jr., Mario B. Lamberte, Mahar K. Mangahas, Felipe M. Medalla, Rosa Linda Tidalgo-Miranda, Manuel F. Montes, Ernesto M. Pernia, and Edita A. Tan. 1986. *Economic Recovery and Long Run Growth: Agenda for Reforms*. Vol. 1, *Main Report*. Manila: Philippine Institute for Development Studies.

Alburo, Florian, and Dante Canlas. 1986. "Balance of Payments, Output, and the IMF." *Philippine Review of Economics and Business* 23, nos. 3–4 (September–December): 275–92.

Balisacan, Arsenio M. 1993. "The Human Face of Poverty During a Period of Macroeconomic Adjustment." In *Perspectives on Philippine Poverty*, 17–46. Quezon City: University of the Philippines Center for Integrative and

Development Studies, University of the Philippines Press, and Yale University Council on Southeast Asian Studies.

Balisacan, Arsenio M., and Majah-Leah V. Ravago. 2003. "The Rice Problem in the Philippines: Trends, Constraints, and Policy Imperatives." Munich Personal RePEc Archive Paper no. 24865.

Ballesteros, Marife M., Jenica Ancheta, and Tatum Ramos. 2017. "The Comprehensive Agrarian Reform Program after 30 Years: Accomplishments and Forward Options." Philippine Institute for Development Studies Discussion Paper Series, no. 2017-34, December.

Batasang Pambansa. 1985. *Record of the Batasan: Proceedings and Debates*. Vol. 5, *First Session: 1984–1985*. Quezon City: Batasang Pambansa.

Beltran, Jose V. Jr. 1982. "The Concept of Urban Renewal in Metropolitan Manila: An Analysis." Master's thesis, University of Tasmania.

Boyce, James K. 1993. *The Philippines: The Political Economy of Growth and Impoverishment in the Marcos Era*. Hampshire: The Macmillan Press Ltd.

Boyce, James K., and Lyuba Zarsky. 1988. "Capital Flight from the Philippines, 1962–1986." *Philippine Journal of Development* 15, no. 2: 191–222.

Clarete, Ramon L. 2008. "Options for National Food Authority Reforms in the Philippines." In *From Parastatals to Private Trade: Lessons from Asian Agriculture*, edited by Shahidur Rashid, Ashok Gulati, and Ralph Cummings Jr., 174–204. Baltimore: Published for the International Food Policy Research Institute by The Johns Hopkins University Press.

Clarete, Ramon L., and James A. Roumasset. 1983. "An Analysis of the Economic Policies Affecting the Philippine Coconut Industry." Philippine Institute for Development Studies Working Paper 83-08.

Dalisay, Jose Jr., and Antonette Reyes. 2010. *Builder of Bridges: The Rudy Cuenca Story*. Mandaluyong City: Anvil Publishing.

David, Cristina C., and Arsenio Balisacan. 1995. "Philippine Rice Supply Demand: Prospects and Policy Implications." Philippine Institute for Development Studies Discussion Paper Series, no. 95-28, October.

Dawe, David. 2002. "The Changing Structure of the World Rice Market, 1950–2000." *Food Policy* 27: 355–70.

de Dios, Emmanuel S., ed. 1984. *An Analysis of the Philippine Economic Crisis: A Workshop Report*. Quezon City: University of the Philippines Press.

———. 1993. "Poverty, Growth, and the Fiscal Crisis." In *Poverty, Growth, and the Fiscal Crisis*, 3–75. Makati City: Philippine Institute for Development Studies, 1993.

de Dios, Emmanuel S., and Katrina Dinglasan. 2015. "Just How Good Is Unemployment as a Measure of Welfare? A Note." *Philippine Review of Economics* 52, no. 2 (December): 234–45.

de Dios, Emmanuel S., Maria Socorro Gochoco-Bautista, and Jan Carlo Punongbayan. 2021. "Martial Law and the Philippine Economy." University of the Philippines School of Economics Discussion Paper no. 2021-07, November.

de Quiros, Conrado. 1997. *Dead Aim: How Marcos Ambushed Philippine Democracy*. Pasig City: Foundation for Worldwide People's Power.

del Mundo, Fe, Thaddeus Evangelista, and Mario Arciaga. 1987. "Trends in the Health and Nutrition of Filipino Children (0–19 Years) in the Decade 1973 to 1983." *Transactions of the National Academy of Science and Technology (Philippines)* 9: 461–94.

Doherty, John F. 1985. "The Philippine Urban Poor." Philippine Studies Occasional Paper No. 8, Philippine Studies

Program, Center for Asian and Pacific Studies. Honolulu: University of Hawai'i.

Dohner, Robert S., and Ponciano Intal Jr. 1989a. "Debt Crisis and Adjustment in the Philippines." In *Developing Country Debt and the World Economy*, edited by Jeffrey Sachs, 169–92. Chicago: University of Chicago Press.

———. 1989b. "The Marcos Legacy: Economic Policy and Foreign Debt in the Philippines." In *Developing Country Debt and Economic Performance*, Vol. 3, *Country Studies—Indonesia, Korea, Philippines, Turkey*, edited by Jeffrey D. Sachs and Susan M. Collins, 371–614. Chicago: University of Chicago Press.

Emery, Robert F. 1963. "The Successful Philippine Decontrol and Devaluation." *Asian Survey* 3, no. 6: 274–84. https://doi.org/10.2307/3023519.

Encarnacion Tadem, Teresa S. 2013. "Philippine Technocracy and the Politics of Economic Decision Making during the Martial Law Period (1972–1986)." *Social Science Diliman* 9, no. 2 (July–December): 1–25.

Ericta, Carmelita, and Emma Fabian. 2009. "A Documentation of the Philippines' Family Income and Expenditure Survey." Philippine Institute for Development Studies Discussion Paper Series, no. 2009-18, July.

Esguerra, Emmanuel F. 1981. "Some Notes on the Masagana 99 Program and Small Farmer Access to Credit." *Philippine Sociological Review* 29, no. 1: 35–43.

Estudillo, Jonna P. 1997. "Income Inequality in the Philippines, 1961–91." *The Developing Economies* 35, no. 1: 68–95.

Francia, Beatriz Romualdez. 1988. *Imelda and the Clans: A Story of the Philippines*. Mandaluyong City: Solar Publishing Corporation.

Francisco, Ruth. 2016. "Essays on the Socioeconomic Consequences of Parental Migration for Children Left

Behind." PhD diss., University of the Philippines School of Economics.

Fuwa, Nobuhiko. 2002. "Evolution of Rural Poverty in Indonesia, the Philippines and Thailand." Unpublished manuscript. https://www.h.chiba-u.jp/lab/mkt/Poverty3.pdf.

Gochoco-Bautista, Maria Socorro. 1999. "The Past Performance of the Philippine Banking Sector and Challenges in the Postcrisis Period." In *Rising to the Challenge in Asia: A Study of Financial Markets*, Vol. 10, *Philippines*, 29–78. Mandaluyong City: Asian Development Bank.

Hartendorp, A. V. H. 1958. *History of Industry and Trade of the Philippines: From Pre-Spanish Times to the End of the Quirino Administration*. Manila: American Chamber of Commerce of the Philippines.

Herrin, Alejandro N. 2002. "Population Policy in the Philippines: 1969–2002." Philippine Institute for Development Studies Discussion Paper Series, no. 2002-08, September.

Intal, Ponciano S. Jr., and Luis Osman Ranit. 2004. "Literature Review of the Agricultural Distribution Services Sector: Performance, Efficiency and Research Issues." In *Special Issues in Agriculture*, edited by Eliseo R. Ponce, 29–100. Makati City: Philippine Institute for Development Studies.

Intal, Ponciano S. Jr., Leah Francine Cu, and Jo Anne Illescas. 2012. "Rice Prices and the National Food Authority." Philippine Institute for Development Studies Discussion Paper Series, no. 2012-27, October.

Kemmerer, Edwin W. 1905. "The Establishment of the Gold Standard in the Philippines." *Quarterly Journal of Economics* 19, no. 4 (August): 585–609. https://doi.org/10.2307/1885290.

Kerkvliet, Benedict J. Tria. 1996. "Contemporary Philippine Leftist Politics in Historical Perspective." In *The Revolution Falters: The Left in Philippine Politics after 1986*, edited by Patricio N. Abinales, 9–27. New York: Southeast Asia Program Publications, Cornell University.

Khush, G. S., W. R. Coffman, and H. M. Beachell. 1992. "The History of Rice Breeding: IRRI's Contribution." In *Rice Research and Production in the 21st Century: Symposium Honoring Robert F. Chandler Jr.*, edited by Walter G. Rockwood, 117–36. Los Baños: International Rice Research Institute Books.

Krueger, Anne O., Stanley Fischer, and Jeffrey D. Sachs. 2003. "IMF Stabilization Programs." In *Economic and Financial Crises in Emerging Economies*, edited by Martin Feldstein, 297–362. Chicago: University of Chicago Press.

Krugman, Paul, James Alm, Susan M. Collins, and Eli Remolona. 1992. *Transforming the Philippine Economy*. Quezon City: APO Production Unit Inc.

Lent, John A. 1974. "The Philippine Press under Martial Law." *Index on Censorship* 3, no. 1 (March): 47–59. https://doi.org/10.1080/03064227408532297.

Lico, Gerard. 2003. *Edifice Complex: Power, Myth, and Marcos State Architecture*. Quezon City: Ateneo de Manila University Press.

Licuanan, Victoria S. 1986. *An Analysis of the Institutional Framework of the Philippine Short-Term Financial Markets*. Makati City: Philippine Institute for Development Studies.

Lindsey, Charles W. 1984. "Economic Crisis in the Philippines." *Far Eastern Survey* 24, no. 12 (December): 1185–208. https://doi.org/10.2307/2644357.

Maca, Mark. 2018. "Education in the 'New Society' and the Philippine Labour Export Policy (1972–1986)." *Journal of International and Comparative Education* 7, no. 1 (April): 1–16. https://doi.org/10.14425/jice.2018.7.1.1.

Manapat, Ricardo. 2020. *Some Are Smarter than Others: The History of Marcos' Crony Capitalism*. Annotated ed.

Quezon City: Bughaw, an imprint of the Ateneo de Manila University Press.

Mendoza, Maria Nimfa. 2014. "Lessons Learned: Fossil Fuel Subsidies and Energy Sector Reform in the Philippines." Global Subsidies Initiative Report, International Institute for Sustainable Development, March.

Mijares, Primitivo. 2017. *The Conjugal Dictatorship of Ferdinand and Imelda Marcos*. Revised and annotated ed. Quezon City: Bughaw, an imprint of the Ateneo de Manila University Press, 2017.

Manuel F. Montes, 1987. "Stabilization and Adjustment Policies and Programmes—Country Study 12: The Philippines." Working paper, World Institute for Development Economics Research, United Nations University, Helsinki.

Orentlicher, Diane, Marvin E. Frankel, and Jack Greenberg. 1983. "The Philippines: A Country in Crisis—A Report by Lawyers Committee for International Human Rights Committee for International Human Rights." *Columbia Human Rights Law Review* 15: 69–129.

Paderanga, Cayetano W. Jr. 2013. "Macroeconomic Policy Regimes in the Philippines." Bangko Sentral ng Pilipinas–University of the Philippines School of Economics Professorial Chair Lecture, Quezon City, 29 October.

Pedrosa, Carmen. 1987. *The Rise and Fall of Imelda Marcos*. Makati City: Bookmark.

Pernia, Ernesto. 1990. "Economic Growth Performance of Indonesia, the Philippines and Thailand: The Human Resource Dimension." Asian Development Bank Technical Report no. 48, January.

Punongbayan, Jan Carlo. 2022. "The Marcosian 'Golden Age' Myths: What They Are, Why They Persist, and How to Dispel Them." In *The Marcos Era: A Reader*, edited by Leia Castañeda Anastacio and Patricio N. Abinales, 293–311.

Quezon City: Bughaw, an imprint of Ateneo de Manila University Press.

Quimpo, Susan F., and Nathan Gilbert Quimpo. 2012. *Subversive Lives: A Family Memoir of the Marcos Years*. Mandaluyong City: Anvil Publishing.

Rachagan, S. Sothi, and Richard F. Dorall. 1981. "The Conflict in Mindanao: Perspective from South of the Border." *Aghamtao* 4: 52–83.

Remigio, Amador A. Jr. 1993. "Philippine Forest Resource Policy in the Marcos and Aquino Governments: A Comparative Assessment." *Global Ecology and Biogeography Letters* 3: 192–212.

Reyes, Celia M. 2004. "An Initial Verdict on Our Fight against Poverty." Philippine Institute for Development Studies Discussion Paper Series, no. 2004-48, December.

Robles, Raissa. 2016. *Marcos Martial Law: Never Again*. Edited by Alan Robles. Manila: Filipinos for a Better Future.

Ruiz, Neil G. 2014. "Made for Export: Labor Migration, State Power, and Higher Education in a Developing Philippine Economy." PhD diss., Massachusetts Institute of Technology.

Salonga, Jovito R. 2000. *Presidential Plunder: The Quest for the Marcos Ill-Gotten Wealth*. Quezon City: University of the Philippines Center for Leadership, Citizenship, and Democracy.

———. 2001. *A Journey of Struggle and Hope*. Quezon City: University of the Philippines Center for Leadership, Citizenship, and Democracy and Regina Publishing.

Samson, Alain, ed. 2022. *Behavioral Economics Guide 2022*. London: Behavioral Science Solutions Ltd.

Sicat, Gerardo. 2014. *Cesar Virata: Life and Times*. Quezon City: University of the Philippines Press.

Simbulan, Dante C. 2005. *The Modern Principalia: The Historical Evolution of the Philippine Ruling Oligarchy.* Quezon City: University of the Philippines Press.

Tadem, Eduardo Climaco. 2015. "Technocracy and the Peasantry: Martial Law Development Paradigms and Philippine Agrarian Reform." *Journal of Contemporary Asia* 45, no. 3: 394–419. https://doi.org/10.1080/00472336.2014.983538.

Takagi, Yusuke. 2016. *Central Banking as State Building: Policymakers and Their Nationalism in the Philippines, 1933–1964.* Quezon City: Ateneo de Manila University Press.

Tan, Edita A., and Virginia Holazo. 1979. "Measuring Poverty Incidence in a Segmented Market: The Philippine Case." *Philippine Economic Journal* 18, no. 4: 450–90.

Totanes, Vernon R. 2010. "*History of the Filipino People* and Martial Law: A Forgotten Chapter in the History of a History Book, 1960–2010." *Philippine Studies* 58, no. 3 (September): 313–48.

Vitug, Marites Dañguilan. 1993. *Power from the Forest: Politics of Logging in the Philippines.* Manila: Philippine Center for Investigative Journalism.

———. 1998. "The Politics of Logging in the Philippines." In *The Politics of Environment in Southeast Asia*, edited by Philip Hirsch and Carol Warren, 122–38. London: Routledge.

Yap, Josef T., Mario B. Lamberte, Teodoro S. Untalan, and Ma. Socorro V. Zingapan. 1990. "Central Bank Policies and the Behavior of the Money Market: The Case of the Philippines." Philippine Institute for Development Studies Working Paper Series, no. 90-24, November.

www.ingramcontent.com/pod-product-compliance
Lightning Source LLC
Chambersburg PA
CBHW031335230926
51848CB00002B/238
* 9 7 8 6 2 1 4 4 8 2 4 6 7 *